Praise for *On the Sponge Islands*

"A gifted prose stylist, Julia Martin portrays the sea and villages and people—and the natural history of sponges—with tremendous sensitivity, absorbing so many perceptions and emotions during her visits to the Greek islands... *On the Sponge Islands* is a beautiful work of travel literature, learned and artful and entirely accessible."
— SCOTT SLOVIC, author of *Going Away to Think: Engagement, Retreat, and Ecocritical Responsibility*

"With a poet's gift for language, Julia Martin transports the reader to these beautiful Greek sponge fishing islands and their brave people. The reader will feel totally present in Aegean island life, both contemporary and historical."
— MICHAEL N. KALAFATAS, author of *The Bellstone: The Greek Sponge Divers of the Aegean*

"Martin writes with deep compassion about lives linked irrevocably to the sea and sponge divers who met mortal danger with a song, risking everything to feed their families. This lyrical meditation on the pace of change, memory, and forgetting is also a prescient warning about what happens when the living sea is stripped for short-term gain. A moving story, beautifully told."
— RYAN MURDOCK, author of *A Sunny Place for Shady People: How Malta Became One of the Most Curious and Corrupt Places in the World*

"Sponges famously can regenerate from a few cells, a fragment, when almost all has been lost. With humility, curiosity, and compassion, Martin considers how communities regenerate from the devastation and transformations of war, migration, exile, and technological change; and how our collective and personal histories both sever and bind."
— ANNE MICHAELS, author of *Fugitive Pieces*

"An empathetic, honest, and vivid story of hard and dignified lives. It is a must-read for all admirers of the resilience of Greek islanders, of their marine, brine-infested joys and sorrows."
— ARI SITAS, author of *Voices That Reason: Theoretical Parables*

"Martin offers readers a series of marvelous excursions into the depths not only of the sea but of our place in the world."
— CHRISTOPHER MERRILL, author of *Self-Portrait with Dogwood*

"A fascinating and troubling tale of the human relationship with 'the living mind of the sea,' superbly researched and told with empathy and insight. I will never look at a sponge, or any other harvested sea being, in the same way again."
— KAPKA KASSABOVA, author of *Border: A Journey to the Edge of Europe*

# On the
# SPONGE
# ISLANDS

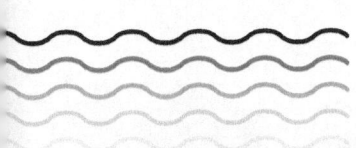

Loss and Restoration
in the Aegean

JULIA MARTIN

TERRA FIRMA BOOKS ◆ TRINITY UNIVERSITY PRESS
*San Antonio, Texas*

Terra Firma Books, an imprint of Trinity University Press
San Antonio, Texas 78212

Copyright © 2026 by Julia Martin

All rights reserved. No part of this book may be reproduced in any form or by any electronic or mechanical means, including information storage and retrieval systems, without permission in writing from the publisher.

Book design by BookMatters, Berkeley
Cover art by Andrew Putter
Cover design by Anne Richmond Boston
Author photo by Michael Cope

ISBN 978-1-59534-332-1 paper
ISBN 978-1-59534-333-8 ebook

Trinity University Press strives to produce its books using methods and materials in an environmentally sensitive manner. We favor working with manufacturers that practice sustainable management of all natural resources, produce paper using recycled stock, and manage forests with the best possible practices for people, biodiversity, and sustainability. The press is a member of the Green Press Initiative, a nonprofit program dedicated to supporting publishers in their efforts to reduce their impacts on endangered forests, climate change, and forest-dependent communities.

The paper used in this publication meets the minimum requirements of the American National Standard for Information Sciences—Permanence of Paper for Printed Library Materials, ANSI 39.48–1992.

CIP data on file at the Library of Congress

30 29 28 27 26 ◆ 5 4 3 2 1

For Michael,

for the children on the islands,

and in memory of the elders

I was sponge, bacterium, an ember among the embers.
—Baptiste Morizot, *Ways of Being Alive*

# CONTENTS

|  |  |  |
|---|---|---|
|  | Prologue: Porifera | ix |
| PART ONE | Evgenia | 3 |
|  | The Gate of the Sea | 5 |
|  | Island of the Angel | 11 |
|  | The Beauty | 52 |
|  | The Felt | 85 |
|  | The Blue | 112 |
|  | The Swallows | 130 |
| PART TWO | The Angel of History | 135 |
|  | The House of Orfeas | 170 |
|  | The Gate | 200 |
| PART THREE | War | 205 |
|  | Restoration | 212 |

| Change | 236 |
| --- | --- |
| The Diver | 269 |
| Epilogue: The Sponge | 279 |
| Postscript | 281 |
| Cast of Characters | 283 |
| Appendix | 289 |
| Gratitude | 291 |
| Notes | 295 |
| Credits | 305 |

# Prologue ◆ Porifera

In the beginning were the sponges. Or perhaps it was the beginning of ourselves.

Sea sponges look like plants, but human beings have classified them as animals. And when scientists at the Massachusetts Institute of Technology found molecules produced by sea sponges in 640-million-year-old rocks from 100 million years before the Cambrian Explosion, it led them to believe that sponges may have been the first of us. This has since been questioned, but whoever was in fact the very first, sponges have been here since almost forever. They are various and extraordinary. And they are, in a sense, our ancestors.

After that early flowering, the primal sponge evolved over unimaginable eons into myriad forms and took on every color. Tube sponges, tree sponges, vase sponges, finger sponges, volcano sponges...deep blues, bright yellows, fiery reds, blacks, purples, pales. But in all this diversity the members of the phylum Porifera retained their defining quality: porosity.

These meekest of animals who live and reproduce without muscles, heart, brain, or nervous system are beings whose entire communication with the world takes place through a multiplicity of pores. This long unbroken breathing of the sponge must far exceed our flighty human attention span. Still, it's where this story begins, in the ancestral sponge beds of the Aegean.

Inhalant pores breathe in the sea. Exhalant pores breathe it out. All day and all night, the tiny whiplike flagella keep the current of water pumping through the body of the sponge as it filters in microscopic nutrients and filters out waste. All day and all night, the ocean flows through, unhindered. Sponges are made of sea, of everything.

# PART ONE

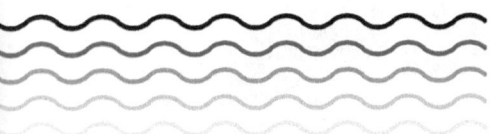

> To dive
> In a peculiar world of weight
> Of power
> Of speed
> With a sense of drunkenness
> Of fear
> Of arrogance
> Of untold power
> —Thodoris Eleftheriou, "PPOINK..."

# Evgenia

The farewell gift from his employer that he carried in his luggage was, he knew, a revolution. The year was 1863 and Fotis Mastoridis had come home to the island of Symi from a job clearing shipwrecks in the East Indies bearing a complete deep-sea diving suit and a hand-cranked air compressor. Sponge divers would now be able to dive to depths they'd never reached before, stay underwater almost indefinitely, and pluck sponges from the bountiful seabed like bunches of grapes from a vine. But as the tale goes, one of many in which the politics of machismo seem inextricable from the culture of sponge diving, the naked divers of Symi had no interest in trying out the new diving suit. It was only when Evgenia—Fotis's wife, who was three months pregnant—agreed to be lowered into the harbor dressed in the full gear that they were shamed into putting it on themselves.[1]

Walking along the harbor wall with my husband, Michael, on our first evening on the island, the water was so clear that you could see every fish. A black-and-white cat sat crouched on a wet step below the bridge watching the shoals intently, every so often dipping in a paw, and I wondered what it had felt like to be Evgenia on that momentous morning. The dare, the challenge, the spectacle, the watching crowds assembled at the edge of the water, the bulky diving suit, the husband who ran the show and fastened the massive helmet over your head, the husband who told you when to jump.

It would be easy to imagine it as yet another story of coercion and fear and old male pride, and perhaps it was all these things. But perhaps, for even just a moment, as she slipped beneath the world she had inhabited all her life, and almost everyone she had ever known stood waiting on the shore, perhaps, as Evgenia Mastoridis descended pregnant that morning into the glimmering clarity of Yialos harbor, and continued to breathe and to walk along the living sea floor as no Symiot woman had done before or probably would again, breathing and walking into the slow tides of blue while her husband cranked the air on deck and waves of curious fishes came swimming by, perhaps it was also a miracle. She returned bearing a stone from the seabed, fifteen meters down.

# The Gate of the Sea
RHODES, 2017

1.

"But what do sponges have to do with anything?"

Our daughter's question had traveled with me. Why cross the world from south to north, Cape Town to Rhodes, to spend a few weeks on some random Greek islands in quest of the near-defunct sponge industry?

The idea of it began when a friend at work surprised me by saying a little ruefully about my forthcoming sabbatical, "So I'll be here and you'll be...in Greece!" Beyond some vague longings, I knew hardly anything about the islands. But his words had me waking early with images of turquoise coves and dazzling white churches and fresh fish markets and donkeys. At last, things converged on the Dodecanese when Michael found pictures of Symi that made it look irresistible, and I began finding out whatever I could about the region. It seemed that, for as long as history could remember, there was one story at the center of its life: the story of sponges and sponge diving.

Because of their wonderful porosity, sea sponges had

always been perfect for a myriad of human uses, and men from the islands had been diving for them and trading them since antiquity. Then, in the late nineteenth century the new deep-sea diving suits like the one Evgenia Mastoridis had first worn on Symi made it possible to mine the seabed as never before and bring home untold wealth. It was a rich harvest that came at the cost of many lives. And it couldn't last. Everything, you could say, flowed through sponges. Until it didn't.

It was enough. A trace. A metaphor, perhaps. I made the bookings.

A few months later, as we crossed the airport threshold to the island of Rhodes, the disheveled sign above our heads announced in faded cerulean paint, "Welcome to Greece, Welcome Home." Impossibly, it felt true. Tired but elated, we put down our bags in the rented house, walked out into the world, greeted the women in black sitting with their cats in the small doorways, found our way through the tiny streets, pushed through the crush of sightseers in the teeming Sokratos thoroughfare, and stepped through the gate.

The Sea Gate was the main entrance to the medieval town of Rhodes from the harbor, a threshold made of rocks hewn into massive blocks. It was built during the rule of the Knights of Saint John in the fifteenth century, but for all the stone solidity of their fortress, the Knights were just one of a succession of foreign powers that came to occupy the island, always by force. When Sultan Suleiman the Magnificent and his army marched through the city gates in 1523, they brought the Dodecanese under Ottoman rule that lasted nearly four hundred years. Then in 1912 the Italians took over the islands after a war with Turkey. And in 1943 Italy was ousted by German military control. During this most terrifying of occupations the old gate was bombed by the Allies. Only in 1947, with the Treaty of Paris, were Rhodes and the other islands of the Dodecanese finally recognized as part of Greece, and a few years later the Sea Gate was rebuilt. By the time we visited in 2017, its great rocks seemed almost alive again with lichen and grasses.

And through the stone gate is the sea. There at the end of baggage checks and passport controls when you find your way at last through the maze of gray cobbles, the ancient streets seething with touts and tourists, hubbub of ice cream and souvenirs, there, at the end of the day, at the end of it all, at last you can stop. Through a space in the limestone wall, you see the sea: Aigaío, Αιγαίο, limitless Aegean.

Past the ferry, the yachts, the sellers of shells and sponges, and the row of massive cannonballs cemented in place at equal intervals, we came to a small square window on the battlements of the fortified sea wall. It was the same view that numberless others had seen as they leaned looking out: this sea, seen through this portal. The limestone wall was porous and resilient, a thing of blood and smoke and war, a wall of stones as tough as words, stones the color of conquest. And beyond the wall, perceived with more clarity because of its frame, was the sea itself. Which is always the sea.

On the small beach of our destination, undertaker crows pecked at rocks and feral cats sniffed for leavings of French fries or fish. A few meters from the Knights' great fortress, a lone boy was building his own castle out of sand with shells for battlements, close enough to the water's edge for the small waves to bring in a moat. I took off my shoes and found a way down from the wall to stand with my feet in the water.

It was late afternoon. The sea was glimmering, made of light.

2.

Our host Renata was working with refugees and migrants at the hotspot on the island of Kos, but she'd left the key to her house in the appointed place. Next morning, I climbed out through a low window and stepped into a realm of abandoned peach trees and fallen lemons in which spring was quietly happening by itself. It was a courtyard walled off from the rest of the world, part of the monastery of Saint Nikolaos whose gates are now closed every day of the year except one, the saint's day. Cerise geraniums sprouted from an ancient grave, early pomegranates were ripening out of sight, and the cobbled walkways of pebbles once smoothed by the slow abrasion of feet were overgrown with yellow dandelions. In the garden of Saint Nikolaos, protector of sailors, fishermen, sponge divers, and merchants, no monks rose early to circumambulate the paths, to pray or sing, or tend the hedges of rosemary and santolina, now dense with buds. No bells rang. No beeswax candles burned. Instead, all day, the ants tracked through. The pigeons called and called in a stillness that seemed to have been made for contemplation. A swallow crossed overhead. New leaves on the tangerine tree were glossy green, and the tiny fruit.

A short walk away in a different part of the Old Town, another place of worship had also gone silent, but its silence was not an accumulation of peace or even neglect.

These days, the building of the Kahal Kadosh Shalom, the sole remaining synagogue on the island and the oldest in Greece, has been restored, and the once busy shul is now mostly a museum. But you can still find a heartrending trace of its vanished congregation in the leaves and spirals of the mosaic floors whose black-and-white pebbles were once smoothed quite flat by the tread of many generations of feet.

They came to the island as refugees from Spain, a community of Sephardic Jews cast out under the Alhambra Decree, a ruling issued in the very month that the same monarchy gave Columbus the order to set sail for the Indies: all Jews who refused to convert to Christianity must leave. Given four months to depart with their children and whichever belongings they could carry, people handed themselves over to the dubious mercy of sea captains who charged exorbitant rates for the voyage. Those who made it safely to Rhodes built a home on the island and passed it all on: the weddings, the synagogues, the shops, the prayers, the food, the remedies, the babies, the stories, the intricate details of ordinary life.

Then came that sunlit Sunday in July 1944 when every Jew was rounded up. This time there was no escape. The soldiers marched them to the harbor where their ancestors had landed five centuries before. Grandmothers, children, parents, bachelors, maidens, more than 1,700 human beings. The soldiers forced them into three overcrowded cargo vessels and sent them on a nine-day trip by sea to Athens. Then came thirteen days in the cattle wagons to Auschwitz. Only 151 people survived the war.

3.

A lifetime later, on a hill overlooking the sea stood a rambling house, brick-red with turquoise shutters. Previously an admiral's residence, its reconstructed purpose was to create a safe space for the life of the imagination. Having read about it online I was curious to visit and had arranged to meet the residence manager, Eleftheria Binikou. In a part of the world where centuries-old animosities still flare into violent conflict or the threat of it, I loved it that the focus of the International Writers and Translators Center of Rhodes was bioregional rather than national: its reach was a geographical area defined not by political boundaries but by ecological systems.[2] Even more wonderfully, its human constituency was described not in terms of land but in relation to the rippling geography of sea. Three seas, in fact: the Black Sea, the Baltic, and the Aegean.

As Eleftheria led us through the rooms she gave a standard account of the good work the center was doing in promoting an intellectual culture and getting local schoolchildren to read. But afterwards, standing on the balcony, she said something more.

"The sea," she said, turning to me with an earnest expression, her voice tender and emphatic, "you know, you *can* be attached to it...because it's always changing."

We'd taken smiling pictures of each other beside the turquoise shutters and were looking out at the lyrical blue Aegean beyond the long pale beach with its rows of recliner chairs and umbrellas. Eleftheria was wearing a powder-blue jersey that matched the aquamarine of her eyes, a color whose radiance had completely supplanted my initial impression of the mustiness of the old building.

"You mean, you can be attached to the sea because it's not a thing?"

"Yes. It's not a thing," she said. "It's alive."

"Thank you! I understand."

I asked her what her name meant, and she smiled, her sparkling eyes.

"It means Freedom."

# Island of the Angel
SYMI, 2017

I.

Our first passage by ferry across the luminous expanse that connects one Greek island to another recalled the seemingly endless traffic of all the others. Early human ancestors and our Neanderthal cousins making it from island to island in small boats, dugout canoes tracking flakes of obsidian across the Aegean seaways from the island of Melos in the last years of the Ice Age, small boats carrying Neolithic migrants and seeds of the first domesticated grains from Anatolia to Crete, timbered galleys with young gods at the oars, imperial warships heavy with cannon and death, fishing boats of every kind, slave ships from Benghazi, pirate ships from the Barbary Coast, tall ships billowing white linen sails woven on the Greek mainland, caïques with painted eyes gone off six months each year to dive for sponges on the North African coast, and in recent years a great parade of steamboats, motorboats, luxury yachts, and high-rise cruise ships packed with merchandise and entertainment like floating malls.

The ferry trip that afternoon from Rhodes to the island of

Symi was a peaceful routine conveyance of locals and visitors. It was early May, the spring air seemed full of hopefulness, and I felt a sort of rippling delight as we sailed over the waves. Yet the arrivals and departures of recent memory were desperate ones. Before the Nazi occupation and the deportation of 1944, which is now remembered as the Longest Journey, two ships packed with Jewish refugees landed on the island on their way to Palestine. One finally made it through, but the passengers on the other were sent to a camp in Italy after their ship caught fire and sank.[3] Now another war, this time in Syria, had reduced streets, houses, marketplaces, gardens, schools, ancient buildings, and all the rich profusion of home to rubble, and sent a new wave of displaced human beings over the same waters. Beginning in earnest in spring 2015, more and more people had begun leaving their devastated homes, risking everything for the chance to step into a flimsy, impossible, overloaded vessel that was never built for the open sea.

2.

After the color-enhanced pictures on the internet, Yialos harbor seen from the deck of the ferry looked like a faded postcard from the days of hand-tinted photography. A few people were waiting on the pier, there were big rich yachts and little boats at anchor, and the buildings were stacked up the hill like watercolor squares painted from a box of Winsor & Newtons: Naples yellow, Venetian red, cerulean blue, iridescent white.

Our rental cottage stood among neatly painted houses and the gap-toothed ruins of abandoned buildings. The little garden was packed with roses and carpeted with green plastic lawn. The air smelled of figs. Our neighbors were a flock

of long-haired sheep. It was late afternoon, and the surface of the water far below was beginning to gleam like polished metal.

By the time we found our way back down to Yialos, the day-trippers had all left and the sponge sellers and trinket stalls had packed away their wares. But outside one of the tourist shops stood a forlorn figure who remained all night looking out to sea when everyone else had gone home. The stained old canvas diving suit had been filled with padding, tied with nylon cords, and suspended from the roof to stand upright like an oversized teddy bear with sad knock-knees and supplicant hands. And where the head should be, a spherical Navy Diving Helmet (SERIAL NO 5123, DATE OF MFG 1/45) was held in place with a chain around the neck. It was a heavy thing made of brass and copper, with small round windows at the front and sides, and a pipe at the back of the head that attached to a black rubber lifeline for air.

*Skafandro,* they named it. The man-boat. The man who is a boat. The men who wore it were called *mechanikoi.*

Once the diver had said a prayer and crossed himself, he'd put on the helmet and his comrades would tighten the brass screws to fasten it down. Then he'd take a lumbering leap from the deck into the waves, consigning his life to the hands of his mates: young men like him who must crank the wheel of the air compressor, turn over the sand glass every thirty seconds to be sure he was not down too long, steer the boat to follow his progress on the ocean floor, and wait for the tug that said he was ready to come up. Even on land, the suit looked claustrophobic.

Stories of sponges and sponge diving were what I thought I'd come for, so it felt auspicious to meet the *skafandro* right away. The deep-diving suit was an invention to enhance human capacities by mechanical means, and while in retrospect the attempt seems tragically clumsy, the new technology was pivotal for the whole region. Once it became possible for a human being to become a boat, a *mechanikos,* everything changed.

Before this, for thousands of years men from the Aegean islands had harvested the sea floor by diving deep on a single breath without masks or any mechanical assistance. Sponge hunters, sponge swimmers, sponge cutters. The ancient Greek texts have many names for them, men of phenomenal stamina and lung capacity who would first say their prayers to the blessed gods who rule the deep sea and then dive naked and open-eyed into the deep with a rope around the waist, carrying only a sickle for cutting and a heavy lead weight for sinking swiftly to the sponge beds.[4] It was dangerous work, but their craft was highly valued, and the skill was transmitted over generations from man to man, and quite possibly sometimes from woman to woman too, through direct experience.[5] The strongest naked divers were island heroes of legendary status, and they could marry the best wives.

In time the divers' prayers may have been whispered to a different god, the sickle was replaced by a small steel knife, and the lead weight became the *skandalopetra*, a smooth flat stone with curved edges, usually marble or granite and weighing up to 15 kilograms, to which the diver was attached by a thin cord, and which enabled him to plunge deep, to steer, and to brake underwater. But the technology for sponge diving in the Dodecanese remained virtually identical until Fotis Mastoridis arrived on Symi with the first *skafandro* and Evgenia put it on.

3.

It was still light as we made our way back up the steep hill to the cottage, but dusk was coming on, and all the painted houses lay reflected in the sea. At a turn in the path near a grove of fig trees, a sound of barking and whining could be heard from a makeshift hovel. Coming closer, I could see two big dogs in a small cage, a white one and a brown one. As I paused to watch, a man approached to feed and shout. A few steps away, almost as disturbing but seemingly unrelated to the dogs, a page of lined exercise book paper covered in Greek and English words fiercely scrawled in blue ballpoint had been taped on a stone step. It looked as though it had been ripped off and stuck down, perhaps several times. I paused again and tried to read it. But even the English was indecipherable and we passed on by, making for the patch of red poppies at the next corner, and the chamomiles coming up through the cracks.

Farther up the hill at the village shop we found red peppers, tomatoes, cucumbers, onions, pasta, pesto, and a slab of halva sliced from a great block. Over the weighing of *graviera* and olives, a man told Michael how he'd once visited Cape Town when he'd worked in the Merchant Marine. And at the back of the shop, looking for chickpeas, I met Zoí.

She'd come over to help me, a tall fair-haired woman with a warm smile who explained in English that you couldn't buy chickpeas in a tin, but there were plenty of dried ones.

"And? Where can we get some?"

"From me!" she said. "I'll make you the best dolmades you've ever eaten."

"Wow."

"They really are the best, you know. But not because it's me. It's a recipe from my grandmother, how she made them."

Ζωή. Zoí. It wasn't just a name you might choose for a child, but the word to use when you want to say Life.

4.

"But how do you paint this sea?"

It was our first morning on Symi, and I'd stopped to talk to one of the group of English watercolorists who'd come to the island on a painting holiday. She looked up from the sketchbook page on which she was drawing a light outline of the harbor, and answered with a serious expression.

"I don't think you can."

The water is clear all the way to the bottom. The colors

of the water shade from transparent gold at the edge to turquoise to an endless hue you might call aquamarine. The water is alive with dark fishes and bright boats that spill reds and whites and greens and cobalts into the sea. The water is suffused with light. Homer did not describe it as blue. I slid in and swam across the harbor, while Michael began talking to a man who was painting the paving stones of a little terrace near a jetty.

"It's a good day," I heard him saying.

The man smiled and said, "Every day is a good day here."

When I joined them he'd stopped painting to talk, brush in air, and was explaining how he'd spent his childhood on the island and recently returned after a long time away. He was tanned, fiftyish, with a baseball cap, dark ponytail, an American accent, and eyes that looked as though they'd seen many things. He said his name was Manuel.

"The water is so beautiful," I said irrelevantly, coming to the edge.

"Yes, it is," he said, "but you watch out for the sea urchins. And there's a little worm too that stings. Lives under the rocks. Best to wear rubber shoes."

Then he told us about a special place we should visit, farther on along the road.

"We go there to swim. Some boulders, going down, and you take the last set of steps…"

"Thank you. I'd love to," I said.

He smiled and then continued talking to Michael about the island, saying, "But commercialization is ruining things."

"Well, surely not entirely?" I said. I didn't want to hear it.

"No, it's true," he said. "The people here used to be so innocent. Can you believe it, there used to be people living on the hill who couldn't even swim, never came down to the harbor? And people down here who'd never been up into the mountain? Mind you, there are still some islanders who've never left Symi."

"Capitalism seems to eat everything," Michael said.

"Oh, it's worse than that," he said.

Then he spoke about the heart, and what contemporary life seems to forget. "What matters, you see, is the heart. The heart. That's what really matters."

As he talked, he touched his hand to his chest and patted it, a gesture we were to see again many times. We were all silent.

And then, as though he'd said too much, he shifted levels. "Well, it's just my opinion. I've been all over the world. Spent three winters here now. It's very quiet, you know. Lots of time for philosophizing."

The men's conversation took a turn towards world leaders, nuclear power, Fukushima, and finally radiation, which Manuel said had been dumped in the Mediterranean by the Mafia. Again, it was not what I wanted to hear, but I couldn't help listening as I watched the reflections of a sky-blue boat tugging at its mooring. I wished they were talking about something else, or not talking at all. I wanted stillness. I wanted the patterns of early light in water, the sky-blue boat…But no island is ever an island. Or it is, and it isn't. The world tracks through.

Still, if there was going to be talking, I needed a change of topic.

"Do you know anyone who was involved in the sponge industry?" I said.

"Yes, me," Manuel said. "My family."

We laughed.

He explained that his family had left Symi for Tarpon

Springs, Florida, in the 1960s when he was a child. It was part of the exodus from the sponge islands that began as early as 1905 when masses of so-called virgin sponge beds were discovered off the coast of Florida and hundreds of spongers emigrated from the Dodecanese to harvest a bounty of wool sponges, less highly prized than the sponges they knew from the Mediterranean but still worth diving for.

"But if you want to know about Symi sponges, then you must go to Dinos," Manuel said. "The sponge shop on the corner. Their stock is authentic, and they can tell you a lot."

"Thank you," I said. "I'll do that."

The image of Greek families leaving Symi for Florida in the previous century brought to mind the recent families of migrants and refugees. Among those who'd fled Syria with a child in their arms, or a single plastic bag, several thousand people had landed on Symi and been taken to Yialos harbor. I'd read that sometimes there were four hundred desperate souls arriving on a single day to join the resident island population of just twenty-five hundred.

"You talk to Wendy," Manuel said when I asked. "She helped set up an organization called Solidarity Symi. They've done good stuff—clothes, food, medicines, all of that. You'll find her at Symi Visitor, or maybe at the laundry. She can tell you about refugees."

We thanked him and said we hoped to meet again. Before saying goodbye, he made sure I'd understood his earlier instructions about the beach.

"Now you remember to take the last path, not the first," he said. "It's a special place."

It was the first of many injunctions I was to receive over the course of our journey, like those directions bestowed on the traveler in an old tale by some human or animal person who knows the territory and also your fate: take this path; you'll not regret it.

5.

In the cool of the day when the day-trippers had left, we made our way there. Walked down the steps from the cottage past the poppies and the fig trees and the white dog and the brown dog barking in their cage, past the scrawled note that had been ripped off the step and taped back yet again with black insulation tape, past the yachts at anchor in Yialos and the people talking in the tavernas, past the Harani shipyard and the painting of boats, on past the little houses with their pots of geraniums and mint, the old woman who fed the cats and the old men on their verandas, the restaurant at the end of the row with its stark gravel beach and rows of umbrellas and sunbeds...

When we found it, Manuel's special place was a pebbly inlet surrounded by high rocks. Thyme and sage and oregano grew wild along the path, and a single small olive tree. In the distance, you could see the mountains of Turkey. From the tiny beach you looked out to an endlessness of blue sea, blue sky, blue mountains. No other human beings. The water was unspeakably clear. A cove. Wild cyclamens. The pink rock roses were all in bloom.

Unspeakable means you just can't find the words. Or that words seem irrelevant. Or that you realize how much easier it would be to describe the flippers and goggles made in China that you bought from an old man who'd once worked in Zaire and now ran a tiny shop in Yialos stacked to the ceiling where you could also buy Neptune's trident for spearing fish, and a thousand hooks and cleats and ropes.

Wearing the goggles and flippers, I swam with tiny iridescent fishes, dark fishes, pale fishes, fish that were blue and green and cerulean, and beneath us a fleet of curious beings that were probably pipefish, dark ribbons of fish with a big eye, small snout, and a tail that ended in what could almost be a sting, slowly drifting horizontally in parallel. While we swam Michael sat on the little beach, looking at the odd shell and writing in his notebook.

Climbing back to the road in the late light, picking oregano and thyme for the evening meal, swallows crossing overhead, pink rock roses at our feet, a single white sail wandering far below, I was reminded of the words of the unnamed artist who is the central character in *Kusamakura,* the haiku-style novel by Natsume Sōseki that I'd been reading in the evenings. On a walking trip in the mountains, he wonders about words and the numinous.

How can I ever convey the quality of peace and beauty that I am experiencing in this moment? he asks. The question preoccupies him for a while, and then at last he writes, "If I were pressed to explain, I would want to say that my heart is moving with the spring."[6]

6.

Next morning as we arrived at the white canvas awnings and sky-blue woodwork of Dinos the Original Sponge Shop, Manuel flew past on the back of a friend's motorbike. He smiled and waved. Thumbs up.

The room was filled from floor to ceiling with golden sponges, among them big shells, a few pieces of coral, framed black-and-white photographs of heroic divers, a highly polished *skafandro* helmet, two model sponge-diving caïques in full sail, and a couple of salvaged Grecian urns encrusted with barnacles. A thickset man with a slow smile came over to talk to us. We introduced ourselves, and I asked whether he could tell me about the sponge history of the island.

"Yes, yes, of course," he said, and told us a story about an archangel. "My grandfather, my father, they had sponge boats. Captains. One time my father was going to Kríti with the boat, and there was a big typhoon, a tornado. The boat fell over. At that time my mother here in Symi was pregnant. So, you know, the boat fell over, and my father prayed. He prayed to Archangelos Mihalis. He said if you save me and the ship, I will name my son after you. So that was me. They called me Panormitis."

"Panormitis?" I asked. "Not Mihalis?"

"Mihalis and Panormitis, it's the same," he explained. "So you and me," he said, turning to Michael with a warm smile, "we are the same. It's the same name."

That was it. He didn't say more.

"What year was that, then?"

"It must have been 1952. I was born in 1953."

At the time, the *skafandro* diving suits were still in use, though the heyday of the sponge trade was already over.

I pointed to the polished helmet on the floor and said, "The *skafandro*? I believe they also called it Satan's Machine. So many died."

He nodded grimly.

Almost immediately after Evgenia Mastoridis returned alive and well from her brief descent into Yialos harbor in her husband's deep-sea diving gear, the ancient Dodecanese sponge trade was transformed. Beginning first with Symi, and soon spreading to the islands of Kalymnos and Halki, the fleets began using the new technology to go deeper than ever before, and to harvest an unimagined bounty of the most luxurious sponges. And while the demands of recently industrialized people in London, Paris, Vienna, and New York for high-quality sponge may have seemed inexhaustible, the *skafandro* now made it possible for the island economies to rise to the challenge. Each year more caïques were built in the shipyard at Harani, more magnificent Venetian-style houses appeared on the hill, the island populations swelled as never before, and in a single season the sponge merchants, the captains, and even the divers themselves became richer than they'd ever imagined possible.

Looking back, the tale of unsustainable resource extraction was bound to be short-lived. It was the golden age of sponge fishing, but the real cost was uncountable. When divers and their families called the *skafandro* Satan's Machine, it was because it killed people or disabled them for life: once the sponge industry had largely relinquished the ancient way of naked diving in favor of the new gear, its magical promise—that you could go down to 70 meters, walk about the sea floor gathering sponges, bring them to the surface, and then simply return for more, several times in a single day—brought with it the shadow of excruciating suffering.

At first the problem was that nobody really understood the physics of decompression. As is now well known, if you're underwater and breathing compressed air, your inhalation includes a high percentage of nitrogen that goes into a supersaturated solution in the body. If you ascend too fast, or stay down too long, or dive too often in one day, the decompressing nitrogen froths out in bubbles that clog the bloodstream and restrict the oxygen supply. This experience of decompression sickness, or the bends, is agony. Like a heart attack, they say, taking place in different parts of the body at once. The Dodecanese divers called it being "hit by the machine."[7] In the early days of Satan's Machine, nobody kept reliable records of how many divers were hit overall, but the impact was devastating. It's said that during the first thirty years after its introduction, from the island of Kalymnos alone, eight hundred men died and two hundred more were heavily paralyzed, while almost all the divers were slightly paralyzed. In another estimate, during the period 1866 to 1915, the *skafandro* claimed the lives of 10,000 men from the sponge-diving islands and caused 20,000 cases of paralysis.[8]

Then, in 1908, physician and physiologist John Scott Haldane produced the first recognized decompression table for the British Admiralty. His work was based on experiments that involved saturating guinea pigs, mice, rats, hens, rabbits, and most especially goats in deep water. For some reason, the poor goats were the best subjects, enduring long lonely hours in compression chambers and painful decompressions, and suffering the ear problems, blindness, paralysis, disability of the limbs (especially the foreleg), and death that accompanied the research. The extent of trauma that the goats experienced in the process is recorded in Haldane's notes in his mention of their continuous bleating. As a result of this torturous work he developed guidelines for safer decompression that involved, in particular, a slow and measured ascent from the deep. But even once this crucial information had reached the Dodecanese, most divers would not follow the recommended rates.

Luckily, Panormitis said, his father didn't have to deal with any of that. By the time he was captaining the caïques, they harvested the sponges without having to employ divers at all. The sponge boat would simply trawl a metal bar across the ocean floor, scooping everything that stood in its way into a great net, including sponges. As he described it I glimpsed for a moment that bar scouring the rippling forests of the sea, tearing out seaweeds, corals, sponges, breaking limbs, crushing heads and fins, snapping the fine sheaths of shellfish, scooping out an entire realm of living beings, the actual living people of the sea shoveled up into the light in a writhing mass, the living mind of the sea raked over in quest of sponge. It's a method that has since been banned, but it sounds about right for the 1950s: naively overconfident technology and no limits to the plunder.

Not that the earlier spongers had many qualms. In the days of naked diving, the minimal available technology set a natural restriction to the quantity and quality of sponges that could be removed from the sea. Yet even so, by the mid-nineteenth century a class of people on Symi and Kalymnos had become very rich and powerful from mining the seabed for all it was worth, and as early as 1840 the Aegean ecoregion had become so depleted that when new sponge beds were discovered along the coast of North Africa, it became lucrative for the sponge captains to make the annual journey all the way to Libya or Benghazi.

After the *skafandro* arrived on the scene in 1863, the opportunities seemed infinite. It was now possible to dive to depths from which no human being had ever returned alive. Critically, this meant the sponge industry began to excavate the sea at a rate faster than the sponge beds could regrow. It was one of those ecological tipping points that is seldom discerned for what it is at the time, until it's way too late. Or perhaps it is in fact discerned, but the interests profiting from annihilating future generations simply do not care.

So, while Satan's Machine is usually remembered as an

instrument of human suffering, the impact of such apparatuses of exploitation is seldom extricable from the suffering of other beings and the devastation of the environment. As the ecological thinker John Elder once said to me rather simply and a little ironically when we parted company at an airport, after an international conference on literature and the environment in Eugene, Oregon, in 2005, "That which is not sustainable will not be sustained."

Yet standing together companionably with Panormitis in a small island shop lit with the pale glow of sponges, I wanted to believe that the golden harvest surrounding us could in fact have become something sustainable, even ethical. Panormitis also wanted me to believe.

"These days," he explained, "you have to have protection for the sponges. You need a permission, and you can only get sponges for two months of the year. April to May, or May to June."

"And where do your sponges come from?" I said.

"Kríti and the North Aegean. Sometimes North Africa. Symi too."

"Really? Not the Caribbean?"

But Panormitis had moved on to describe how the sponges feed on plankton. Like a filter, like the kidneys, he said, explaining that when you cut the sponge from its stem, you always leave a little to grow back again in maybe three or four years.

"If you don't cut the sponge," he said, "it grows big and in the end it breaks off. It's washed away. So it's good to cut."

It was probably his standard patter, but at least this version of sponge fishing was a world away from his father's metal bar trawling the ocean floor. I felt a little reassured, but suddenly he was talking about Chernobyl, and how after the explosion in 1986, the Aegean sponge beds were all killed by radiation. It was, he said, the end of the local industry.

"It's like cancer," Panormitis explained. "Radiation. The sponges were like dust."

Then abruptly, seeing my expression, he changed tack again. With a broad smile he took one of the high-quality sponges harvested at 70 meters, dipped it in a bucket of water, and put it to my face to smell.

"It smells good," he said. "It's good for you. Good for your breath. These ones inside the shop last ten years. The cheap ones outside...it's no good."

The touch of the sponge was a gentle relief. The soft golden fronds caressed the skin. I could see why for many centuries people may have given much to feel that delicious texture on the cheek.

"Breathe it in," Panormitis said. "It's the sea."

"It is. It's beautiful."

I explained that in our currency, the cost of his sponges was high, and we'd have to think carefully about buying. Yes, yes, he said, he understood. He'd been to South Africa when he was in the navy. He'd been nearly everywhere, he said.

"That's Dinos," he told us, pointing across the room to where a man of about the same age had been sitting so quietly at a table near the door that we'd hardly noticed his presence.

"It's his shop," Panormitis said, and explained that they had worked together for twenty-something years after they'd left the navy.

At that, Dinos called me across. With a gentle smile, he handed over some pieces of the apple he had just peeled and cut up to share with us.

"For your husband too."

During the half hour or so that we'd been in the shop,

a young couple had come in and bought two thirty-euro sponges. The two men were philosophical about the day-trippers. Clearly the tourist category was not a single thing, and the distinction between foreigner and local was not always straightforward. There are the day-trippers, the people like us who stay for some time, the regular visitors who have been coming back every year for decades, the Symiots who now live elsewhere but return home when they can, the expats who live permanently on the island, the superrich yachties moored in their superyachts, not stepping ashore if they could avoid it, croissants and bikini girls on the deck. And then there are the refugees, people who wash up on the island and stay for a short while, desperate and hungry and uninvited.

"But Symi without tourists is dead," Dinos said with a shrug.

I pointed out that we were tourists too, but the two old friends seemed quite uninterested in trying to sell us anything. Instead we ate the apple together, and Dinos peeled an orange. We talked about Turkey and Erdoğan and nationalisms.

"We are all just people," Dinos said. "It doesn't matter where we come from. We're the same."

"Yes," I said.

By the time we left the shop, with a small sponge and a promise to return, our body language had become a sort of gentle patting and holding of arms. Dinos explained that he lived not far from where we were staying.

"So if I stand outside my house and call 'Julia!'" he said, "you'll hear me."

7.

When Dinos's father Kiriakos opened the shop in 1939, the synthetic sponge had not yet been invented and sea sponges were still highly prized. Once stripped and cleaned, the densely fibrous skeletons of the three species of *Spongia* used to make the so-called bath sponge become fabulously soft and luxurious, while the sponge's rubbery animal protein remains robust, elastic, absorbent, long-lasting, versatile. And for thousands of years, this is what made sponges such an indispensable tool. For all the cleaning, mopping, decorating, and caring for the body that enabled human culture to flourish in the Mediterranean and beyond, there was nothing like it. More recently, with an emphasis on cleanliness that coincidentally began to escalate around the same time as the appearance of the *skafandro*, the sponge became an object of industrialized desire.

Sponges may be too ephemeral to endure in the archaeological record, and like all the ropes, needles, spades, cooking pots, and soap that support human civilization, they don't feature either in the big narratives of history. But a sponge was such a handy thing, a precious thing in daily use, that occasionally its presence may be discerned at the edges of other stories.

After Odysseus and Telemachus slaughter the suitors who have been gathering around Penelope, the servants use sponges to swab down the banqueting tables and chairs. In the *Iliad*, the soldiers pack flat sponges under their greaves. Hephaestus wipes the face and hands of Thetis with a sponge. And Jesus on the cross is offered a sponge dipped in vinegar. At the Minoan palace at Knossos the walls were decorated by dabbing the paint on with a sponge, just as designer house painters still do for faux painting finishes. And in texts from the later Classical period, sponges are used for polishing shoes, to suck up water from a spring, to separate water from wine, as a protection from heatstroke, to line battle helmets, to wipe bottoms, and for removing or revealing the written word. You could also erase writing from parchment with a dry sponge or soak a sponge in water to dab on a letter written in invisible ink to make it visible again.[9]

Most of all, though, the soft tough skeleton of the sea sponge was perfect for the human body. In the apparatuses of medical care and personal hygiene, nothing else was so absorbent and robust, or so soothing in its touch on the flesh. For diseases of the head Hippocrates advised applying a soft, large sponge squeezed out of hot water to stop the pain, soaking a small sponge in honey and placing it inside the ear to heal discharge from the ear. Or you could twist a sponge into a spiral shape, wind it with linen thread, insert into the nostril, and tug on a thread through the mouth to dislodge a nasal polyp. Sponges were also used for cleansing, drying, and binding up wounds, as a plug for an enema, for the treatment of hemorrhoids, for relief from pains and tiredness, and for a variety of gynecological conditions. For pains of the uterus, a sponge might be squeezed in oil or hot water in which olive leaves or roses had been boiled. And for intense blood flow, a drink was made of toasted and ground sponge tissue, mixed with wine.[10]

During the Medieval period, doctors began using sponges for anesthesia. The thirteenth-century Arabian doctor Ibn al-Quff writes about the advantages and risks of the so-called soporific sponge in *Al Omdah*, his book on pain relief. Before surgery began, he explains, the patient must inhale the vapors from a sponge that had been soaked in an impressive mixture involving hashish, Papaver, and hyoscyamine juice, probably from datura. Once the patient was unconscious, an assistant to the surgeon would continue holding the sponge to their nose during the operation.[11] This anesthetic method, *Al moukkhader*, traveled swiftly across the trade routes, and Arnold of Villanova, a contemporary alchemist, astrologer, and magician, reports that versions of *Spongia somnifera* were common in Europe from as early as the ninth century.[12] In Europe, the potion for saturating the sponge involved a different but equally convincing concoction of opium, hemlock, mandragora, ivy, and unripe mulberries.

By 1522 when the Ottoman conquest of Rhodes was imminent, Aegean sponges were so highly valued that when Symi managed to preempt its own conquest by offering the island's voluntary submission to Turkish rule, the message was carried to Suleiman the Magnificent by a delegation of women laden with loaves of white bread and a great trove of luxurious sponges.[13] The fate of the Symiot women themselves in the transaction is not recorded, but the island's strategic offering of three objects of sensuous pleasure had the desired effect. Symi was awarded self-government by the sultan and given the exclusive right to fish for sponges in all the seas of the Ottoman Empire.[14] In exchange for this relative freedom and major stimulus for trade, Symi would each year send four thousand precious Turkish Cup sponges to the sultan's harem as tribute.[15] The fine-grained, elastic, sometimes cup-shaped body of this species, *Spongia officinalis mollissima*, made it one of the finest (and therefore ultimately most exploited) bath sponges of the Mediterranean.

Perhaps the sponges were some comfort in that dazzling prison. For the hundreds of women who lived behind the locked doors of the Golden Cage, the walls tiled with Iznik leaves, tulips, and flowering trees glazed in gleaming cobalts and reds, the annual haul of high-quality Symi sponges would have been valuable for a range of tasks, and for the intricate rituals of cleansing that the life of the harem required. More crucially, the sponges were essential in the harem for contraception. The paranoia that stalked the Topkapi Palace around the issue of imperial succession meant that if one of the concubines became pregnant, she would be sewn alive into a sack by a eunuch, loaded into a rowing boat, and dumped in the Sea of Marmara.[16] So, it was critical to do whatever possible to avoid pregnancy. The most effective method involved inserting a sea sponge soaked in lemon juice into the vagina before sex.[17]

By the late nineteenth century, when the new deep-sea diving gear had become generally available in the Aegean, the seemingly unlimited hoard of bath sponges the *mechanikoi* began bringing to the surface could not have been more perfectly timed. Through a confluence of plantations, mechanical looms, relatively affordable cotton clothes, the large-scale manufacture of soap, and perhaps even a certain anxiety about the sooty grime of industrialism, wealthy people in Europe had begun bathing regularly, and cleanliness was emerging as a defining characteristic of civilization.[18] Even Queen Victoria was using Pears Soap, and the aggressive marketing of that most certain guarantee of a fair complexion was designed to assure the new class of consumers that a cake of one particular recipe of transparent soap was what the whole world needed.

In this way, the Victorian virtues of cleanliness, godliness, social progress, and the brutal imperatives of the imperial project were all brought together in an extraordinary manifestation of early brand advertising. If Pears was the very thing for half-dressed middle-class white women and peachy English babies blowing bubbles, it was also recommended for children of the London poor. And it was not long before the particular brand whose purity was said to produce soft, white, beautiful hands at home was being promoted as the first step towards lightening the so-called white man's burden abroad, "brightening the dark corners of the earth as civilization advances."[19]

In this heady environment, the perfect companion for the first mass-market soap was a high-quality bath sponge, and the Aegean merchants were ready to supply them in great quantities: bleached lemony pale and trimmed to a satisfying shape for holding in the hand.

8.

Meanwhile, the horrifying human cost of the new technology began to spark protests on the islands, and delegations were sent to the Ottoman ruler to ban the *skafandro*. By 1903, when Metrophanes I. Kalafatas, a school principal from Rhodes, made his own passionate appeal to Sultan Abdul Hamid II in the extraordinary form of a twenty-two-page poem, several bans had already been issued. But each time, sponge merchants and captains in collusion with local Turkish police would find ways to ignore the ban, or the fleet would set off for the seven-month summer season early enough to be out of reach of the news. And again, each time the pressures of the market forced the ban to be revoked, and things continued as before.[20]

Kalafatas called his poetic rant "Χειμερινός όνειρος" or "Winter Dream." Furious with grief, he describes the *skafandro* as the pivotal technology that changed everything, a devilish harbinger of a mechanized way of life and what we might now call commodity capitalism. The new diving gear made people abandon their traditional ways, he says, and when the islanders gave up local handcraft for foreign commodities it broke down the guilds. Because of the *skafandro*, house painters and tailors have become idle, European dress reigns, and Symiots have lost their characteristic honor, their pride, and ethics. The key agents of this social perversion are the ruthlessly profit-driven captains and merchants, and the cost of their luxurious lifestyle is all too apparent. Many men die on deck, and their corpses never return home. Many others are disabled. For Kalafatas the only way to eradicate the toxic delusion that has the whole community in its grip is a return to the beautiful purity of naked diving with the *skandalopetra* that has always been at the heart of island life. So, when he appeals to the sultan to ban the new technology, he is also calling on the islanders to return to their senses.

In all, Kalafatas's rage against the *skafandro* is also, more generally, a rage against the machine, and his great hope is to bring both the island and the spongers back to the old ways. Where the industry was now pursuing riches at whatever the cost to human lives, he writes that the true wealth of Symi is a priceless treasure. This treasure is to be found in safe ports, serene places, skillful shipbuilders, beautiful churches, enchanted views, monks who tirelessly build cells and tend orchards, priests who flood the people's gentle hearts with gifts and feed the hungry with the sky's own bread, and also in the work of professors, doctors, pharmacists, libraries, schools, girls in girls' schools with their teachers, and in the provision of free health care and education to everyone.

Nostalgia aside, the list reads as a compelling image of a functioning community. But Kalafatas goes even farther. He imagines the sultan's wished-for ban of the diving gear as having the power to turn back time to a golden age. If the rumor of it is true, the divers say to the sponge boat,

> the gear will cease,
> your nails turn gold and silver,
> your sails to silk, your ropes to steel,
> no engine nor its shame[21]

The urgency of the school principal's heartbreak was palpable. But to read these impossible words downloaded onto my iPad more than a century later as I sat alone on a warm afternoon on the balcony of our holiday rental in Horio with a cup of chamomile tea made of flowers picked from a crack in the path, to read the poem at that particular time of day when the air around the cottage was thick with the voices of sparrows and the scent of fig leaves and the massive Blue Star ferry was powering into the harbor far below laden with people and cargo, and the island breathed in and out in its wake, to witness from the location of this present moment the hopeful rage of the twenty-two pages of his "Winter Dream" was to catch a glimpse of the angel of history trying to make whole what has been smashed.[22]

## 9.

It was early May and the island was ever more brimming with spring. On the hill above our cottage, the ruined stone fortress once built by the Knights of Saint John and bombed during World War II was surrounded by a mass of waist-high bushes of wild oregano in full flower, and the world was all swallows and wide sky, wide sea and wild herbs, the air alive with pale-orange butterflies and bees, and a deep red pomegranate on our table. Some days before sunrise I'd run along the edge of the sea towards Nimborio, and even at that early hour when the yachts were asleep at their moorings, the Romanis asleep under blankets on the harbor wall beside a small van laden with garlic and infant chairs, and the greengrocer's fruits and vegetables still trustingly stacked in rows and mounds outside his little shop, even at that moment when the full moon was just setting and the sun had not yet quite lifted over the Aegean, the woman selling morning pastries would be standing at the corner with a fresh stack of *koulouria* and *tiropitakia* in a glass case, and the street sweeper would be setting out for work with his thin white-spotted harbor dog beside him. Always we would greet and smile, and once an old man out walking with his friend in a pair of striped pajamas called to me in English, "Run for your life!"

After meeting Panormitis in the sponge shop, we kept receiving intimations of what it could mean to live on an island that dwells in the bright gaze of an archangel. Symi is dedicated to the powerful angel-warrior Saint Michael, and many of the old gods' temples now bear his name, most famously the monastery at Panormitis on the other side of the island, a site once sacred to Apollo that is still a pivotal place of pilgrimage and miracles for the whole Dodecanese.

In this sacramental landscape Michael's name had magic in it. The mighty Mihalis Panormitis who quells Lucifer with the power of his name is also the beloved guardian of sailors and sponge divers. When we introduced ourselves, the woman selling olive-wood spoons kissed Michael on both cheeks and showed us a picture on her phone of her grandfather Panormitis who had died the previous week. The young baker we bought *koulouria* from each morning, and whose eyes filled with tears when he heard Michael's name, said to him, "It's the same, we're the same, both Panormitis!" And after that conversation he always made sure there were fresh *koulouria* for us, even once stopping on his bike to come back and put two in the oven, promising just a few minutes' wait while we sat with his mother, Irene.

During the sponge divers' long months at sea, the comforting miracle of the archangel's presence would sometimes appear in encounters with another animal. In one story from a little book that I found in an island shop, Manolis is on his last diving trip in Egyptian waters when he meets a mortally injured dolphin. Once he's bound up his wounds he names him Mihalis for the archangel, and as Mihalis recovers he returns every day to the caïque to play. Then one evening at sunset Manolis is preparing to make his very last dive. The perfumes and dates and embroidered slippers are packed and ready for the journey home. And he's ready too. He's fifty-five and it's been a long haul. For the last time he puts on the *skafandro* and dives below the surface, descending with practiced ease to the place on the seabed where his hands do the work they know, cutting the sponges from their roots.

Suddenly out of the deep a shark appears. It lunges, shakes him, and tries to flip him over to pull into its mouth. Manolis panics. Instead of detaching the rope of sponges from his waist for more freedom of movement, he unties by mistake the rope that holds the waist of the diving suit in place. It flies up and covers his eyes. The air hose breaks. He has a few minutes left. Everything goes black. He's going to die. "My Mihalis," he whispers to the archangel. On deck, his mates see the broken hose and despair. There's only one possible outcome. But then they hear splashing in the water. It's Mihalis the dolphin who has lifted his friend away from the shark, carried him up all the way to the surface, and is signaling to the crew. Miraculously, Manolis is still warm. Nobody can believe it, but it's true.

Whether it was the archangel who rescued him or his unwitting kindness to a magical being, the miracle doesn't end there. A secret dimension comes to light when Manolis returns to Symi. Like the other old divers whose sea voyages are at an end, he enjoys sitting and having a cigarette with his mates on the quay. But there's something different about him that everyone recognizes, a certain mystery. Every day in the darkness before dawn he's seen walking to the end of the pier and looking out to sea, as though waiting for someone, and it's said that every morning, the dolphin comes. This is not something that Manolis explains to anyone.[23]

These divers' tales might be finely tuned to the sentience of cetaceans, yet land animals seemed to be another story. Each day when we walked down the steps to the sea from our cottage, the dogs were still barking in their terrible cage. And at the top of the hill near the church built among more bombed-out ruins from the Knights' occupation, just below a little cave where you could rest and gaze forever at the shimmering radiance of an infinite sea, a lone donkey was tethered to a short rope that was continually becoming tangled in rocks and between his legs. He would tolerate you patting his nose and disentangling the rope, but his eyes were weary and plagued with flies, and he seemed to reside in that depressed stupor you see in some animals whose lives have been utterly overpowered by human beings. It was as though someone had deliberately staged a reminder of entrapment right at the threshold of blue spaciousness. Right there where you pause near the summit of the hill, breathing in the vastness of sea and sky, right there stands the tethered donkey beside you.

It was all unrelentingly intense.

Then a message came in from Vassilis Stavropoulos, Gary Snyder's Greek translator, that gave a hint of what was taking place. Writing from Athens, Vassilis, who practices the Greek Orthodox way of life with an awareness of interconnectedness, wrote warmly: "I feel proud for you that you can get the feeling of the place and the people, despite being a non-Hellene. Be careful, you might become one of us!! Also, do not overlook the fact that we are living the post–Easter Resurrection period and all this power and sweetness permeates the universe. You are there at the best time possible! The islands are great in spring!"

Power and sweetness. That was it. His words invoked not just springtime but also the sense of things I'd been experiencing: that metaphor had become indistinguishable from the real. On the islands Eleftheria is freedom and Zoí is life. Michael and Panormitis are the archangel. The archangel works miracles and his messenger is a dolphin. The dogs of Hell bark all afternoon from their cage at a bend in the path, and God's donkey is tethered below the church with a short piece of rope. And Harani, the little shipyard where the men still paint and mend their boats, is the place where Symiots built the *Argo* for Jason's voyage, and the great ships they sent to Agamemnon's fleet.

As Panormitis the sponge seller explained it, next time we saw him, "We sent three ships to Troy, you know, with King Nireus." And then, putting his arm around me, he said, "It was because of her, because of the lovely Helen."

Everyone smiled, but he insisted it was true. After all, we'd entered a present moment saturated with symbol, a place where spring is the best time possible, a season when Christ actually returns, alive in the buds and the orange butterflies, and even Persephone may still come back from the dark, her forehead garlanded with oregano and rock roses, pomegranates on the kitchen table.

## 10.

And then at times it felt like a place caught in a mist of forgetting. The hills still bore traces of abandoned terracing, but whenever I asked what used to grow there, the responses were vague.

"We did use to have our own fruits," Sofia the young museum assistant said, a little wistfully, "and make them dry for the winter."

We were standing in the courtyard of the Symi museum at the end of a labyrinth of little streets in an old mansion built with sponge money. Most of the exhibition rooms were closed for reconstruction, likely indefinitely because of EU austerities and budget cuts. But a few visitors still came to see the encrusted amphorae and Byzantine plates salvaged from shipwrecks, and the young woman was glad to talk. When I asked about water, she said the original house had no fewer than seven cisterns.

"It doesn't rain all summer, you see, so they had to store the water."

Then she showed us the great oven and explained how neighbors used to come to bake their bread in it. And the fruits, where they used to dry them.

"Does anyone still do that?" I asked.

She thought a bit and then said, "I remember my grandmother used to make something with grapes and flour. She would dry the grapes, and we'd eat it in the winter. In the old days, they would farm every square centimeter of land, you know. In the Byzantine period, we even used to export wine."

"And now?"

"Now," she said, and smiled, "at the supermarket we can get everything."

"Of course."

Manuel had given me a book about the neighboring Chatziagapitos Sala, now also a museum, and said to take a look.[24] It was the most magnificent of the island's Venetian-style mansions built in the late eighteenth century with profits from the sponge trade. Though it was closed when we visited, Sofia was happy to show us around.

It seems that the four-story house had been built on the instructions of the widow Chatzidoukissa in the 1870s. After her wealthy husband died, she took on the management of his trading interests and probably expanded them, making trade deals with Venice and building a shop at Yialos. Unlike most of the houses on the island, which tended to have no view and were set huddled together in deliberately mazelike streets for fear of pirates, her house was distinguished from its neighbors by its spectacular view, and also by a particular orientation to sunlight which meant that the visitor entering the mansion would be drawn inward to the most brilliantly illuminated heart of the *sala* where the prosperous host awaited him.[25]

It was on just such a sunlit morning that we entered that bright space with Sofia, the museum attendant, a large hall once used for dancing and parties, with an upper level for musicians to stand and play. After years of decay the ample rooms had been reconstructed, but at the time when we visited, the state of funding in Greece for inessential sectors like the Arts meant that the *sala* was closed most days, and very few visitors ever came. So, as we trod through the quiet spaces of the great house, pausing to admire the murals of lovers and flowers, and peering in at the threshold of the entrepreneurial widow's bedroom, I felt a simultaneous sense of presence and absence. She had designed it to adjoin the office where her son Chatziagapitos Chatzioannou took over the work of tracking the progress of his cargo ships. From the balcony you could see all the way down to both Yialos and Pedi, voices of goats in the distance.

At first, the sponge business did well for Chatziagapitos. He traveled to the Holy Land in the company of other wealthy Symiots. He became mayor of the island. And in his magnanimity, he built schools and an isolation hospital. But by the time he was drawing up his will in 1856, the wheel of fortune had turned once more. He'd spent three years in Ottoman jails as a result of the War of Independence in 1821 and his mercantile ventures never really recovered. After his death, the great house became increasingly difficult to maintain, and though his sons continued their father's trading interests as best they could, by the early twentieth century the mansion itself had partially collapsed.[26]

In its heyday the great house was iconic in its grandeur, unrivaled in beauty and opulence by any other on Symi. But in its decline, the Chatziagapitos story came to be cited on the island as an instance of the cautionary proverb: "God cuts down the arrogant and destroys the domes and knows how to dismantle the large vessels."[27] In this version of the perennial tale of ruin that follows overreaching power, the sponge trade was the engine of wealth, and the sponge mansion the most visible site of its destruction. But what I found most poignant about the *sala* were the things it seemed almost, yet not entirely, to have forgotten: traces of orchards and vegetables, cisterns.

In the courtyard of the mansion in its present incarnation were ancient grapevines, a few lemon trees, some loquats, pomegranates. Chatziagapitos would have been glad to know they had endured. By the end of his life, his priorities seem to have been infused by a realization of impermanence, and he appears more concerned to secure his legacy through cultivation of the land than by means of property or trade. After a brief mention of the ancestral house, his will, written at the age of eighty-nine, goes on to stipulate in detail how his son Konstas should inherit the gardens. He shall have the rights to half the fruits planted in the bottom orchard, he wrote, and to whatever vegetables should be grown there. Konstas is also to water the trees, pick vegetables, sow seeds, and plant more trees. Similarly, in the orchard at Avgerinos, "he shall dig and plant in the proper season and shall repair the cistern that it collect water, and those who need may take and forgive, and if there be any damage he shall repair it without delay or ill-feeling." The will ends with the injunction that Konstas perpetuate his father's memory through the offering of fresh produce. "And he shall bring in the year...the fruits from this same orchard to my tomb that I be remembered."[28]

This poignant sense of a life memorialized in the cultivation of food and the conservation of water seemed strikingly different from what we witnessed for the most part on the island. Whatever business deals were negotiated at the Chatziagapitos sponge mansion in its glory days, its daily life was sustained by orchards and vines and fruits and vegetables, and the building was constructed with enough cisterns to collect rainwater for the needs of a large household and the watering of their gardens. Though the *sterna*, the cistern, is now dry, you can still see the alcove where the water was drawn up from below to pour into a basin. And having just come from Cape Town where anyone who could afford a rainwater tank was installing one against the drought, I was impressed.

These days, by contrast, on one of the hottest and driest of the Greek islands, the old cisterns were no longer in use, and fresh water came either from desalination or on the water boat from Rhodes. While there were still fig trees growing in every street, the tomatoes, cucumbers, green beans, red peppers, zucchini, and strawberries on sale in the little shop we enjoyed in Horio had arrived that morning by ferry. And though some people did grow their own food and collect substantial amounts of rainwater during the winter, the general assumption seemed to be that the island was arid (what the tourist guides called it) and that self-sufficiency of any kind was out of the question.

So while Chatziagapitos wanted to be remembered in the fruits of his orchard, by the time we visited, the recent past in which such things were still possible seemed to have been forgotten, as though the thriving island community that Metrophanes Kalafatas had anxiously and correctly perceived in 1903 to be on the brink of destruction had now been entirely effaced in modernity's amnesia about the recent past.

"When the ships used to come with wind, it was more difficult," Sofia explained, when I returned to the question of self-sufficiency and supermarkets. "But now it's every day from Rhodes. The food comes on the ferry. Water too."

When the ships used to come with wind...It was a lovely, nostalgic way of putting it, a billowing multitude of sails setting forth from the island and returning. The museum display reminded us that since ancient times, Symi had been famous for shipping. Together with sponge diving, the islanders' skill in shipbuilding was crucial in linking its economy to wide-reaching networks. Michael Kalafatas, grandson of Metrophanes, notes that Symiots were known for building the fastest ships, so the Ottomans called the island Symbekir, the island of the lightning-fast boats, and gave them the contract to convey all military correspondence across the empire.[29] This meant that until steamships took over the trade routes at the beginning of the twentieth century, the powerful Symiot commercial sailing fleet enabled merchants like Chatziagapitos to trade back and forth across the Mediterranean, connecting the island to the economies of London, Paris, Genoa, Berlin, Constantinople, Venice, Benghazi, Syros, Smyrna, Odessa, their ships filled with figs, currants, wine, and—more than anything else—sponges. From Yialos they set sail laden with masses of golden sponge and returned with all sorts of commodities and worldly ways, collectively supporting a much higher population on the island than it would otherwise have sustained.[30]

What I wanted to know was where the timber came from. An island doesn't become legendary for shipbuilding without a good supply of trees. I'd read somewhere that as early as the sixteenth century, Symiot shipbuilders began buying timber a few miles away on the coast of Turkey, or Asia Minor as they called it. And before that? Surely it was a crucial element in Symi's history: a once densely forested island denuded for timber to build the best ships. Surely the place had not always been what the guidebooks called arid. But nobody I spoke to seemed to know, or even to care.

When I asked Sofia she said, rather vaguely, "Yes, it seems there used to be more trees on the island."

"And what happened to those forests?" I said.

She really didn't know.

While we were talking, the neighborhood cat had been winding herself so urgently around Michael's ankles that the bottoms of his black trousers were covered in white hairs. We all bent over to look at her.

"I have a little dog at home," Sofia told us, smiling. "The cat can smell him on me."

The intimacy with which she spoke about him made me feel I could ask: "Why do we see dogs kept in a cage, or tied up with a rope around the neck?"

Her dark eyes looked sad but resigned. She was silent for a while and then said, "It's a...different way to think about animals. An old way. They tie them up, leave them alone in the sun."

She shrugged, then went on: "We think differently now, but that is the old way."

And then, coming back to the earlier conversation about subsistence, she said, "You know, farming is hard. Our industry is tourism now. Five months of the year."

"People like us," I said.

"Yes."

Michael and I were part of the industry that now fed the island. And the "old way" of treating animals was a vestige of the very agricultural lifestyle whose loss I was regretting. Keeping house pets was part of being globalized.

"Modernity is complicated," I said.

We all laughed.

## 11.

When I asked Manuel about trees, he sent us on a walk. We were to take the path over the hill to the church of Agios Georgios and then down to Nimborio, kingdom of Nireus, king of Symi, he whose beauty was second only to that of Achilles, and whose three ships sailed to Troy to fight with Agamemnon.[31]

"There are some good trees up that way," he said.

"Is it a nice walk?" I said.

He looked surprised, almost offended. "It's a lovely walk. You must do it. And you must go into the church. I'm not religious, but it's wonderful."

Tracking up the hill from the harbor, the wide marble path led through olive orchards to a land of rock and grasses, old groves of cypress and holly and oak, dry stone walls on either side, swallows overhead, and the smell of goats. Drakounta, they call it, a place older than the gods, since only dragons, or possibly Titans, could have hewn and set in place the great blocks of stone that still rest there. It was early, the air fresh, no other human beings about. The next day we were leaving for Kalymnos and Patmos, returning in a couple of weeks, when I'd arranged to meet with someone who could tell us about refugees. But for now, our last day, I was content with beauty. Trees.

And then we saw the horse.

In a tiny enclosure to the side of the path, a chestnut horse was walking back and forth. Walk to one end, turn. Walk back, turn. Walk back, turn. Repeat, repeat, repeat. I tried to talk to him, but he was oblivious or mad, and seemed to have given up on our species, caught as he was in the desperate repetition of walking back and forth, back and forth.

It was agonizing to watch and eventually we left him, making our way up the hill in the bright morning through the remnants of old groves, my heart aching with the ambiguous joy of our freedom.

A little farther on we met the goats. They were more cheerful and engaged than the horse, hopping onto their stone wall to bleat at us and lick my fingers through the fence. At least they had each other. Mothers, fathers, children. And they were goats. Resilient, canny, pragmatic, and ready to take whatever was on offer. Still, the daddy goats' front and back legs had been tied together with a short rope. Hobbled.

We poked some grass to them through the fence and then continued to a place with some sparse memory of forests, the scent of trees.

At the summit of the hill the path reached the little church of Saint George. It was the perfect location for a shrine, and perhaps it was no coincidence that when the old god who used to reside there was displaced by the new religion of Christ, the saint from the Orthodox firmament chosen to occupy the holy site above Drakounta was Agios Giorgios, the Dragon Slayer. Without Manuel's earlier insistence, we may simply have walked on. The island is packed with churches and chapels, and from the outside this one didn't look that significant. But stepping through the gate we entered a courtyard enclosed by whitewashed archways that drew the eye out to the sea and the sky and the distant mountains of Turkey, and a quality of spaciousness that was something to do with the interaction between constructed limits and blue infinity, stone walls built to frame great windows into limitlessness.

Within, the courtyard enclosed another order of immensity: two great holly oaks, a tabby cat stretched out in their shade, and the church itself. The trees' proximity to the shrine must have protected them from logging for hundreds of years, and their presence gave a glimpse of the old ones who'd been present on the island before shipbuilding.

As we entered through the unlocked door under the gaze of the surveillance camera, my eyes took a moment to adjust. Outside in the brilliant morning light of the courtyard everything looked outward, and the beyond was glimpsed in the beyond, the blue expanse beyond the frame. But the church was a scented darkness lit by beeswax candles and the gold halos of saints, a small room built for interiority, a space of prayer and contemplation constructed for the believer to look into the depth within. Above our heads, the All-Seeing Eye, a brown eye of God with a neatly painted eyebrow, looked out of a triangle of blue. *Sub specie aeternitatis*, under the gaze of eternity, I lit two candles for our mothers and blew them out again, as instructed by the sign. Then we stepped out once more into the temple of great space.

Back on the path leading down from the church to the shimmering sea on the other side of the hill towards Nimborio, we saw the dog. He was a big golden dog, utterly alone, tied to a small tree on the hillside, and he was pulling as hard as he could at the end of the rope and barking savagely. It was a lovely morning and the dog just kept barking.

It's an old way of thinking about animals, the woman at the museum had said. An old way, yes. A brutal, thoughtless, terrible way. Dogs are social beings, for god's sake. Like horses, goats, donkeys. Like us. Nobody wants to be tied up. My heart was crying. Since arriving on the island, I'd felt the absurdity and outrage of human cruelty to other beings more strongly than ever before. The intensity of this feeling was heightened by the beauty of the place and the generosity of its people. Symi opened the heart.

I wanted to do something, but I didn't know what. Instead, I said goodbye to the golden dog, uselessly apologized to him for *Homo sapiens*, and took the way down the hillside with Michael to the old realm of King Nireus.

On either side of the path, thyme and sage and oregano grew wild. Our destination was a few stone houses and churches, goat bells calling on the hills, more goats skipping along the street, two children on the side of the road selling shells and stones, and an old man rowing in from Yialos with boxes of tomatoes for the taverna. The woman behind the counter looked surprised to see guests in spring. But she served us a bowl of yogurt and honey, and we sat out under the awning beside the long slow drift of the Aegean.

Gazing out to sea that still morning from our table at the taverna, Nimborio felt a world apart. But the coast of Turkey was just three miles away, close enough for a strong swimmer. And probably ever since the beginning, the arrival of the earliest settlers on Symi had meant boats and communications, gods and sponges, pirates and prisoners, trade. Now that the terraced vineyards are no more, and the sponge boats have been abandoned, the island's trade is in itself. Or an idea of itself, for people like us. The Symi Dream, as one blog calls it. The most beautiful harbor in Greece. The shimmering sea. The perfect getaway. Across the empty sky, a white contrail tracked through the blue, traveling north.

Walking back over the hill, we once more passed the dog, the church, the two great holly oaks, the goats, the memories of cypress and oak, and the horse. The single other human being on the path was a tanned young woman wearing a white bikini and an Apple watch who strode past quickly without greeting.

As we came down the hill to Yialos, a church bell began ringing, on and on, ding-a-ding-a-ding!

It was a Thursday morning, no saint's day, but soon other bells began joining in, the boats in the harbor sounding their horns, the cars hooting, people shouting. Was it war? A disaster? Perhaps it was the end of the world. We wouldn't know. We hadn't been reading the news. Perhaps the end of the world had come, and we were on Symi. But everyone looked delighted.

I found Panormitis at the sponge shop and asked what was going on.

"It's the little boys," he said. "They won the football. The under-eleven boys. They won the Dodecanese Finals."

Just then the victorious team themselves burst through, running and strutting through the streets, small boys in shiny yellow soccer uniforms shouting in triumph, plastic gold medals banging around their necks and each child carrying a freshly cut rose.

# The Beauty
KALYMNOS, 2017

1.

On Kalymnos, our next destination, they make hard bread. The *koulouria* baked each morning on Symi are rings of white dough coated with sesame seeds, crisp on the outside, soft in the middle, and stale by midday. But the distinctive bread of Kalymnos, *krithini kouloura* or *paximadia*, is a rusk made of tough barley flour fermented with anise and mastic, and slow baked to an unrelenting hardness to last six months at sea.

The people also have a reputation for being tough, divers especially. Much of the mountainous island is rock, and in the Kalymnian stories of sponge diving there's a special pride in qualities of extreme endurance. Since the divers had always been champions whose manhood was intimately linked to acts of daring, once the *skafandro* became available, the modern dangers of the new diving technology were easily assimilated into an old code of heroism. Or at least this was how it seemed to the cultural anthropologist Russell Bernard when he studied the Kalymnian sponge fishing industry in the 1960s.

# The Beauty

A century after Evgenia Mastoridis, it was another transitional moment. Satan's Machine was still in use, but it was soon to be replaced by the first scuba diving suits. At the same time, the recent invention of the synthetic sponge was severely impacting the demand for sea sponges. In 1950 more than a third of the male workforce of the island had been directly involved in the sponge trade, but by the mid-1960s this was dwindling.[32] Still, Kalymnos remained home to fifty sponge merchants and a range of artisans, and several hundred men were employed in sponge fishing. A few were naked divers who harvested sponges in the ancient way, but nearly everyone was using the now-battered old *skafandro*.

Before leaving for Greece I'd written to Russell Bernard in Arizona, and though we'd not had any contact before, he'd responded immediately, signing himself as Russ and kindly sending me all his writing on the subject, together with the documentary *Matadors of the Deep*. The film was made by Bengt Börjeson in collaboration with Russ, and offers an irreplaceable record of the sponge diver's craft.[33] In what must have been an extraordinary research trip for the young PhD candidate, in 1965 Russ spent a month traveling with the Kalymnian sponge fleet off the coast of Libya. His records are full of images of the sponge divers' daily life: the lack of sleep, the sunburn, the seasickness, the longing for home, the diver crossing himself three times while the deckhand is dressing him in the diving suit, the jump from the bow of the boat into the sea, the comrade on deck timing the dive with a half-minute sand glass and shouting "*torna*" at each turn, the cigarette the diver must smoke on surfacing since if he couldn't inhale the smoke he'd be sent down again to recompress, the crew working together to tend to him if he began to feel the pains. Only at dusk, when all the dives were done, could they eat. The single meal of the day was shared on deck, several men squatting around a bowl of *fasol* beans with tomato sauce, or macaroni and tomato sauce, or lentils with lemon and vinegar, or rice pilaf, or *fasol* beans with olive oil, sometimes with meat and sometimes not, always with olives and *krithini kouloura*.

Back on Kalymnos, the careful count Russ made of the community of artisans and shops on the island in 1964 reads like a poem about the diligent self-sufficiency of local craftsmanship: twenty-five cobblers, fifteen barbers, eleven bakeries, nine distillers, eight furniture makers, five tanners, three goldsmiths, three salt grinders, three knitting shops, two weavers, two coffee grinders, a paint maker, a soap maker, a blanket maker, a kerchief maker.[34] Fifty years on, the lists of names invoke an entire life on the brink of dissolution, though at the time nostalgia at the imminent impact of transnational modernity was not his concern.

What Russ wanted to know was why so many Kalymnian sponge divers were dying or becoming disabled. Even decades after Haldane's decompression tables had been widely available, the *skafandro* still claimed a devastating number of men's lives. During the single month he traveled with the fleet, out of just nineteen divers, one man died, two were paralyzed, and at least nine suffered more minor cases of the bends.[35] And in the year of 1965, an astounding 7 percent of the divers who set out from Kalymnos harbor after the Easter festivities in the spring never came home, or returned to their families permanently disabled. And these were only the most severe cases. More than 90 percent of all the diving accidents, Russ explains, were treated at sea.

Why did this happen? The men lived an extraordinarily difficult life on a small wooden vessel for six months at a time, far from family and community, in conditions of extended sleep deprivation, inadequate food, and constant exposure to the elements. The diving gear was obsolete, and the divers tended to know little about the medical dangers of diving. Instead, Russ says, they had their own theories and folk remedies relating to the bends.[36] Also, and most significantly, they took risks. "Kalymnians as a group employ extraordinarily risky methods of diving," he writes.[37] All too often, the divers would linger too long on the sea floor, ignore the commands from on deck to return, untie the lifeline, and finally ascend too quickly to the surface. They knew the risks, but they did it anyway. Why?

The situation he describes was a seemingly intractable one in which economic pressures became entangled with a prevailing code of masculinity. Knowing they may never return from the diving trip, Kalymnian divers insisted on being paid all their wages in advance. This put huge pressure on them to fulfill their debt to the captain by bringing up enough sponge, and the only way they could do this was by rapid ascents and repetitive dives. At the same time, Russ says, this economic trap had become enmeshed with the status of the divers on the island as folk heroes, men who were not afraid of anything, young men who took risks. As he put it, "the hallmark of manhood among Kalymnian divers is intrepidity to the point of defying death."[38]

Of course, it was not only the men who had to be tough. Generations of running the household while their husbands were away at sea had given women a powerful social role, at least for half the year. And once the new diving technology brought heartbreak to the island, the women of Kalymnos found in themselves a different sort of power in the fury of grief.

The first protest against the *skafandro* took place in May 1885, with the early news that many Kalymnians had died at sea. It was a Sunday, and keening women poured out from churches all over the island to stand in circles, touch stones to their foreheads, and fling them into the center of the circles. The curse was an ancient one, performed now on the merchant captains and the *demogerontia*, the island senate, who'd sent their young men out to die. Afterwards the women streamed down from the old capital to Pothia, the port recently built from the new sponge profits. As Michael Kalafatas describes it, writing about his grandfather's poem that was in itself such a protest, "the women wanted their rage to be seen and known at the new center of money and power."[39]

It is not recorded what lasting impact, if any, these or the many protests that followed may have had on the authorities. But eight decades later when Kalymnian women marched on the mayor's office in 1963, the sponge industry was sufficiently in decline, and the divers' mythic status in the community sufficiently weakened, for him to give in to their appeal. This time, their demand was quite specific: that the city close down its only brothel and force the divers to stop the notorious wild spending and lavish lifestyles that the wealth from the *skafandro* had made possible. It was a victory of a kind, and Russ thinks it spelled the beginning of the end of the island's sponge-fishing days.[40] Still, the terrible injustice of the industry remained a deep wound to the whole community and rippled through the generations. As one sponge diver's wife says to the camera in the prize-winning documentary *The Sponge Diver's Dance*, "It is a job which gave us comfortable bread," and then, wiping away a tear with a rueful smile, "but bitter bread. Lots of bread, but bitter."[41]

These days only five sponge boats leave from Kalymnos

in the spring, and the diving technology is safe enough if you follow the rules. But the memory of collective trauma is fresh, and one particular dance from the island, the *Mechanikos*, enacts it explicitly. It begins with the wailing song of a violin and a group of men taking the first graceful steps of a Syrtos circle. Then the main dancer enters, leaning on a cane, and shatters the symmetry of this ancestral form. Like the cloth-capped young men in old Kalymnian movie footage who lean on the shoulder of a small boy or walk with difficulty along the harbor wall with the help of a cane, the man at the center of the dance is disabled by the bends. He shakes uncontrollably, his steps are desperate and slow, and he uses his hand to lift a paralyzed foot, halting, falling at the feet of the others, painfully getting up. It's shocking and astonishingly direct. When at last the music changes and the main dancer tosses down his cane to join the circle, his terrible stumbling remains in the memory even as it is transformed.

2.

It was with a mass of such images in mind that I stepped off the ferry from Symi. I wanted to see the place they still call Island of the Sponge Divers and perhaps to hear some stories. It was early in the season, and we were the only guests at the restored sponge mansion now called the Hotel Apxontiko, pronounced "Archontiko."

"The internet translates *archon* as ruler, magistrate, big man?" Michael said to Henrik, our Danish host.

"Yes," he said, and laughed. "House of the big man. At one point, it was the home of a major Ottoman dignitary. Well, I'm a small man."

Small man or not, I appreciated the humility with which he took care of bookings, welcomed visitors, conceptualized the design of the hotel, and single-handedly cleaned the rooms, made the beds, and did all the laundry. As he led us up the marble staircase and into a sunny room that commanded a fine view of the harbor, the faded grandeur of the place was a reminder of the sumptuous lifestyle that used to be possible for the island's elite.

I'd hoped for a closer glimpse of the remnants of this sort of affluence at the neoclassical house of Nicholas Vouvalis and his wife, Katherine. He was the wealthiest sponge merchant during the *skafandro* boom, and the Vouvalis Mansion has been preserved for the public as a museum. The dazzling opulence of chandeliers, gilt-framed portraits, and rococo furniture were visible online, but like the Maritime Museum, the place itself was closed. Well, I thought, so be it. I was not trying to be a historian or to write an exhaustive study. Instead, we took a walk along the harbor wall and met a larger-than-life bronze bust of the big man himself.

Vouvalis's particular success was to link the Kalymnian sponge trade to the industrial networks of the British Empire and the middle-class desires it nurtured. So, even if the deep beds of ancestral sponges must be cut beyond their capacity to regrow, and fleets of young men must die or become disabled in procuring them, once Vouvalis set up the headquarters of his business in London, mountains of high-quality sponges harvested from the deep began to arrive in the dockyards of an empire primed to use them.

Today, the great sponge boss is memorialized on the island as a benefactor. Having amassed a considerable fortune during that brief window of opportunity for unrestricted exploitation of the seabed and of fellow human beings that the *skafandro* made possible, he became a philanthropist. He built schools.[42] Still, the impervious bronze face gazing down at us from his marble plinth wore the look of disdainful ruthlessness that unbridled supremacy inevitably gives to a man's features. It was a curious relief from the despondency that such a face always seems to evoke in me to see a weathered old man in blue overalls quietly appear from the harbor carrying a wooden box filled with lobsters. I watched him place the box carefully on the back of his battered red scooter, squirt the lobsters with water, cover them with an orange towel, secure the box in place with two bungees, and drive off.

3.

From Henrik we had directions to a shop near the silver dome of the municipal offices where we'd find a man who knew all about sponges. There was also, he said, a very old man who walked along the harbor each morning.

"He used to be on the sponge boats, and he knows everything. You ask about him too. There are also various sponge factories. You'll see."

Kostas the sponge seller, big and balding, was stationed beside a mound of sponges.

"I have two wives," he said, putting his hand to his heart in that direct gesture I had now seen over and over. "One that makes children, and the other wife is this—the sea and the sponges."

With a friendly smile he introduced us to the different sponges at his stall. Immense sponges and small ones, elephant ears and the branching fine ones, sponges that would last for just a couple of years and the high-quality sponges you might use for eight or ten, he said, if you looked after them well. Then he spoke the old names, and for a moment the utterance recalled the vanished centuries when sea sponges were not holiday souvenirs or the commodities of an industrializing empire but highly prized essentials of human culture, the precious golden fleeces of the deep, finely distinguished from one another for their different qualities. *Matapas,* the fine silk sponge, its texture soft and yet resilient, the smooth pores plush and perfect for face and body. *Kapadiko,* the honeycomb sponge, the maze of its pores less fine, a sponge highly prized for its absorbency and gentleness, and the durability of its beautiful form.

The contemporary sponge industry is not shy of using powerful chemicals to make sponges more marketable, but Kostas said this made the sponge weak. He explained that he never uses bleach to change the color of a sponge or puts the sponge in chemicals to dissolve the stones that get stuck in its branches.

"If it has small stones or shells in it, I hit the sponge with a rock to break them up," he said. "The sponge is strong. Just try. Come, squeeze it."

He soaked a dry sponge in a bucket of water and gave it to me to wring out. I was tentative but he insisted: "No, no, more. Squeeze it harder. It can't break."

I'd read that most of the sponges sold near the Kalymnos harbor are now imported from the Caribbean and the Gulf of Mexico, but Kostas assured us that his were Aegean.

"Yes," he explained, "they used to go to the coast of Libya, but not anymore. You can't get the permits."

When I asked about the harvesting of sponges these days, whether it's being done sustainably, he answered by talking about the sponge as a marvelous creature that seems to slip through whatever categories we try to ascribe to it. I was reminded of Aristotle's insight that the elusive indeterminacy of sponges challenges our analytic classification systems. Presciently, he categorized sponges as animals by including them in his zoological works, but he also believed that the transition from plants to animals was continuous. As the sponge biologist Eleni Voultsiadou puts it in her study of sponges in antiquity, this is because sponges are among those sea organisms that "raise the question of whether they are animals or plants since they grow attached on one hand, but they exhibit a kind of sensation on the other."[43] For Kostas, the wonderful ambiguity of the sponge manifested in a combination of mobility and rootedness, and in its sexuality.

"Look," he said, "sponge is hermaphrodite. Not male, not female." He went on, "You see, worms make the sponges. When you cut the sponge, the worms all run away—I've seen it when I'm diving—and each one makes a new sponge. So it's no problem to cut."

"But the old caïques, didn't they take out too many sponges?" I said.

So far nobody I'd met was prepared to say outright that the sponge beds had been overharvested. But his response gave a hint of it, in his reassurance that things were now different.

"The way it's done now," he said, "there are not so many ships. There's no problem to take sponges. They are growing again every year. The sea—there's no way you can fish in it naturally and make a problem."

I must have looked dubious because he added, "It's the big boats and the big nets. They destroy everything."

"The ones that come with a metal bar and scrape everything living on the seabed into a net?" I said.

"Yes, it's not good. Destroys everything."

"And pollution is the problem," he went on, his kind face filled with concern. "The sponge is a filter, very sensitive. You know, after Chernobyl poisoned the water, the sponges were like dust. But if it's just diving, no problem."

Once again, someone was making the link between contamination from the nuclear disaster in April 1986 and the widespread sponge death in the Mediterranean later the same year that turned entire sponge beds to dust, devastating the industry. It was not a conclusion I'd seen confirmed in any of the scientific papers I'd read about the catastrophic sponge death of that year, but it had a lot of traction in the popular imagination.

We stopped talking then to look at the sponges heaped at Kostas's stall like a mound of porous gold. *Matapas, kapadiko*...Each golden sponge was its own quiet form, branched and once-breathing, neither male nor female, the soft bones of an animal that looks like a plant, a creature that inhales and exhales the sea. The sponges were soft and tough and beautiful. I wanted to hold them, touch them to my cheek.

Was it ethical to buy them? I'd begun to wonder. The question was a twenty-first century one that implied the possibility of a straightforward answer. But human beings' association with Porifera was such an ancient and intractable story, entangled with many others, and filled with people like Kostas who loved the sea and was doing what he could to make a living, and people like us who desire what he has to sell.

I agonized a bit, and then we bought four. Three for gifts, and one for me from Michael. It was Mother's Day. Kostas went back into the grocery shop to find a special *matapas* sponge he said he'd been saving.

"This is the one for you," he said, placing it gently in my hands. "You keep it separate, so you remember." It was fine-grained and silky, soft on the cheek yet elastic and strong.

Then he told us about the old man they called Latari who walked through the harbor each morning. He used to work on the sponge boats, Kostas explained. Not as a diver but as the pilot, the man who steered the caïque following the diver as he traveled along the seabed. It was a crucial task as the diver's life was literally in his hands. If he made just one mistake, the air pipe could snare or break. Latari's other job was to clean the sponges on the boat and then to count and weigh them once the fleet returned to Kalymnos. It was another essential role, the intermediary between sponge boats and merchants. His special skill, Kostas said, was to be able to assess the value of the sponge simply by looking at it. So that was his work. But the main thing everyone knew about Latari was the story of the shark.

"His grandfather was the diver who was bitten by a shark, but the shark couldn't eat him," Kostas said.

I'd read about it somewhere. One of the last naked divers was swallowed by a Great White somewhere off the coast of North Africa and then spat out again because of the heavy diving stone he was carrying. Kostas said the old man would be walking past around nine the next morning, and we could come over and meet him. He'd let him know.

4.

Later that afternoon we met Aphrodite, a woman of about my age. She had a forceful voice and a direct gaze, and she occupied a shop filled with shells and sponges, the front house of what is called a sponge factory.

Aphrodite explained that when the sponge boats arrive in August or September, maybe only five or six these days, her husband chooses the sponges, buying them by dry weight. The thick black layer, the animal's living tissue, has already been cleaned off on deck, but the sponge still needs more cleaning, sometimes bleaching. They use potassium permanganate and a mild solution of hydrochloric acid.

"Doesn't that affect the sponge?"

"Oh, yes, it's not good for it. Makes it not so strong. But you know how it is. Some people don't like the natural color of the sponge." She shrugged. "They want the pale ones. They say it looks cleaner."

The shop was piled to the ceiling with sponges. Some were the original golden brown. Others had been bleached to a lemony yellow, the perfect thing for a curly blond toddler stepping into a Victorian bathtub with a glowing cake of soap. In a sense the bleached sponges were beautiful, and they did look clean. But they no longer smelled of the sea.

"Oh, you know," Aphrodite said, smiling ironically, when I asked why people prefer them. "It's light and bright. What people want."

I mentioned the museums we'd hoped to see and said, "I guess the EU doesn't want to fund culture, so they're closed? Culture's not profitable?"

"Yes, exactly," she said. "And education. Teachers are getting reduced pay, and sometimes even no job. The EU requires a school to have maybe thirty children in a class. But here on the islands, it's sometimes just three or four. Children live far apart, but they still need a teacher."

So far, nobody had spoken directly about the debt crisis in Greece, but we'd met young men with degrees in computer science working as touts outside restaurants or waiting on tables.

"They used to grow many things on the islands," Aphrodite went on. "Food, beautiful things. Not so much here, but on Kos. Now they don't anymore."

"Why is that?" I said.

"It's since we joined the EU. Or maybe it's just that our generation became lazy."

Like Manuel on Symi, Aphrodite had left her island as a child and returned as an adult. Her family had gone to Australia, a popular destination for Kalymnians in search of work after the decline of the sponge industry. But the trope of leaving and returning must always have been part of the islands: people who step into boats and cross the sea, to return home with languages, stories, and international opinions, coming back to the intimacy of a place that is, and is not, home.

I said how glad I was to talk to a woman. I knew that women on Kalymnos had been especially outspoken in protesting the *skafandro*.

"Have you read *Bitter Sea*?" she asked. "Faith Warn's book. It's all in there. I used to have copies in the shop, but they're sold. I could bring you mine from home."

I said that I had, and that the single most extraordinary image for me from the book was the black shawls. Faith Warn tells how, when the bells began ringing to announce the return of the sponge fleet at the end of the season, everyone on Kalymnos would stop what they were doing to run down to the harbor to greet them. If you were the wife of a diver, you'd grab a black shawl, just in case. Nobody knew who would still be on the boat, or whose wife had become a widow.[44]

"Yes," Aphrodite said. "The women are very strong. And it's not just that the men used to go off on the sponge boats in the past. Now lots of the young men still go away. They become seamen, and they're away for many months of the year. It's a way to earn money. So yes, we are strong."

She was quiet for a bit, and then she said, with a wry smile, "But we don't let the men realize it. They still need to feel that, you know, the man is the head of the household. As we say in Greece."

5.

Henrik was in the foyer when we returned to the hotel. He talked about living in Greece, how he'd made the break from a high-stress life in Denmark at the age of forty-five to settle on Kalymnos, and about the rich bastards on their yachts who don't even step off the boat to have a meal in the town.

"The locals call them *skata*," he said. "It means shit. I'm sorry for the word."

Michael gave him a poem he'd written that morning on the ferry:

MOTHER'S DAY FERRY TRANCE
SYMI, KALYMNOS, MAY 14, 2017

In the blue ferry
On the blue water
Rocked in the arms of
A vast blue mother

Right, the rough coastline
A single white lighthouse
Left, the perfect level
Blue, meeting blueness

Steeple of azure
Axis of distance
Dozing, a baby
In the lap of a mother

Mare, Maria, Mother, Marina
Misty the blueness
That blurs all distinction

*Dodekanisos*
Endless Aegean

"It's so, so beautiful," Henrik said. "I'm going to frame it, have it translated into Greek. I'll get my friend to do it."

For a moment we simply stood together in the foyer, held in the intimacy of the poem's spell. Then I remembered that I wanted to ask him about the Syrian refugees who came to the island. How it happened.

"You know, I will never forget this," he said. "Two young girls. They said they were eighteen, but I'm sure they were younger. They arrived with just a plastic bag! I put them in a room, and they closed the door. They just cried and cried. When I knocked to ask if they needed anything, they opened the door just a tiny bit to peer out. They were terrified. I mean, here they were alone with just a man in the hotel. A gay man, but they didn't know that. I said to myself, I'm never going to complain about anything ever again. Afterwards we became friends, of course, but when they left and I asked them where they were going, they just said 'I don't know.'

"There was also an old grandfather," he went on. "All that people had was a plastic bag. In the beginning, I would ask, 'Where is the mother?' But then I learned not to ask. They don't know.

"We started an organization, Hands of Kalymnos, and people would come here with blankets, food, everything. Just opened their hearts. The local people are poor, but they just gave. As a northern European, I know how rich those countries are. And they didn't help. I'm embarrassed. I'm really embarrassed."

We were all close to tears.

"It was 2014 to 2015," Henrik continued, "from autumn 2014 into the spring of the next year. We took them in, of course. I had just come to the hotel, and I literally opened the place. I mean, it was like a movie! They came in little dinghies. In winter! All the people came in here.

"And some terribly sad stories too. Did you know that seventeen children died in the sea? The authorities brought the bodies in in plastic bags. They had to. But what can you say to someone whose child has died?"

The terrifying photograph of the body of a single child, two-year-old Alan Kurdi, washed up on a Turkish beach that September came to mind. The image had traveled around the world, and its publication catalyzed a shift in global responses to the refugee crisis. As his aunt, Tima Kurdi, said of the image, "It was something about that picture. God put the light on that picture to wake up the world."[45]

"I just tried to be friendly," Henrik said. "Talk about ordinary things. And again, everyone in Kalymnos helped."

He said his friend Nika who had a restaurant nearby would come to the hotel every day with a big pot of food. Take care of them.

Then Michael told him about Nikos Vassilaris, whom we'd met on Rhodes, a fellow jeweler who was the last in ten generations of goldsmiths. During the war, before such things became impossible and the whole community was rounded up and sent to Auschwitz, his father rescued Jews from the Nazis. He would set off in his rowing boat at night from somewhere on the island and quietly row people to safety on the Turkish coast. Now the refugees were coming the other way.

Henrik nodded. "I must say, to me, it's uncomprehendible. How people can turn to hating one another. Nazism, ISIS, Trump..."

"It's war," Michael said, and quoted what Benjamin Ferencz, the last Nuremberg prosecutor still alive, had said in a recent interview. "War makes murderers out of otherwise decent people. All wars, and all decent people."[46]

"Yes," Henrik said. "I think it's important to realize that it's a human being that went that way. Maybe they had a good childhood, everything okay, and then they became a Nazi. I don't know what you do about it...I feel—it may sound soft—but I feel you need to give them love."

So many of our conversations in Greece came back to the heart. Michael described to Henrik the young man we'd seen walking on the harbor wall, clearly mentally disabled, and how the older man with him had just stopped and given him a big hug.

"I thought, whatever else, he knows that someone loves him. He's getting love."

"I know him," Henrik said. "There is no support system in Greece for someone like that, but they are accepted and taken care of. In the developed countries, it's all very organized and they put you in an institution."

"You know," I said, "visiting the islands, I keep feeling it, more clearly than usual, that we in the developed world have lost our way."

"Yes," he said. "The developed countries *have* lost their way. I think how rich they are but how poor they are in compassion. The poorer the society, maybe, the more the compassion." And then, after a pause, he said, "It was so vulgar, you know, seeing the rich people sitting in their boats in the harbor, drinking champagne, and the refugees arriving in their dinghies."

6.

Later that evening we met Henrik's friend Nika at her restaurant and toasted our mothers with red wine during a meal of dolmades and halloumi and salads. She was a powerful woman and a formidable cook, and when Michael painted a sea of faces in black ink with his brush-pen on the brown paper tablecloth, she loved it.

"We're going to keep this," she said, coming to our table. "It's something special."

Then he painted the head of Orpheus, a young man with his eyes looking to the side, and beside it the words "Don't look back."

This time Nika simply shook her head in a kind of disbelief.

"You know," she said, "this is what I've been wanting to tattoo on my arm. If I get some money. Don't look back."

All the staff came over to look, and as Nika returned to the front of house, an older woman from the kitchen said quietly to Michael, "This was for Nika. What she needed to read today."

Afterwards we walked out to the edge of the sea. The tide of refugees was over, at least for the moment. But there on the jetty were the shelters the UN had built for them, just meters from the big rich yachts and the old sponge caïque lit up with fairy lights in the dark.

## 7.

Old man Latari was waiting for us the next morning at a table beside Kostas's sponge shop. White hair and beard, he was dressed all in black, and wearing a smart black admiral's cap. I noticed immediately his youthful stance, the lithe strength of his straight back.

Kostas introduced him with the words, "He's eighty-seven years old, and he never takes even one pill. Not like some old people who take handfuls of pills just to live."

Latari laughed.

There was an unmistakable gravitas in his bearing, but he laughed a lot as we talked, with Kostas translating. He had brought a book about the sponge divers in preparation for our meeting and used the photographs as a catalyst for the conversation, which began as soon as we'd sat down.

First, he showed us pictures of divers and captains. "All kaput," he said, with a laugh, waving his hand across the page.

He was born in 1930, he told us.

"What month?" I asked.

"February."

"My mentor was born in the same year, in May," I said. "He's a writer, in America. I'm very happy to meet you."

It was not just his age that reminded me of Gary Snyder. There was something about his beard, his demeanor, his strong spine, his debonair confidence. Both had about them the reckless humor of an old man who is well acquainted with suffering and is looking death in the eye.

Kostas said to me, "Well, Latari is my mentor. He's been sad since his wife died. That's why he wears black."

Then he went on translating. Like all good translators, he put himself aside, so it felt as though Latari and I were talking directly.

At sixteen, he said, he went to work on the sponge boats off the coast of Egypt for five or six months a year. It was 1946, just after the German occupation had ended. After the war there was no food, so he had to leave the island to find work.

"And what did you do on the sponge boats?" I said.

"His job was to watch the diver," Kostas explained. "He

was a pilot, keeping the boat following the diver, staying close to the diver."

"That must have needed a lot of skill. And what did you eat during all that time at sea?"

Latari laughed. I sensed that he was glad of the conversation but knew that whatever he might say would just be words to me. You'd have to have been there.

Later in Cape Town when I was writing up this story, my friend Ari Sitas together with his friend Costas Joakimidis tracked down the account of the Kalymnian sponge fleet by Giánnis Mangklís and helped with translation. The book was recommended to me on the islands, and the glimpse it gave of the *skafandro* days, the hellish conditions of the divers' lives and the horror of their deaths, was terrifying. Mangklís calls the men the Kolasmenoi—the Damned.[47]

"They ate fish," Kostas began, translating. "Salted meat. *Galeta*."

It was yet another name for the tasty hard bread we'd bought at the bakery, slow baked from a tough flour to last six months.

"He says they had to eat the bread, even if it was rotten."

Latari continued paging through the book quickly, stopping at pictures to explain. He showed us a photograph of divers surrounded by giant sponges ("*Spongi, spongi*," he said), a trident used for spearing sponges, a collection of the *skandalopetra* that the naked divers used to sink to the ocean floor, a picture of himself as a younger man, photographs of the different kinds of sponge, and a picture of his grandfather, the man who was eaten by a shark.

"Jonah!" Michael said.

Latari nodded. We all laughed.

"Can you tell us the story of your grandfather?" I asked.

"He had three sisters," Kostas began, translating. "Normally a man had to marry off his sisters before he could get married himself. But he did opposite. He was afraid he was losing his wife, and he married her. His mother—she was angry. It was like cursing him. She said, 'Go and don't come back!' So he went away, and the shark bite him."

"He had scratches all over his body," Kostas went on. "And people said, 'We can make you famous.' Even the king of Greece, Giorgios, he wanted him to make money from it, but he thought it was bad to show his body like that."

"Hold on," I said. "The shark couldn't swallow the *skandalopetra*, so it spat him out with it?" I wanted to hear more about the Great White and the miraculous escape.

"Yes."

"And where did this happen?"

Latari looked in the book. It said the shark swallowed his grandfather off the coast of Tripoli.

"Did your grandfather think it was because of his mother's curse?" I asked.

The story had been told so many times that what I'd imagined to be its moment of highest drama had become less important in the telling than the intricacies of human culture.

"Yes, he thought it was because of his mother's curse. But he wrote a letter to her and said that his wife had no father, so he had to marry her. That's why God saved him."

"And his mother forgave him?"

"Yes, his mother forgave him. And they took salt and water, to make the curse go away."

"It's a wonderful story," I said. "It must be an important story for the whole community."

"No, not the community!" Kostas said emphatically.

The people I met were never hesitant to correct me.

"No," he insisted, "It's a story for the whole of Greece. At that time, the sharks were used to eating human meat. Many divers."

"And your grandfather, when did he die?"

"He died in 1944 or 1945. He died with the Hunger."

On the islands, the memory of the war was always just under the surface. During the occupation of Greece, the Nazi army controlled the distribution of food, and hundreds of thousands of Greeks starved to death. Where they could, people picked wild greens to eat, ate donkey heads, sometimes grass and flowers. Black-and-white photographs from the time show Nazi soldiers looting food from a local store, skeletal children and adults queuing at Red Cross soup kitchens, and the first grain finally arriving on Rhodes in May 1945. As one British officer described it, "The police had to keep the crowds from swarming on to the ships. Even so the starving would eat flour and grain as it spilt from the sacks."[48]

"What a terrible time," I said. "You were just a young teenager."

"Yes. No more dogs and cats on the island! Eat them all!"

Latari laughed heartily as Kostas translated.

Then he started paging through the sponge book again, pointing out pictures of naked divers like his grandfather and of other men wearing the *skafandro*.

"The *skafandro*," I said, "so many people died."

For the first time, Latari simply stopped talking and shook his head. No more laughter. This seemed to reach the heart of it. A silence.

"Oh," he said, and shook his head again.

Then he said something to Kostas, who explained, "The *skafandro*. He says that many men died in his arms."

At first I thought he did not want to talk about it, and that my naive questioning must have transgressed some threshold. But then he paged through the book until he found a picture of two young women veiled in black and seated on either side of a photograph of a young man, flowers in a small vase.

"You see," Kostas said, "he says the divers were buried on the island. So the women had to cry on the photographs."

I'd read about the island. This was not Kalymnos or anywhere inhabited by the living, but an unmonitored place off the coast of Libya known as White Island where the bodies of divers were dumped. It was a desperate place of rocks and white seabirds, littered with white skeletons. A man's comrades who remained alive on board might threaten not to dive unless his body was returned to home soil, but it's said that the captains often found it more convenient and profitable to deposit the dead men on White Island than to make the long trip back home.[49] So, when the sponge boats returned with crew members missing, the women had only photographs.

We were all silent. My own life seemed to have nothing in it with which to respond. Latari wordlessly showed us the cover of his book whose title, *Sfoungári I Tomári*, could be translated as *Either a Sponge or a Body*. In the photograph he wanted us to see, a young man in the joyous pride of youth is being carried off the caïque by his comrades. Raging about exactly this condition, Metrophanes Kalafatas wrote:

> But many beautiful young men are lost,
>    hale and strong as lions.
> They end up beggars, impotent,
>    miserable, awful, they walk the streets.[50]

In the picture on the book cover, the diver's right arm is around one man's shoulder. In his left hand he holds a cane.

His shoelaces are tied, his socks neat, and his legs are being supported, paralyzed from the bends.

"It was a terrible thing," I said.

Latari bowed his head briefly. Then he looked up and said with a firm smile, "Okay."

It was a clear signal that the meeting was over. Through Kostas, I said how wonderful it was to have met him, and he replied that he was happy to have met me too. Then Michael took a picture of us together, we kissed on both cheeks, and he set off to continue his daily walk.

Afterwards Kostas said, "He's my teacher, you know. He

walks past every day. And when the sponge boats come in, he comes with me to tell me what's good to buy. I don't come from a sponge family, so I had to learn from him."

"You're lucky," I said. "He's amazing. So young and strong."

"Yes, he is amazing. He is. He is a good guy."

Our ferry was leaving soon, but I felt some need to explain what I was trying to do.

"It seems to me," I said awkwardly, "that if you look at a sponge, it's like a key to this whole region, the heart of it. The history, the environment, the people. Everything flows through it."

Kostas simply stared at me for a bit, and I was about to try explaining again what I meant. But it was a stare of recognition.

"There's a painting you must see," he said.

"I'd love to, but our ferry is about to leave..."

"No, you must see it."

It was another of those clear instructions: unambiguous, emphatic, and impossible to ignore.

"It's in a taverna in the next street," he explained. "The picture is a dream the painter had, like a vision. It's a painting of a sponge and an angel, and the sponge is giving birth to Kalymnos."

We said goodbye then, with kisses.

"I'm so grateful to have met you," I said.

"Yes," Kostas said, touching his hand to his heart. "Me too. Only mountains can't meet. People can always meet. I love people. Be happy."

8.

The taverna was down a narrow alley, with a couple of men at a table outside.

"*Kalimera*," I said. "Is this the place with the painting of a sponge?"

"Yes, go inside. Please."

The historical artifacts were like others we'd already seen: the photographs of divers and boats, the carefully made model caïque, and even the collection of giant mussel shells, or *Pinna nobilis*, harvested by women divers on Sardinia to obtain sea silk.[51] But the paintings were a portal to another realm.

In the picture Kostas had sent me to find, a massive sponge rests on rocks in the sea in a glorious dream of sea and clouds and wings. A smiling woman or angel or goddess with magnificently long hair rippling down into the water is rising over it on a great white dove with an olive branch in her beak, or perhaps the woman is herself the dove, the dove who is flying above the sponge, while above her head someone holding a lyre, surely Apollo, soars by on a dolphin. In the far distance are the masts of the Kalymnos harbor, but these are tiny, peripheral, and the mystery of the sponge that, as Kostas said, is giving birth to the island, is taking place at sea and radiating into the sky. The mood is serene, even ecstatic, and the entire painting is suffused with a light flooding from the great sponge at the center, as though the object of desire that people would risk their lives to bring home had transcended its materiality as commodity to become a radiant image of the precious, a sort of Grail. It was something I'd intuited, but this was the only time I ever saw it represented: the living sponge at the heart that powered the islands for centuries and is now almost vanished.

Across the room a naked diver with the athletic limbs, sculpted features, and curly hair and beard of a Greek god stood forever gazing at a magically illuminated underwater world alive with sponges, seaweeds, and shipwrecked treasure.

Over his groin he held the white *skandalopetra*, while the rope that ties it to the boat was a fine line of paint reaching up across the canvas into the blue above. In another painting a diver wearing the *skafandro* is harvesting sponges with a knife from an ocean floor alive with fish, starfish, seaweed. And in the last picture a sponge caïque sails happily in a blue sea, white sail aloft in a blue sky dappled with clouds, with the Greek flag flying, blue and white.

Held silent in the midst of this shimmering celebration, I realized how little I knew about sponges or the people who dived for them. The pain and terror and tragedy of the industry were one story, but what about the joy of the dive, the mythic power? The paintings called up a radiant world inside of this one: invisible until you make the voyage.

"These pictures are very wonderful," I said to the man who had spoken to us in English from the small green table where he was sitting outside. "I'm interested in the stories of sponge diving. I'm trying to write something about sponges."

I didn't know what his English was like, so I found myself gesturing with my hands, making the shape of a sponge about the size of a large ostrich egg.

"No, no," he said firmly. "That is not a sponge! *This* is a sponge."

He made a shape in the air like a great round cheese.

"Okay, I understand," I said.

We all laughed.

"Come and sit," he said.

We explained that our ferry would arrive in a few minutes, so we couldn't stay long. But the moment was too rare to lose.

Sitting together at the little green table, we spoke about the paintings and about the sponge at the heart of Kalymnos.

The other man was a weathered old diver who nodded at us but let our new friend do the talking. He told us he'd written a long poem about it all, and when we showed interest he called for a copy from inside the shop. A woman came out with a meticulously produced volume of poetry. In Greek of course.

"It looks beautiful," I said. "Where could I buy one?"

"No, not buy," he said. "I give it to you."

He explained that the first poem in the book was the one about the sponge. I said I'd ask someone to translate it for us and send him a copy. He was glad.

"Have some ouzo!" he said.

We really had to leave soon, but who cared? The woman brought out a glass for us to share and a plate of olives, tomatoes, *kouloures*. It was our first ouzo. He said to sip it.

"You are so kind," I said. "Thank you."

When I told him Michael had written a poem about the Aegean on Mother's Day while we made the ferry crossing, he wanted to read it.

Then he explained, "In English I can understand, but I can't hear the music. So I need to read it in Greek."

"Sure. It's all in the music, isn't it?"

I said we'd try to get him a translation, and he told us his name: Thodoris.

"It means gift from God."

"I think you are our gift from God," I said.

He smiled, and we kissed and said goodbye. It was time for the ferry. As Thodoris remained sitting in his chair, I realized he had only one leg.

## 9.

In performances of the *Mechanikos*, the capacity to turn extreme suffering and disability into a dance gives a richer interpretation to the Kalymnian reputation for toughness than a simple notion of bravado or physical endurance. Once I was able to read it, the fifteen-page poem "ΠΟΪΝΓΚ…" (or "PPOINK"!) by Thodoris Eleftheriou had some of the same quality. I'd sent a scan to Ari Sitas, and soon a generous email came back with his translation.

Ppoink, ppoink, ppoink…There's a ball bouncing from one stanza of the poem to the next, and as the sound of it keeps punctuating the story of the island's history, Thodoris asks a question that doesn't go away either: How did we end up like this? How did I end up aimlessly kicking a plastic ball around by myself under a streetlight at Kalymnos harbor? How did the island lose its ancient and lucrative sponge fleet and become instead a place visited only by cruise boats, tourist boats, and ferries? How did a tough and energetic community become reduced to a spectacle for the globalized gaze? They "are full of curious eyes / And strange languages / they want to take photos of us."

Michael and I were part of it all, of course. Our photographs show Thodoris seated beside me outside the sponge-diving *kafenion*: wooden chairs with grass seats, little wooden table painted green, white tablecloth printed with a map of the island, old stone wall hung with a big wooden fish painted red and blue, a bottle of water on the table, Coke ads on the drinks fridge. The white-haired old diver sharing the table with us is looking away, but Thodoris, cloth-capped and bearded, has his arm around my shoulder.

I realized he'd wanted me to read the poem because it puts sponge diving at the heart of the island's story: the "great danger, sacrifice and honesty" of the naked divers' quest for the black sponge, the maddened shark who head-butted the caïque for a long, long time after Latari's grandfather escaped (afterwards he was known as the Fisheaten), the captains and the people who could afford high-quality ouzo and became rich from the invention of the *skafandro*. The new technology was supposed to be an improvement, Thodoris writes, but all the safety rules were unknown or breached. Part of this was ignorance, but it was also a story of pain and injustice in which unscrupulous captains forced men to dive in all conditions. Yet having written this, he also makes a point of saying that some captains were deeply caring.

As for the divers, he is awed by their epic struggles and imagines the extraordinary qualities of mind and body that their work demanded:

> To dive
> In a peculiar world of weight
> Of power
> Of speed
> With a sense of drunkenness
> Of fear
> Of arrogance
> Of untold power[52]

The poem honors the lyrical force of their lives and the misery their deaths left behind. Thodoris writes that he hopes through his words to save "the lithe body of the diver" from oblivion and to admire the beauty of the island's luckless men.

What he does not do in the poem is answer the question asked near the beginning. How did we end up like this? How did the divers' craft become so diminished? Perhaps the answer is painful to face, entangled as it is with overfishing of the sponge beds that increased so dramatically from the 1860s after the appearance of the *skafandro*, the departure of many spongers to Florida in the early twentieth century, an exodus that escalated after the Italian occupation in 1912, the midcentury appearance of the synthetic sponge, the impact of the massive sponge death that took place in 1986, and the growing and seemingly inexorable currents of international trade.

Instead, having celebrated the divers and retold the tragic tale of lives sacrificed for profit in the name of an ancient heroism, in the last lines of the poem Thodoris remarks that very few seamen are left who can sit sipping coffee and telling stories that recall past glories. These days, he writes, the community is drowned by new problems. In such a condition, "The world is fast and loud / And full of shiny modern things / Cars and new machines." The island fills up with tourists, and with the fraternity of serious rock climbers who in recent years have begun to arrive equipped with special shoes and colorful gear to conquer its cliffs, sprawling like ants across the rocks. If Russ Bernard's research on Kalymnos in the 1960s recorded the tenuous life of a traditional community on the cusp of irreversible change, Thodoris's poem is a quiet witness to the contemporary space the island has since become. The tone is sad, even elegiac. But not entirely so.

Right from the first word, there's a hint of something more. "Ppoink!" The presence of the ball bouncing against the stone wall of the quay throughout the story of the sponge-diving island is playful and ironic—even more so since the ball is a plastic planet Earth!—and it transforms nostalgia into something more present and alert.

"Time has passed on," Thodoris writes towards the end, and the primordial morning is now peopled with modern humans:

> And I can see the rose-fingered dawn
> And a ship coming in to dock
> Pouring out tourists
> Tourists and climbers.[53]

Bitterness, cynicism, despair, anger. These could be obvious responses to the brutal abuse of young men in the name of company profit or the more recent occupations of the island by foreigners. But the point of view towards the end of the poem is more subtle.

Since tourists and climbers have begun visiting Kalymnos, Thodoris writes, "Laughter and joy has returned!" It's an ironic moment. Whose joy? At whose cost? But still, it acknowledges the presence of joy. And though the speaker himself, having told as much of the story as he wishes to share, says he's tired and off to bed, his tale of bewilderment and tragedy and loss in the poem is presented not as melodrama but as a calm and resilient witness to change.

It was an attitude I'd glimpsed in Thodoris himself. When we visited two years later, our friend had passed away. But in the photographs we took that morning, he faces the camera with a gentle mixture of irony and friendliness. And then there were his final words as we set off for the ferry, and he remained seated because of the leg.

"Life goes on," he said, with a nod. "That is the beauty."

# The Felt
PATMOS, 2017

1.

They were golden and desiccated. The thick black outer layer, what was in fact the living body of the animal, had been beaten out, so all that remained was the skeleton. When I gave them water to drink, they soaked it up. This is what sponges do, and I felt forlorn.

The sponges lined up on the windowsill were a reminder that their wondrous porosity, that defining quality so useful to human endeavors and so metaphorically evocative, was just the faintest memory of the breathing animal body of the sponge: inhaling and exhaling, breathing all of the sea, interconnected. It seemed fitting that Ernst Haeckel, who had a special love of calcareous sponges and produced a mass of drawings of these beautiful creatures, should be the first person to coin the word "ecology." In 1866, just three years after Evgenia Mastoridis first put on the *skafandro*, he defined the terms of a new science he called *Oecologie*. By this, he wrote, we mean the whole science of the relations of the organism to the environment including, in the broad sense, all the conditions of existence.[54]

By contrast, the Porifera we had bought from Dinos, Kostas, and Aphrodite were discrete items with names and prices. And they were dead.

It was not the fault of the kind people who sold them to us, or the divers, or even the few remaining sponge bosses. In fact, the idea of fault was too small to make sense of the living mesh of processes that had, over millennia, brought the bath sponges into our hands. And the painful dilemma of their lovely skeletons was not just mine and Michael's, but all of ours, our inextricable entanglement with other beings.

We'd just arrived on Patmos, and it was not just the sponges in our room that I found unsettling. The island was the farthest reach of our journey, the heart of Eastern Orthodox spirituality, and a beloved spiritual destination for people from all over the world. Yet after the radiant sea of Symi and the complex social world of Kalymnos, I was not finding it easy. We were staying in a bed-and-breakfast peopled with gentle humans and rescued cats, and there was a little beach just a few steps away. But the sea was dark and deep with water grasses, the sands were swept with the prevailing winds from Ikaria, and as I watched the crows and the high gulls soaring over the black rocks that edged the beach, songs of grief kept sounding in my head.

Why had we come? I couldn't remember.

Patmos had nothing to do with sponges, and though people had been living on the island since at least the Late Neolithic, its contemporary life all seemed to be constellated around the Revelation of Saint John. The landscape was dominated by the dark fortress of the monks on the hilltop, and when I asked about refugees, our host told me that when they'd landed on the Sacred Island in their makeshift boats, they were sent away at the port. After a couple of days, I realized we'd probably never understand anything about the island until we'd visited the cave up on the hill where the revelation took place. The road sign read "1.5 km to the Apocalypsi." We took the stone path.

Once it was a rock shelter where you could sit and gaze out forever at the sea and the sky. But the mouth of the cave had long since been enclosed by huge stone slabs that turned the place into something dark and sacred: an environment constructed to withdraw the believer's consciousness from the daily world. We arrived early, before the tour bus, and sat quite still. Nobody else was present except the priest with an iconically long white beard and long black gown, walking his rounds, silently checking on us, tending a thousand years of candles and incense, entering and departing from darkness into light, back and forth. Sitting quietly beside the very place where he once lay, John of the lavish visions, around the year AD 95, it felt like being inside an El Greco painting, a smoky darkness lit with candelabras. In the chiaroscuro, a vase of fresh flowers gleamed, the space of the cave was encrusted with sacred art, and the little niche in the rock where the saint put his hand to steady himself when he'd stood up after his dream was plated with silver.

It's known that spiritual vision is a capacity of the human mind, and it may take myriad forms. But what did feel exceptional that morning were the centuries of devotion and power and art that had arisen from John's particular visions. At the same time, sitting in the candlelit silence among the painted record of the fabulous images he'd once seen, I could not help wondering who was there before. Who came to the cave before John lay down one day on the stone floor, prostrate to the voice of God? The site gave shelter from the prevailing winds, a place for solitude and practice where you could make a little fire and look far down into the hills, the bay, the wide beyond. Sitting in its enclosed space, as the priest tracked back and forth, my impulse was to escape. Instead, for half an hour until the next visitors appeared, we sat there drenched in ancient holiness. Outside in the blue daylight beyond the tiny window, a rooster crowed, sparrows chattered, and there must have been swallows tracking across the sky.

Afterwards I found the textiles. Among the dense assemblage of icons, amulets, holy words, and Orders of the Sultan written in black ink on thick parchment in the nearby museum of the Monastery of Saint John the Theologian, was a collection of fabrics whose intimacy and vividness made me weep. Fragments of Coptic tunic bands woven like tiny kilims and preserved for fifteen hundred years in a desert grave, cloth of gold embroidered with the finest stitching of pink roses and leaves, great vestments sewn with golden babies and angels, the palest creamy silk embroidered with green leaves and gold, red velvets stitched in gold thread with wheat and flowers, bells around the hem, and at the heart a depiction of Jesus and Mary, their robes encrusted with tiny pearls.

That night I dreamed of felt. On our walk up the donkey path to the Apocalypsi, a piece of white sheep's wool had snagged among the stones. Now in sleep, the dream turned the wool into felt, and the felt became an image of religious belief. The idea of personal belief, the dream said, was a delusion. Like a single thread of sheep's wool that is nothing much on its own. Instead, the way belief takes form in a community like Patmos or any of the other islands is more like felt: a mass of threads, interwoven with all the other threads by time and repetition to make that meshed fabric of practices we call religion.

In the dream, the friendly old woman down the road with

dementia and a tiny church in her garden, the clinic on the way to the Apocalypsi with its shrine cluttered with saints and remedies where Michael was given a free antibiotic for an abscess, the young woman who walked out of her hardware store to unlock the tiny baptistry for us at the edge of the sea where Saint John had baptized the first people on the island, the way she kissed each saint's picture before locking it again, the taxi driver who crossed himself whenever he passed a shrine... In the dream they were all meshed in the island's deep felt of incense, monks, robes, texts, golden candelabras, the cave itself, the tenderness of embroidered vestments, and somewhere perhaps even the living traces of the old gods.

2.

Once properly awake, I wondered if the mesh of felt could be an image of entrapment. But in the dream it was a web, a sentient network, a mind. And over the next few days, we met three women who each instructed me in the ways of threads and paths, the living mesh.

Katerina Mourati was the friend of a friend, an artist with the air of a high priestess, a cosmopolitan person whose work had been exhibited around the world and who had in recent years returned to live on the island where she was born. Her shop was a little art studio up in Chora, the old village on the hill, where for centuries people had built their whitewashed houses in a meandering maze of cobbled streets clustered around the monastery. In those days the spiritual function of the structure was reinforced by its great oven, which had ample space for the villagers to bake their bread, and by the massive stone walls, which gave refuge to the community when pirates raided the island.

"You feel it's a sort of oppressive presence that dominates the island, don't you?" Katerina said with a smile.

I'd not said anything, but she knew.

"In fact," she said, "the monks are very open-minded, very spiritual. I've never been a member of *any* specific religion or political party, but some of them are my friends. We have good conversations."

"It's a contemplative practice?"

"Yes."

She explained that the heart mode of prayer in Greek Orthodox practice (*kardiaki*) was a lot like Buddhist meditation, a mantra that goes around and around in the mind.

The morning sun began to pour in through the open door, and she showed us her art: great bright swirling pictures made of her own past work that she'd cut and torn up and reassembled with words and fragments, magic sculptures made of colored threads, arteries of pain and joy, nerves of woven string, networks, networks. In conversation with the sunlight it lit up the shop.

"So, it's spiritual environments that you're making here, isn't it?" I said.

"Yes, that's it. The net."

When we said we'd been to Symi and would be returning on our way back, she nodded. "Symi and Patmos, these are the most beautiful islands."

"Oh," I said, "do you think so?"

"No," she said emphatically. "It's not that I think so! That's how it is."

The other two women we met were mother and daughter. Despoina Vakratsi was a writer and theater person. I'd tracked her down after reading her book, *Footpaths of Patmos*, which is many things at once: a practical walker's guide to the network of old paths that thread across the island, a reminder of premodern modes of inhabiting its different regions, a witness to the diverse plants and animals that remain, and an imaginative contemplation of place.[55]

Despoina had agreed to meet one evening in the shop down near the harbor where her daughter Ariadne sold embroidered cloths from India and one-off designer garments from Greece. Like so many women on the islands, both mother and daughter wore black. They also had black hair. The idea was that Ariadne's role was to translate our conversation, but over the hours we spent together things became a little more entangled. It turned out that Despoina could, in fact, speak English, and that Ariadne did not always share the opinions she was being asked to translate.

"She had a passion for it," she said, as we began by talking about her mother's writing. "My mother spent seven years gathering stories from Patmos. Stories for the people and from the people. We couldn't do anything with her! Not even talk!"

"And the book about paths?"

"It's part of it," she said, "a piece of a bigger book. The paths...became the stories of roads, small churches, flowers..."

"Yes, I understand," I said. "You start with a particular thing, a place, a path, and it opens out into everything. And the old paths, why is it so important to make them known?"

"It's our history!" Despoina said fervently in English.

"The small roads are vanishing," Ariadne explained. "Nobody walks there. You see, archaeology came to the island. Patmos is protected and controlled by UNESCO, but they haven't done big research. The original path to the Apocalypsi—it's gone."

"Some of the paths must be very, very old," I said. "People have been walking them for thousands of years. What changed?"

I was expecting to hear through Ariadne some sort of general answer to do with modernity. But once again Despoina responded, and what she said was very specific.

"It all changed in 1960."

"What happened then?"

"The cruise boats."

"And globalization?" Michael said. "The container ships. A supermarket where you can buy whatever you want to eat."

"Yes."

He asked Despoina the same question we'd raised on Symi about cultivation. "When I look at the hills here on Patmos, many of the slopes are terraced. So many stone walls and terraces on the island. They were cultivating it all in the past, but now most of the terraces have been abandoned and the hills look wild. What happened?"

The two women talked back and forth to each other for quite some time, without much translation. Once again, as on Symi, it seemed especially difficult to speak about the agricultural past.

Finally, translating for her mother, Ariadne said, "For a long time, people were going out from Patmos and coming back with language, food, and culture from other places. It was very rich. Patmos is a very old place, very important as a port. There were really rich people here."

"And therefore very poor people too?" I asked.

"Yes, of course. Poor."

She then went on to explain that during the Italian occupation, which began in 1912, many people left, and cultivation stopped.

"I see," I said.

"After 1960, it stopped completely," Despoina added.

"Okay, that was with the cruise boats," I said. "The same with the paths. So, in your book you write about walking on paths that go past what used to be orchards. Places where you used to pick fruit as a child. Something I've wondered about during this visit is that we've seen quite a lot of fruit on the trees, and people are not picking it. What is that about?"

"Yes," Ariadne said. "It is like that. But now with the Crisis, if people have a small land they use it. Growing vegetables."

The Greek financial crisis was present as a shadow to many of our conversations, but nobody so far had spoken of it directly or for long. Instead, Despoina had Ariadne tell us about a group of women who had asked her to take them walking on the old paths.

"It sounds wonderful," I said. "Can you tell us more about women? I believe they're a powerful presence in the community."

Despoina was pleased to be asked. "Yes," she said. "This is a very interesting question. It's very important to me."

"You know," Ariadne explained, "Living on an island, you have to make your own decisions. I've lived in Athens and here on Patmos. Here there are only three boats out per week. So living on an island makes you strong. Autonomous. Okay, so women are very strong in all Dodecanese. The Aegean islands and Crete are not patriarchal but matriarchal. Even now. Even from the ancient times. Even the first people living in the ground we now call Greece, they were worshipping the Great Mother."

Despoina would not have put it this way, but mother and daughter both enjoyed the story Michael then told of a meeting we'd recently attended in Cape Town, where Nesrin

Abdullah, the commander of the YPJ, the Kurdish Women's army fighting ISIS/Da'esh in Syria, had said to a room full of activists: "After five thousand years, we are bringing back the Goddess."

"And ecology?" I asked, "Is the *Footpaths* book a way of raising awareness about ecology?"

"Of course!" Despoina said.

I said that I'd read the Greek Orthodox Ecumenical Patriarch Bartholomew's decree that harming the environment is a sin.

"He's sometimes called the Green Patriarch, I believe. Do you think this way of seeing is having an impact on Patmos?"

"It's slow," she said. "We are trying to recycle."

"I understand. My sense is that…your book wants to wake people up to the living world. So many creatures and plants."

"Yes."

"But from the outside, it seems there's a lot of work to be done. People wasting water, treating animals badly." I was hesitant to say this, hyperconscious of being a visitor who had flown in to Greece from the other side of the planet.

"Oh, yes," Ariadne said. "I think the older people are more cruel to animals. But it's not just about age. My grandmother never had animals in the house, but she was not cruel."

This seemed to be the reminder Despoina needed to go home and check on her mother, but Ariadne was glad to stay and talk. She spoke about her life, her shop, her aspirations.

When we asked what she would do on Patmos if she were us, she thought a bit and then said, "You know, I love getting lost in the old streets of Chora. Just getting lost. It's a labyrinth."

"Oh, but you must!" I said. "You are Ariadne."

We laughed. Then she talked about how she was studying ancient Greek culture through the Open University, and about all the Ariadnes now living on Crete. I had the strongest sense that in her experience the old myths were alive and well.

"Where are you staying?" she asked, as we were leaving.

"Near Merika Bay," I said, adding vaguely, "It's different."

"Oh, I know," she said at once. "It's melancholic. The sea is different there. The color. And it's somehow heavier. And the winds. It's melancholic. I lived there for two years. I had to move."

Melancholic! No wonder I'd been singing sad songs. I thanked her for the word and we said goodbye. It felt as though she'd slipped me a ball of thread.

3.

The black rocks, the black crows, the slate-gray waters, the tangled water grasses, the restless winds.

Like Ariadne I found Merika Bay intense, and our stay there had opened up a well of inconsolable grief. But after she had given me a name for it, the island began to reveal itself as a landscape of many moods and qualities, highly charged, a realm whose ancient gods of cove and rock and tree had never quite been eradicated, either by the saints that came to supplant them when John began casting out demons and baptizing believers, or even now by the new gods that arrived with the cruise ships.

Then one day I dived into the dark. Beyond our melancholic beach was a cavern you'd only be able to reach on days of relative calm. There was something enigmatic about it. So, on a quiet afternoon I put on goggles and flippers and swam out, wading through the water grasses and into the cold unwelcoming sea.

And there they were: families of sponges living on the rocks. My fingers touched the springy tough skin of their bodies, which felt like sentient rubber. The sponges were alive. They were black as ink. The waters of the cavern were dark and chilly, and I felt astonished to have encountered them: native inhabitants of that region of the porous in-between that endures outside of all our attempts to categorize it.

For the rest of our visit, whenever the sea was gentle enough, and for as long as the temperature of the water would allow, I'd return to swim among the ancient ones, diving into clouds of tiny fish, seaweeds, and white sea flowers, the dark rocks marked with mauve and orange and red lichens. A crab appeared, and sea snails, and we'd all flow under the wave that was rocking through the cavern, rocking the fish back and forth, rocking my body, slapping us all up against the rocks, drawing blood. Is the sponge an animal or a plant? Stationary or mobile? Male or female? Form or space? Their home reached far into the rock and ended in darkness. It was deep with sponges, deep beds of black ink bodies, breathing the sea in and out, ingesting tiny plankton, filtering, filtering.

Luminous blue beaches are easy to love, and the black rocks of a jagged cavern can tear your skin. But calling the place melancholic was a kind of gateway, a recognition of the inconsolable, and a bow to the old gods as a matter of etiquette and humility. When you dive into the cold waves beyond the beach where the rocks are deep with inky sponges, their plantlike animal bodies interpenetrate form and space, being and nonbeing. Perhaps sponges are our ancestors. Perhaps they are ourselves. But who or what they are exists in a place before words, where our categories become irrelevant and our notions of identity simply give up.

Before male or female, plant or animal, sadness or joy,

the families of ink-black sponge are older than all the gods: breathing in the living sea, breathing it out.

4.

The day after that first dive into the sponge-dark cavern we met Sarandis, he of the white mustache and generous smile who sang and played five different stringed instruments without having been taught, and who for many years traveled everywhere around the world as a ship's engineer until one evening in some random café in Brazil he was called back to Patmos by a photograph of his mother's house on a tourist poster and left for home the next day, to arrive at the Arion Café in the harbor at Skala where on his first night back he met a woman who happened to be visiting the island briefly from France and became his wife.

"After four hours, that was it," he told us. "Boom! I met my wife. Right here in this café where we're sitting."

"It makes you see how one could believe in the Greek myths," Michael said. "That the gods guide your fate."

"I believe it," he said.

It was a morning brimming with light from the sea. We sat at one of the Arion's outdoor tables and talked about the violin, the lute, the bouzouki, the sazi, the quarter-tone intervals of the old Orphic sound, and about what happens when you improvise.

"What we have comes from the heart," Sarandis said, generously including me because I also like to sing and to improvise.

"Yes! It's not about a performance, or about you at all, is it?" I said. "It's about opening your heart to the hearts of the people listening. The task is to become transparent to the music. To let it speak."

"Yes. That's just how it is."

Sarandis was a maker of things as well as music, and he and Michael had much to say about their work with hand tools, and about what is lost to the craft when everything is computerized and 3D printed.

"I don't like it," Sarandis said. "I want to *make* my mistakes. I want to make my mistakes."

When I explained that I was writing about sponges, he said, "Well, then, you must meet Lefteris. He used to be a sponge diver from Kalymnos. He is also a musician."

It was another clear injunction: you must meet Lefteris. Sarandis said we'd find him in the workshop at the Diakofti shipyard and agreed to meet us there that afternoon.

5.

It was a small collection of buildings on the azure side of the island, not far from the site of Aphrodite's shrine, where the long lineage of Aegean shipbuilding was alive and well. Near the jetty we found Sarandis inspecting the workmanship of a young man who was following his instructions in painting and sanding the hull of his sailing boat. The winds were still and the sea was the bluest blue I'd ever seen.

Sarandis was completely absorbed in boats. He took time showing us the details of his, which was clinker-built without a single nail or bolt. Teak beams, over a hundred years old, Norwegian. Then he pointed to the boat resting beside his at the edge of the water: "If you are in the mentality of shape and stability, and all that," he said, "this white one has perfect shape."

In the warehouse he showed us the great wooden vessels standing silently among piles of timber. They were painted, sanded, almost ready. I thought of the graceful sponge caïques, built for the six-month voyage to North Africa.

"They build them from zero," he explained. "And you know, the carpenters will not follow the orders of the owners! They follow what they feel. Their hearts. The main idea to build a boat is to start with a plan, but really they follow their hearts. Sometimes they have papers, but mostly it's models, pieces of wood. They make lines on the ground, and you won't understand those lines. They will look crazy to you."

A young man with a long golden ponytail was sanding a tall mast of Oregon pine with such complete concentration that our watching presence seemed quite irrelevant to him.

"He's my carpenter," Sarandis said.

"It's beautiful," I said.

"Yes. He's beautiful too." And then, touching his heart, he said, "My heart carpenter."

He led us through a great ecosystem of workshops filled with pieces of boats and all the tools and timber of the ancient craft to arrive at last at the place where a big man in blue overalls and a little hat was grinding a hole for a bellpull and making the wooden frame for three huge church bells.

Lefteris straightened up and looked me directly in the eye. Then he took my hand and smiled.

When Sarandis told him I was writing about sponge diving, he laughed. "Tell her it's a very different thing to write about it and actually to do it."

He stopped what he was doing then to talk, speaking to me directly with big gestures and without waiting for translation, while Sarandis followed on with a few words in English as best he could. Lefteris was a tall man with a strong back, the clearest blue eyes, and a great open chest.

"His cardio got to pump very strongly," Sarandis explained, "Because of the diving. He says that when you stop diving, it's like an amputation."

"Wow," I said.

"Yes."

Now at seventy-seven, Lefteris the sponge diver worked all day as a carpenter. I took off Michael's silver pendant that I was wearing to show him that he also knew about hand tools.

"He does very fine work," he said. "We do big rough work."

Everyone laughed.

While he finished what he was doing, the three of us went to sit at an outside table at the taverna and watch the men painting their boats and a woman negotiating with one of the fishermen over an octopus.

"This sea right here is just so incredibly beautiful," I said to Sarandis.

He shook his head and smiled. "I'm telling you, I've been everywhere, on the boats. This water. There is nothing like it. Anywhere."

"I feel as though there's some sort of special healing quality in this particular wavelength of turquoise. Something that goes right into your brain and makes you feel restored."

"Yes."

Then Lefteris appeared from the workshop to join us. He was laughing.

"This guy is crazy," Sarandis laughed too as Lefteris sat down. "I think he'll live a long time because he's crazy."

Lefteris laughed even more at that, drilling his index finger into his temple and then pointing at Sarandis. He ordered a chocolate milkshake.

"It's his nephew's place," Sarandis said. "He doesn't pay."

"He's wonderful," I said.

"Oh yes, you don't get people like this now."

A great dark bird flew over our heads. It was an eagle, Sarandis said. No big deal.

Then Lefteris began to talk. He talked and talked in Greek without a pause about sponge diving, with Sarandis translating as much as possible.

They'd only have one sardine with a little olive oil and a *galeta* in the morning, he explained, before going out to dive. Just a sip of water. You can't eat too much before you dive. Each man did three dives a day—by then it was scuba—with a two-hour break in between. At the end of a season they'd come back to Kalymnos with five to six tons of sponge.

"That's a lot," I said. "How many in a day?"

"Fifteen to twenty kilograms per diver, once they'd been cleaned."

One time near Kríti, Lefteris said, the captain told him to make a dive, and he went down to 55 meters and only came up with one small sponge. He was nervous about that, but later, sailing near the coast, he suddenly knew exactly where to dive. "I'll go there!" he said. Underwater he found many, many sponges. It was only 18 meters deep, but they were very good quality, and for two and a half months they all worked the area, filling the boat.

I asked if they could have gone back to the same place in a couple of years, hoping, I suppose, to hear that the harvest was sustainable. But the question was lost in translation, and Lefteris kept on speaking. He spoke and spoke, and his words made long, musical sentences, as though somehow if he spoke directly to me in Greek, talking and laughing a lot, gesturing with his hands, his eyes the color of the sea gazing into mine, I would understand. I tuned all my senses to listen.

"*Spongi spongi!*" he said, gesturing with his arms the shape of a huge sponge the size of a great tortoise. This was the quality they were getting.

Then he turned to Michael, tenderly calling him "Mihalis, Mik-i," laughing and patting his hand, and saying something about Patmos and erotica.

"He's warning him about the island," Sarandis explained. "That he may fall under its erotic spell."

We all laughed.

Then Lefteris told us how he dived from the age of thirty-five to forty-five, fifteen of them living on the boat.

"Working together like that, you must have all been comrades?" I said.

"*Ne ne!*" he said emphatically. "Yes! You can't be in a boat like that with people and fight."

Inevitably, the conversation turned to the *skafandro*. It was just before his time, Lefteris said, but in those days, fifteen men would set out in the spring, and only eight returned home.

He laughed. Sarandis translated: "If they got sick, they would put them in a sack and go down with a stone."

By the time he was diving, Satan's Machine was obsolete. But it was still six months at sea each year, and each time he came home, the children had grown bigger. Finally, he stopped and became a carpenter.

"The diving doesn't just paralyze you," Sarandis explained. "You start getting pains in your joints and your back. That's when he decided to stop."

It sounded like a sensible decision, but Lefteris was looking wistful.

"He says his memories from the time he was diving—that's what keeps him alive."

Lefteris smiled and continued to speak in an uninterrupted stream. His words sounded like poetry, and I could discern from the intonation that he was back in a vivid underworld of *spongi*, fish, lobsters. A rippling forest of color and form.

Sarandis simply summarized: "It was paradise."

Lefteris nodded.

"Before the pollution of the sea," he went on. "Before Chernobyl."

At that word, Lefteris pulled a face, grimacing as though he was smelling something rotten. But in a moment, he was back in the glimmering memory of the deep.

"He says it was really life," Sarandis said.

So much was taking place in the conversation that after a while I simply gave over to listening to Lefteris's voice. The long musical flow of words, waters, islands.

"What's he saying now?" I said at some point.

Lefteris had become simultaneously humorous and mournful, and Sarandis responded to him quite firmly, then turned to me to explain. "I say to him, we must not be so pessimistic. Why? Because, okay, we are not so well. But we are alive. Others are not."

Lefteris said that when he was younger, much older people would tell him, "As you are now, we once were. As we are now, you will be too."

"He was not understanding the meaning then," Sarandis said. "But now he understands very well."

"That's really old," Michael said. "It's what the dead say to Orpheus."

A while back, he had written a cycle of poems inspired by the Orphic texts in the Derveni Papyrus, a scroll burned in a funeral pyre around 340 BCE that was found in a nobleman's grave near Thessaloniki in the 1960s and painstakingly reconstructed to assemble what is now Europe's oldest surviving manuscript. As he mentioned it, the thought felt significant, but the conversation with Lefteris had already rolled on.

"He says his life was very good," Sarandis said. "He was satisfied with his life. The life he lives."

Living and dying together beside the limitless blue, sitting together at the taverna, it felt like a perfect day. Lefteris recited to me the words of a song while Sarandis translated:

> I would like to build a boat to travel around the islands,
> And I will take you around with me.
> I will take you to many islands and you will be the captain.
> But when we arrive in Patmos, I will be the captain.
> In the night with the moon, you will be the captain.

"He was working as a musician for many years," Sarandis said. "In this area, there are thousands of songs about the sea and about love."

Next was a love song the sponge divers would sing as they were leaving Kalymnos harbor.

"It is very hard," Sarandis explained, "the time of separation when they leave the port."

Lefteris uttered the old words tenderly, blue eyes looking out to the sea.

> When you say goodbye, you get dizzy
> And the welcome is a great pleasure.
> The engine that is giving air to the diver, it is like my mother
> And the wheel they are turning, it is like my sister
> The guy who is receiving the messages from the rope

# The Felt

My life is depending on him.
For you, I am wearing the *skafandro*
For you, I am carrying the pipes for the air,
For you, I am wearing the metal shoes.

When the song was done, Sarandis left us to go and work on his boat.

At first I felt stranded without our translator, but as Lefteris just kept on talking I realized he was naming the different islands and speaking about their music, and I joined in saying the names together: Patmos, Symi, Ikaria, Naxos, Kalymnos, Rodos, Lipsi. I asked him to sing one of the songs for me, but he said he couldn't sing without his instruments. I sang an Irish love song for him called "The Singing Bird" instead. He smiled and clapped, and then he took my notebook and wrote his full name on the back page: Elefterios. The one who is free. Then he drew a picture of a sailing boat with the words "Julia Patmos" inscribed on the prow.

The eagle appeared again, and when Sarandis returned, we were all smiling.

"You see," he said, "sometimes life can be very simple."

## 6.

On an island where all roads lead to the ornate cave of John's Revelation, the shrine of the goddess is not much signposted. But the big rock called Petra or Kalikatsou is still marked on tourist maps, and the site that some people call Aphrodite's temple can be found in a network of caves down there at the coast near the Diakofti shipyard where we met Lefteris. The place is out of sight of the monastery on the hill, and when you climb the small rough steps hewn in the rock, pulling yourself up to sit facing the dawn as it lightens over the Aegean, there is only stone and sky and bluest sea, a few quiet marks of human work that might reach back to the Neolithic, and a little wax from a recent candle.

If Merika Bay was melancholic, then Aphrodite's realm on the other side of the island was palpably ecstatic. After meeting Lefteris we kept returning to her azure shore between Diakofti and Petra to swim or walk or simply to sit under a tamarisk tree listening to the voices of baby goats crying on the abandoned terraces of the islet across the water. After the goat, the desert, as they say, and you could see the line of their destruction even at that distance: green plants on one side of the wall, bare hillside on the other. At first I wanted the sea to remain forever the same limpid perfection we'd seen that first afternoon. But over the days, as the wind stirred up the waves and the waters darkened, I began to understand what Eleftheria had said to me on Rhodes at the beginning of our journey: you *can* be attached to the sea, because it's always changing.

It was on one such windy morning that we were driven away from the beach to the relative shelter of the taverna at Diakofti. Men were building and repairing boats near the water, and for a while Sarandis's blond heart carpenter stood talking at the quay.

"I feel as though I'm in a dream," Michael said. "Only in dreams can you go back to childhood. Being here is like going down to the harbor with my dad when I was a boy."

We both felt a sense of relaxed and focused workfulness about the place, a sense of focus without stress.

"There's none of that hopelessness you often see with workers at home," he went on. "If you're building something from your heart, as Sarandis says they do, then surely it's better?"

We were just getting up to leave when Lefteris appeared.

"Mikey!" he called, and came over to join us in his blue overalls and small hat.

This time there was nobody to translate, but Lefteris insisted that we stay and have something to drink with him. When I said I'd like chamomile, he snorted and fetched me a can of iced tea from his nephew's place and one for himself. Mine was peach flavor and he had lemon. I took out a nectarine from my bag.

"*Mandarina!*"

This set us off on an exploration of fruit. He asked what fruit we have in Afriki, and so with pictures and gestures he and I began talking about bananas, pineapples, and strawberries, and how on Patmos they grew prickly pears, lemons, mandarins. And grapes? I drew a picture. I knew there used to be vineyards on the island. Many, in fact, and some still remain.

"*Ne ne ne!*"

"And they were growing here?" I asked.

I pointed to the abandoned terraces on the hills around us, our recurrent question. I knew that Grikos, not far away, used to be an important wine-growing area. I drew a wine bottle.

"*Ne!*" Lefteris said.

I showed him a picture on my phone of our twins and explained that we were mama and papa. He was pleased. Then I found a photograph of Sophie running ("*Athletika,*" he said, "*bella*"), and told him Sky was a *musiki*, like Lefteris himself. He smiled. When I asked about his children he said he had four, *tessera*, and named them, holding up four fingers. So, I asked him to teach me to count, and we said the names for the numbers: *éna, dío, tría, tésera*. Next I drew a little house and asked him where he lived. This led to an extended explanation of a neighborhood somewhere beyond Kampo. I took out a map and he showed me exactly. Looking at the map together, we spoke about places where you can swim. I showed him my goggles and flippers and said I'd been swimming near Petra. Did he still swim?

"*Ne.*"

On the back of the map were pictures of tourist sites. I'd heard from Sarandis that one of Lefteris's sons had been involved in reconstructing the old mills up on the hill. I asked him about it, and he said it was Jorge, and mimed grinding flour.

"*Pano?*" I asked.

"*Ne.*"

"*Fourno?*"

"*Ne.*" Then he pointed to specific places on the map and started talking about Vesuvio, miming eruptions and shaking the table.

After quite some time, Michael thought of asking Google Translate on his phone for a sentence. He typed in the few words he wanted to say and showed the translation to Lefteris: "μπορούμε να καταλάβουμε χωρίς λόγια!"

"*Ne!*" Lefteris said, very emphatically. He smiled.

In English it said, "we can understand without words!"

Afterwards I thought of it as a jam session. You keep trying things out, and it's all about the relating. Communication rather than content, just staying open. For over an hour Lefteris and I talked with no translator present, except towards the end, some suggestions from Google. For the rest, we were on our own: playing, improvising, surfing the wave of the interaction, wherever it led. The force of our mutual fondness was enough to make it work. Fruit, children, volcanoes, swimming.

## 6.

Two nights before we left Patmos it began to rain and the island was wracked by a storm powerful enough to call up that sky which is the realm of Zeus who hurls lightning to the earth from his great hand. Michael found a picture where the bolt he is holding is a perfect *dorje*, the same thunderbolt of diamond clarity that traveled to India and beyond.

The next morning at breakfast we talked about it with our fellow visitors at the guesthouse, some of whom were Greek. I asked whether anyone thought that over time there may have been an etymological slide from the name of Zeus to Theos. Nobody knew, but Michael said that by the end of the Orphic period, Zeus was already being acknowledged as the name of a single God. Early monotheism.

"The other gods wouldn't agree with that," said Herbert, an urbane and sensitive man who spoke many languages, worked at the heart of the EU in Brussels, and came to Patmos every year for a complete break, walking alone in the hills.

Everyone laughed, and the conversation moved elsewhere.

After breakfast Michael and I walked up the donkey track for a last meander in Chora, getting lost in the mesh of Ariadne's labyrinthine streets. As we started to climb the hill, rain and thunder began lashing the island once again. We joked about how unfortunate it would be to get struck by Zeus on your last day on Patmos, but by the time we reached the village, the sun was shining on a world washed clean: blue window frames, white walls smoothed over stone, the round belly of an oven extending from a wall, a pink rose bush in lovely bloom, a few cats stretched in the sun and, at the end of a narrow street, a tiny inert scrap of wet fur and ears.

There were so many cats on Patmos, many of them stray, but our friends at the guesthouse loved them relentlessly. They had helped organize a regular sterilization program, they constantly took on cats in need and found new homes for them in Europe, they tried to save cats that had been poisoned, and when I found a black-and-white kitten lost in the nearby reeds, they rescued him and brought him to live in their house. But this tiny cat in Chora had drowned alone in the storm. The mother sat close by, gazing.

At breakfast the next morning, Herbert said, "I don't think Zeus liked us talking about him. All that thunder and lightning."

We laughed. "I think you're right," I said.

Later, on the long ferry trip back to Symi, Michael and I found him standing alone on the prow of the ship. We joined him for a while to watch the sea in silence, and in the last moments of the trip, just as we were passing through the narrowest and shallowest strait between Symi and the islet of Nimos, where the water is brightest turquoise and the skipper of the ferry must use all his skill to navigate the great boat through, Herbert told us what had happened the previous day.

"I was out hiking yesterday when the rain came," he said.

"Lots of rain?" I said.

"Yes. But more than that. The lightning. I had to cling to a rock, try and get under it. The lightning came very close, right past me."

"Wow!"

"The next one…" He seemed almost apologetic. "I'm afraid it hit me. I lost consciousness. When I woke up again, I was shaking all over and half of my body was paralyzed."

"*What?*" I said. "That's astonishing."

"I know. As I said, I don't think Zeus liked us talking about him."

"And then?"

"Well, gradually I was able to move. I think perhaps it hit the rock and then traveled into me."

"And how did you get back?"

"Pretty slowly. It was an hour and a half to reach the road. You can imagine! If I had stayed paralyzed, it would have been tough to get back. Crawling. And in the rain."

In the distance the painted Yialos harbor came into view. Returning to its sanctuary felt like coming home, and already the irreducible mystery of Patmos was settling into story. But it wasn't quite over yet.

"And now?" I asked.

"Well, it burned through my clothes," Herbert said. "My jacket, my shirt, right through to…my bum. And my side, it feels a bit stiff. But I'm fine."

# The Blue
SYMI, 2017

I.

Manuel was cleaning a sponge when we found him. He'd painted a piece of the harbor wall blue while we were away, a particular shade with a bit of violet in it. His cousin told me it was the quintessential blue of Symi, but Manuel shook his head and laughed and said it was just blue. Then he turned back to the sponge in his hands.

"I don't like doing this," he said, "but it's for my friend." He said an Italian guy he knew had found the sponge when he was diving around the bay beyond the cove.

"So this is something unusual?" I asked.

"Yes. Very!"

The sponge was black, and he was washing it in the sea. Over and over, squeezing and scrubbing and rinsing out. It's what you have to do with a sponge if you want to use it. Clear out the living animal. Reduce the breathing rubbery living being to a dry skeleton. On the sponge boats they'd do it on deck, treading the sponge with their feet and beating it out.

"And you feel bad about doing it?"

"Yes, I feel bad. But my friend didn't know. I'm doing it for him. He didn't know. It will take a few days. It's something between a plant and an animal. You know that?"

"Yes."

"See, it's dying now," he went on. "This milk that I'm squeezing out, this is its milk. It's toxic. So the fish won't eat them. It will burn your skin if you don't wash it out."

The sea gleamed metal in the late light, in the most beautiful harbor in all of Greece, and Manuel explained that it was a wild sponge, not a high-quality bath sponge like the ones in the shops. His brown hands continued to squeeze and scrub.

"When sponges reproduce, they squirt out white stuff like this milk, and it makes more sponges," he explained. "They can farm them too these days. Cut one like this up into squares, keep them under water, and they start to grow again."

A young boy came over to watch. He lived on the island but had never seen a sponge being cleaned before and was full of questions.

"Will it sting me? Is it dead? When will you be finished?"

Manuel answered him gently, translating for us every now and then. For a long time we remained together on the blue harbor wall, rapt in the quality of the evening and the action of Manuel's hands. It was poignant and reluctant work, and he seemed glad of company.

"You wouldn't cut them like this," he said again. "But he didn't know. You'd leave something to grow back."

His ancestral heritage in sponge fishing meant he knew what to do. And he was doing it for his friend. But he felt quite acutely the hurt of the living creature in his hands, even as he was rinsing it out.

"Look, it's dying now," he would say every so often. "You can see it."

The evening light rippled in the water as the sun tipped behind the horizon.

"Do you still see the beauty, Manuel?" I asked. "For us, the island is inexpressibly beautiful."

"You know," he said, "sometimes I feel like a bird in a gilded cage when I'm here. But it's a perfect place for a childhood. Really. You all run around together, and people are kind. At anyone's house, the mother or the grandmother always makes sure you can't leave without being fed. We used to swim naked, and I had a little boat. I was only six. At some point, as you grow up, you do have to leave. But in the beginning, it's perfect. Safe and free."

He was looking tenderly at the little boy, smiling.

"So anyway, you leave. And then you come back. Well, I did. Many people do. Being back on the island, I've come to feel…my connection with nature much more. In the winter I walk in the mountains a lot."

The sponge cleaning was done for the day, and Manuel got up to leave. Then, as an afterthought, he said, "You must go to Panormitis. It's nice. And, you know, I'm not religious, but many people have experienced miracles. Actual healings of different ailments."

2.

The minibus trip to the Monastery of Panormitis took a winding road over mountains of rock and mist, ravines whose dense conifers recalled the island's forgotten trees from a time before shipbuilding. It was raining softly when we arrived, the water in the tranquil harbor a milky blue-green shadowed by cloud. Our little busload were the only visitors: two other tourists like us and a couple of Greek women carrying pots of sweet basil and a red hibiscus.

Inside the Byzantine sanctuary of Saint Michael, we joined the other pilgrims lighting candles before the mighty archangel whose suit of armor was beaten out of silver by the ancestor of our jeweler friend Nikos on Rhodes. Beside us the faithful sank to their knees before it, weeping among the offerings of green herbs and red flowers and beeswax tapers, praying and weeping and praying.

After placing our lighted candles with the others, we moved to the other rooms around the heart of the shrine that housed a profusion of sacred objects in one part and an assemblage of implements of daily life in another: a bishop's vestment woven with roses, manuscripts illuminated with peacocks and gold, multitudes of angels young and old, precious icons, shining swords offered to the archangel in gratitude for a miracle, and also millstones, cartwheels, massive copper pots, a shepherd's crook with a ram's horn at the end, a saddle decorated with leather stars, goat bell and cow bell collars decorated with bright plastic beads (one marked with the date 22/5/04), and a pair of traditional leather boots made with car tire soles.

When we stepped outside the rain was over, and the mosaic courtyard made of black and white pebbles in spirals and flowers had filled up with the voices of sparrows. Like the Kahal Shalom Synagogue in Rhodes whose well-trodden floors were paved with the same pebbles, Panormitis had been pillaged during World War II. But while nearly the entire congregation of the Rhodes shul had been murdered, soon after the war the monastery had come alive again, and it remains a place of pilgrimage and healing for the whole Dodecanese. On the morning of our visit, a great accumulation of roses, geraniums, Dipladenia, bougainvillea, hibiscus, and cyclamen were flowering all at once in a late spring rage of scarlet and blood-red petals that illuminated the overcast day, and an ancient priest with a long beard and gray hair that flowed down his back crossed our path with black robes flapping, bent over his plastic shopping bags.

Afterwards, writing notes on my lap in the minibus as we drove back through the mountains, the wonder of the place came together for me in a room that housed a collection of prayers lodged in tiny sailing ships. One small boat had been sent all alone to Panormitis from the island of Lipsi in 1998, two hundred kilometers away, with a little cargo of oil and beeswax candles. Many smaller yachts bearing secret prayers were stacked around the room, and a rowing boat resting on the floor was laden with even more prayers folded into bottles: glass wine bottles, plastic Coke or 7UP bottles, a big olive oil tin, a mayonnaise jar, messages in boats and bottles consigned to the blue waves of the Aegean and the power of the Archangel Michael, and washed up at last on the blessed shore of his monastery. Many never reach this haven, but for those small craft that do, it is evidence of a miracle. Each new prayer that lands at Panormitis is taken to join the installation of all the other tiny vessels, along with some taxidermied crocodiles and a large sea sponge.

3.

The harbor is often described as the most beautiful in all of Greece, the lovely houses stacked up the hill like a watercolor exercise by Paul Klee and the wide sea luminous as an angel in the afternoon light. But two years before our visit when the small unseaworthy boats kept landing at the port like prayers, and the *kámpo* and the area around the clock tower were continually crowded with desperate people, the heartbreaking beauty of Yialos was also discernible in pots of lentil soup and rice, fresh fruit and clean clothes, showers and toilets, conversations, emails, diapers.

"They were just inflatable dinghies, designed for a smallish lake," Peter said. "But they were coming across from Turkey. A boat for ten would have seventeen people in it, and they were being charged a thousand euro per person for the passage."

Peter Vidal, a retired Englishman who'd been living on the island for some years, was happy to talk and suggested we have a coffee at one of the harbor *kafenia*. Wendy, the person Manuel had originally said I should speak to, had put me in touch with him. Now at last I was hearing about the refugees.

"Who were they paying?" I asked.

"People traffickers. Human traffickers. It's rumored that the Islamic State were involved, using the money for armaments. But that's a rumor."

Peter was tall, dark, and slender, his bearing serious and self-effacing. "The people arrived with nothing," he explained. "There was nowhere for them to stay. Just sleeping on the streets and in the square."

"And then?" I said.

"Once they had some papers, they'd stay two or three days and get the next boat out to Athens."

"What were they leaving behind in Syria?"

"There was nothing for them there. If they hadn't left… Their homes had been flattened."

People on the island would happily make up extra portions of food, he said, and businesses would either give people breakfast or only charge them costs. But there wasn't enough to feed hundreds every day.

"The suppers were enormous. And by the end of it, people were getting very tired," he said. "So Wendy and Andrew set up Solidarity Symi to raise money for food, showers, and so on. It was a way for people from all around the world to contribute. And they did."

After that, Peter's sister and brother-in-law in their village in Suffolk saw the unfolding tragedy on the news and began collecting secondhand clothes. Within days, boxes of clothes began arriving at the house, and soon the three of them formed a UK charity, Next Stop Symi. Together they bought a van and began driving vanloads of sorted and folded clothing in through Europe. After March 2016, when the EU signed an agreement with Turkey that drastically reduced the numbers of people coming across to islands like Symi, they continued to collect clothes and deliver them to wherever they were needed. Meanwhile, Solidarity Symi began to focus on supporting the poor on the island.

"But Greek people are a very proud nation," Peter said. "Many people do not want it known that they are in need."

"And what did it feel like, when the refugees were all landing on Symi?"

Peter was a wonderful reporter. He was precise about the details, and his story felt completely reliable. But I was hoping for more sense of the emotional tone of the experience. Everyone I'd spoken with so far in Greece was full of strongly voiced opinions and intense feelings, but he was simply focusing on the facts.

"What did it feel like?" he said. "They were so happy to be in a safe country. Though it's true that some local businesses were concerned about the effect on tourism."

I tried again. "It must have been an emotionally powerful experience for you."

"It was. A very emotionally powerful experience. People put their hearts and souls into it."

Michael said, "A friend of ours here told us that there's a characteristically Dodecanese tradition of openness to strangers."

"Yes. *Philoxenia*. Or as some people now say, *xenophilia*. It's a modern coinage, the reverse of xenophobia."

He then went on to explain how the EU agreement had designated certain refugee hotspots, one of them on the island of Kos, where people had to remain until their application for asylum had been resolved. Then he told us about the vanload of clothing he'd just driven over in April, all the way from Suffolk.

"There were one hundred and twelve boxes of clothing in that van," he said, "and each one had been sorted and labeled by my sister. 'Men's trousers,' that sort of thing. When I arrived in Kos, they saw the box and said, 'Look! We've got men's trousers!' Doing it that way made their life so much easier."

"And why do you do it?" I said. I was still trying to get below the surface, the statistics, the information.

Peter laughed. "Why shouldn't I do it?" He added, "They are desperate. They are taking desperate measures. Giving them a little bit, it makes a big difference to them, even if it's only a change of clothing."

"The only really important thing in life is kindness," Michael said.

"Yes, that's it."

4.

"Rosemary or chamomile, you can't find them growing wild on the hills anymore," Stavros the herb seller said. "Because of the goats. The EU gives farmers money if they have a lot of goats. But they don't use the money to feed the goats, so they strip the hillsides. The oregano is too strong for them, but they eat the thyme down to a small bush."

To Michael and me it was a rare gift simply to walk out of the cottage and pick herbs for a meal. But for Stavros, the island's present biodiversity was a much-diminished trace of how things used to be, and his daily collection of plants involved a continual war with goats.

"The EU thinks they know best," he said. "Oranges too. People could be growing oranges here on Symi. But if there are too many, they have to dump them. The EU doesn't want them to flood the market and make the price of the oranges in Spain go down."

"It sounds crazy."

"It is."

His shop in Yialos was a small stall hung with great bunches of oregano and rosemary and salvia and lavender. There were nutmegs and cinnamons and saffron traded from the mainland, many little labeled drawers, garlands of red and green chilies, and strings of garlic from the Romani's van. We bought chamomile and mint and said we'd think about the saffron. With a wink, he slipped Michael a packet labeled *Sex Tea*. Next time we saw him he agreed that the red flowers were, as we'd thought, hibiscus.

"It breaks the ice, you know," he said. "Makes a connection."

Like many men we'd met on the islands, Stavros had spent his youth at sea. By the time he returned to Symi and took over his mother's herb business, he had a fluent command of English and an astute sense of the market. Talking with him about goats and plants over several visits, it was clear that his inheritance of the ancient craft of herbs had made him an environmentalist. His knowledge of leaf and shrub and flower was intimate and very precisely situated, and it gave him a view of the island as a living ecosystem inextricably permeated by global flows. And by the sea. On an island the size of Symi, it's easy to recognize the land and the sea as one ecological and social system. For all beings in the region, the experience of island life is tracked through with seafaring, and the condition of the marine ecosystem is permeated with the impact of land-dwelling *Homo sapiens*.

This interpenetration is very clear in the work of Aegean spongiolist Eleni Voultsiadou. Among the papers she kindly sent me, one intensive study of marine extinctions in the region reads as a lament.[56] The authors describe the Aegean Sea as a wonderfully complex region of more than three thousand islands and islets, a realm of richly diverse habitats that are home to myriad creatures, and at the same time an environment that is now under threat from a range of high-impact anthropogenic activities: tourism, urbanization, industry, agriculture, aquaculture, intensive exploitation of fishery resources, the effects of climate change, and biological invasions.

In presenting this picture, Eleni and her research team use historical and even literary sources as the backstory for scientific research into contemporary conditions. So, when they write about the beings whose lives are now endangered, the authors remember the great herds of monk seals from the *Odyssey* that came forth in throngs from the sea to sleep on the beaches. Now the monk seals are close to extinction, and those that remain of a species that was once gregarious and docile have become solitary and shy. Also at risk are the ancient families of loggerhead turtles, green turtles, and leatherback turtles whose nesting grounds have been disturbed, the many diverse kinds of dolphins, whales, and porpoises, the particular shark species that breed only in certain areas of the Aegean Sea, the Mediterranean red coral, the oysters and scallops. And among these precious and vanishing lives are the communities of bath sponges whose exploitation has been, as they put it in the characteristic understatement of the academic article, extensive historically.

From 1910 to 1940, they note, the Kalymnian fleet was processing around eighty tons annually. Since this refers to dry weight, each kilogram probably corresponded to more than a hundred individual sponges. This would bring the total harvested each year during this period to about eight hundred thousand individual animals. Before then, it seems no accurate records were kept of the devastation.[57]

That ravaging boom is over now but, writing in 2012, Eleni and her team make it clear that what remains of the great Aegean sponge reefs is still at risk from overfishing and disease. Though the sponge sellers we met were keen to believe that contemporary harvesting was being done sustainably, the authors comment that the remaining five Kalymnian sponge boats "exhaustively exploit every sponge bed that appears lucrative, excluding only the smallest cluster of individuals."[58] And though all commercial bath sponges are now protected under the Barcelona Convention, the present situation is still reminiscent of the days of the *skafandro* when safety was subordinated to profit. In practice, as they fiercely put it, "little or no control is enforced by Greek authorities over sponge fishers or merchants."[59] As for sponge disease, though many of the people I met on the islands saw Chernobyl as the culprit in 1986, neither this paper nor any of the others that I've read consider it to be a factor. Instead, the scientific consensus seems to be that mass mortality events like the great sponge death of that year, and other subsequent disease outbreaks, are "associated to environmental temperature anomalies that promote stress."[60]

In other words, sponges are a kind of climate change indicator. As the seas warm, there will be more sponge deaths.[61] There will also, for separate but related reasons, be more refugees. In recent years, the term "climate refugees" has become widely used for people who are displaced from their homes by climate change and global warming. And the extent to which climate change—specifically a prolonged drought—has been a factor in the Syrian refugee crisis and civil war has been a matter for considerable scholarly debate.[62]

Eleni the spongiolist does not track these resonances explicitly, but like Stavros the herb gatherer she perceives the condition of the Aegean ecosystem with a chastening awareness of loss. Towards the end of the paper on marine extinctions, the authors allow themselves to imagine how different it would have been to dive in the Mediterranean waters two thousand years ago among great red forests of coral, dense populations of black bath sponges, and large herds of seals lying fearless on sandy beaches.

This leads to a single shocking sentence that summarizes the conclusion of their research. "Thus," they state, "we could argue that the major extinction that has taken place in the Mediterranean is that of the physiognomy of the marine ecosystem as a whole."[63]

5.

Our time was short, and the fleetingness of it all made everything more precious. From the cottage in the early morning, you could watch the fishing boats returning from Turkish waters, their wakes a wide V across the sea like the long reach of migrating birds. As the sun came up, sparrows filled the garden with chattering sound, and the swallows swooped and soared. A month before, you could pick chamomile flowers for tea on the side of the path to our cottage, but now they were gone. The last red poppies were beginning to set seed. Figs were ripening in every garden. On the hillsides, the rock roses were almost over, and the mountain thyme was all in flower. As we stepped out of the gate the air was fragrant with wild oregano. By 8:30 it was already hot.

As the days became warmer, everyone was painting. Up in Horio a tall young man, one of the Argonauts in a previous life, was painting the steps of the *kafenion*. At the cottage, our host Takis was sanding and painting a piece of wood. In the shipyard, men in overalls were tenderly painting the prows of old ships. All along the harbor, a new group of English water-colorists had come to paint the island and the sea. And in the late afternoons while I swam, at the cove Michael would paint tiny faces in black ink on the pebbles and in the pearly interiors of small shells, placing them in niches on the rocks to last until the next tide. I painted nothing but swam with fishes the color of oak leaves in spring, or silver, or iridescent red and blue, and I could not stop taking photographs of the sea with my phone. Our twins in wintry Cape Town would receive image after image of the late light over the harbor or the view looking out across the hillside of thyme and rock roses to where the water shades from clear to green to shimmering blue, and reaches all the way to the mainland.

"You've taken that picture before," Michael would say.

"I know."

On the last day of our journey, we walked up early to Agios Giorgios: the sacred inner darkness of the little church and the whitewashed portals of the courtyard through which the heart reaches into the endlessness of sky and shimmering sea, and the mountains of the territory they call Asia Minor.

"We never call it Turkey," Ariadne had said to me on Patmos. "And Istanbul sounds strange to us. We say Visantium. Or Polis, the City. For us it is still the City."

And yet for a moment up there on the hill the centuries of empire and war and dispossession seemed to dissolve into blueness. The distant mountains are all blue. And the sea is blue, and the sky. And then once again, in the vastness of that wide view, sensitized by the beauty of the island and the anticipatory nostalgia of imminent leave-taking, the pain of things registered acutely.

The golden dog was still tied up under a tree, far from other dogs or people, weeping and barking with the terrible rage of his isolation. The horse was still pacing his yard as we passed, eyes refusing to make contact. The two dogs were still trapped in their cage at the bend in the path on the way back to our cottage. Someone had yet again taped the scrawl of crazy ballpoint words to the stone on the steps near the fig trees. And down in the harbor outside one of the sponge shops, the hapless figure of the *skafandro* was still standing alone.

**6.**

All day, we said goodbye. Goodbye to Stavros, the environmentalist herb seller. Goodbye to Panormitis the baker and his mother, Irene, whom we bought our last *kouloures* from so that we could sit on the harbor wall beside the clock tower feeding crumbs to the sparrows, who fed them to each other. Goodbye to Panormitis and Dinos at the sponge shop who called us in to talk and look at pictures. Goodbye to Dinos the hardware man who'd sold me diving things, and whom we found that afternoon in the garden of his holiday house at Harani, tending pots of pink roses. Goodbye to the manager at Paxos who, after weeks of coffees and ouzos, was touching his heart and kissing us on both cheeks. Goodbye to the supermarket owner who said he would wait right there until we returned.

To describe the islanders as friendly would be too easy. And yet they were. For all the real stresses of contemporary life in Greece, people on Symi and the other islands that we visited smiled and laughed a lot more than they do back home, and the warmth we experienced, over and over, felt real. Or perhaps it was a pervasive friendliness that was at once both real and performed. It made obvious business sense for Irene at the tiny bakery to greet us with a smile. But the look of joy when she exclaimed "*Kalimera!*" whenever she saw us, and her halting determination to communicate though she spoke no English, made the economic transaction seem like a chance to articulate a condition of openheartedness that longed for expression.

Now that we were leaving, the kisses, the eye contact, and the hand that involuntarily moved to touch the heart combined with the beauty of the island to fill me with an overwhelming sense of longing in which anything at all could make me weep, even the day-trippers. Seeing some of the visitors really for the first time when we were buying a few last gifts in Yialos, I came to imagine the package tour as the manifestation of a society that has so thoroughly alienated and exhausted and disempowered its citizens while giving those who have jobs just sufficient means to escape for a few days during their annual leave, that all they long for is a break and to be looked after. Who cares about antiquities or cultural specificity? Go somewhere warm. And so the island becomes a place to shop and eat.

That evening we walked down the small steps to Manuel's little cove, and on either side of the mountain path the thyme was flowering in the late light in patches of lilac, alive with bees. The cove was always empty of other people, but this time someone had placed a great big pinkish-red shell on the sand, the wing of a huge mussel, and beside it a row of pebbles, little shells, and sea-washed glass.

For the last time I swam, gliding through flocks of colored fishes, diving through clear water into the edge of blue, ears feeling the pressure, bubbles streaming out of mouth, flying and soaring in the blue like a bird like a fish like a being made of water, dancing and gliding in the deep transparent blue, sunlight shafting in, the surface a glittering rippling skin of molten glass, breaking through into air and the long reach of sea, far mountains beyond and the other islands, the hills at my back alive with thyme all flowering purple and humming with bees, land of sage and oregano and rock roses and the little olive tree, pink cyclamen growing among stones. While Michael painted faces on tiny shells to wash away with the next tide, or set painted pebbles in niches on the shore, I swam in the wide sea rippled by small winds, rocked by the wake of the ferry from Rhodes, floating and gliding and diving again, the azure sea so blue it feels like freedom, diving and rising, soaring like swallows in the bright air, like seagulls that skim the surface, swimming like flying fish, land of water and silence, land of so much space where everything is made of space and flow, stones glittering at the edge like jewels, this heart a jewel, this mind dissolved to ripple and flow, swimming in the slow lapping reach of blue that shades to green and turquoise at

the shore, this sea that still, for all pollutions and extinctions, feels like eternity.

When I came out of the water Michael read aloud his entire Orpheus cycle of poems. I'd wanted to hear the story of Eurydice and the Man with the Lyre uttered on that particular shore, facing that sea. He took a pomegranate from his rucksack and put six of the jewel seeds into my palm.

It was the end of the day, and the only person we'd not seen was Manuel. But later as we were walking back from the cove, he appeared near the blue harbor wall outside his cousin's taverna and held out a plastic bag to me.

"It's oregano," he said. "I picked them for you. All buds."

"You are so kind."

He smiled and said, "And when the figs are ready, I'll sundry some and send them to you in South Africa."

I found myself telling him about the dogs and the horse, and the little canary I'd just seen hopping to and fro in a cage on someone's veranda. I tried to explain how much it hurt to see the bird in the cage, that it was something to do with the beauty of the light over the sea. All I wanted was to open the door, but I didn't have the courage.

"They catch wild canaries," he said, "and put them in a cage. You know, I made people cross one day. I opened the cages. I paid for them all, the birds. But they were still cross with me. I opened the cages."

He shook his head. Laughed. Shrugged. We said goodbye.

# The Swallows
## RHODES, 2017

Just one Grecian urn would have been enough. But the old hospital of the Knights of Saint John, now the Archaeological Museum, was stacked with hundreds. Things buried and dug up, things made with sadness and fine craft, things made of this clay world to carry across the great water to the next, beauty that becomes visible only because of death.

Other animals may mourn their dead, but we human beings make bowls and vases and urns and vessels of all kinds for them, and centuries later others of our kind collect them together with names and numbers: cremation burial of a young woman in the form of a female bust, vase in the shape of a duck for an infant burial, pedimental grave steles, the birth of Aphrodite on an urn (inhumation of an adult), Man with Lyre and Woman with Clappers (inhumation of an infant), urns in the form of a monkey (cremation burial of a young woman), faience vase in the form of a hedgehog for a child's burial, offerings to the goddess Athena at her temple on the island, vessels made and broken and reconstructed, strings of beads. I found the ode on my phone and read it to a roomful of burial urns. And all the time the swallows in the great stone courtyard swooped and whistled. Alive, alive, alive.

We were staying once again in Renata's house while she herself was still away on Kos, helping her refugee friends prepare for their asylum interviews. Her goodbye message spoke directly to the abandoned terraces we'd seen on the islands and the questions I'd kept asking about agriculture.

"The very sad," she wrote, "is that Pakistanis (the main refugee population in Kos) are a max 10 percent to take asylum. But from all refugees they are the most needed for Greek economy because they are land workers and this is the lack in Greece."

I'd seen her called the Angel of Kos because of her work with these young people, and perhaps she had a gift for making one feel at ease. For even in her absence, the Magic House welcomed us back: a pause of quietness before the long flight home, and a chance to exit the journey through the portal of the garden.

It was late afternoon when I climbed through the window into the pomegranate courtyard where daylight turns to evening, and the scarlet stars of the flowers are turning to green fruits. In the forgotten garden fat green pomegranates grow deep seeds so quietly that nobody knows in the cobbled streets beyond the old stone walls of the Saint Nikolaos garden. Each peach growing on the ancient tree ripens tenderly in the sun, the golden lemons fall to the ground with a thud, and the herbs grow thick along the paths, visited by bees. Not even the pomegranate flower knows it is turning from scarlet to green, and that someday the deep rich fruit will become a crimson belly packed with jewel seeds. All afternoon the swallows track through the blue, calling to one another, twittering and whistling, as the day cools. In the forgotten garden nobody knows Persephone or thinks of a realm beyond or beneath, or imagines the possibility of winter. In the garden of the Magic House, not even the swallows imagine that day when the wind begins to bite and everyone finds themselves gathering in the sky for the long journey south. Not even the swallows remember it, not even the pomegranates imagine death.

In the quiet space of the Saint Nikolaos garden, forgotten by everyone, the pomegranates grow fat, and the peaches ripen, and the hedge of yellow santolina is flowering out of sight. In the quiet of ancient walls and forgotten trees, all stories slip away, even time itself. In the garden of the Magic House, past and future arise and dissolve in the single moment of the pomegranates growing. Sunlight moving through leaves, and the swallows calling.

# PART TWO

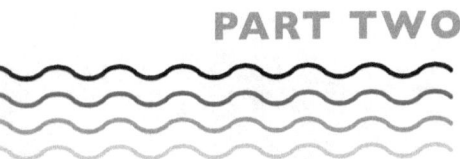

Ας είχα από την κράμπια κρύο νερό
Από την κάτω γη σταφύλι,
Κι από τους δυο λιαότες σκάρο.

> I wish I had fresh water from the cistern at Krambia
> Grapes from the Kato Ghi vineyards at Zies
> And parrotfish from Liaotes.
>
> — Mario tou Mousi, to the sponge divers

# The Angel of History
HALKI, 2019

I.

After months of Cape Town's winter cold, Michael and I sat in the summer shade drinking orange juice, while a middle-aged man in shorts took his three white ducks for a swim in the sea.

It was two years since our last visit and in the intervening time death had appeared twice, unannounced.

First Michael Wessels, the best friend who'd first given me the idea of visiting Greece, drowned in the campus swimming pool on one of his daily swims. On the Wednesday he and I were talking about how the water was so shallow because of the drought that you could walk your hands along the bottom like a coelacanth. And on the Thursday he was gone.

The following year, cancer took me to the brink.

Now after six months, it was twelve whole days since I'd rung the bell in the chemotherapy ward to mark the end of my treatment, while friends around the world rang bells and gongs of many kinds. Tired after navigating airports and crowds and taxis, with me wearing a surgical mask to reduce the chance of infection, Michael and I had come at last to a stop at Kamiros Skala, the tiny bay on the island of Rhodes where the ferry leaves for Halki.

Turtles dived and came up for air and dived again. Three white ducks bobbed in the radiant blue. We sat there with nothing left to be done but wait for the ferry. The sound of the small waves lapping on the shore was like the slow unceasing breathing of the world.

At last I was warm. My ears were no longer sore. My chest was not sore. We were drinking freshly squeezed orange juice. We had made it through.

2.

Panos was deeply tanned, a mustache and graying hair, sandals and a cotton shirt. He greeted us with a relaxed smile. He'd moved out of his own home to lease it to summer visitors like us, and the place was equipped with a good blender, an extensive record collection, and a cluster of model boats. In recent years he'd returned from Athens to live in the family home on Halki.

He told us, laughing, "My friends asked me, what are you going to do there in the winter? I said, I don't know...maybe read a book?"

The island was tiny, a destination the tourist guides call heavenly, complete with seafront tavernas, brightly painted fishing boats, Venetian-style villas, remote monasteries, and jewel-clear sea. The house of Panos stood at the far edge of the cluster of inhabited buildings near the harbor, at the end of a bougainvillea alleyway past fig trees, cats, and stone walls. It faced east, with a balcony over the sea. Our part was the upper floor of what must once have been a sizable villa.

"Was it a sponge house?" I asked.

"Yes," Panos said.

Michael and I had not managed to visit little Halki the first time, but together with Symi and Kalymnos it was one of the three main sponge diving islands in the Dodecanese. Panos said his grandfather had been on the sponge boats, a man from Kalymnos who'd fallen in love with a Halki girl.

When I explained that I was interested, he said, "You must meet Petros. And the other Petros too. Petros One is the shopkeeper. He has the grocery store at the harbor. Just go down and introduce yourself. He knows a lot about the history. And Petros Two, he was a fisherman. You should speak to him too. I'll arrange for you to meet."

Panos went on to tell how when he first came to the island to live, a few years back, he soon found himself managing a number of places as holiday rentals. Things went well, in business terms, but it was becoming stressful.

"Then I realized, that's not why I came here! I didn't come to Halki to make money."

So, he downscaled to just a few.

"And now," he said, and smiled, "I have found my peace."

The house was built at the edge of the sea. Each morning we watched the sun rising, a red ball of fire over distant lands. The sea was wondrous. It was bliss.

Yet for all its beauty, Halki was a husk of its former life. Houses and little shops had been freshly painted for the season, but many of the buildings were in ruin. The roofs, doorways, and windows of once-grand sponge mansions were open to the sea and sky, fig trees grew through the rooms where human beings once slept and ate, and sparrows chattered in their branches. When the place was still a key node in the Aegean sponge trade, there were 3,600 human inhabitants or more living across the island and it was densely cultivated.

Now the single industry that mattered was summer tourism, and the winter population was 240 human souls. Everyone lived at Emborio, the port. There was just one baby.

3.

Petros the shopkeeper was a man in his eighties, neatly dressed in black. He had a sensitive face, a straight back, and an interest in archaeology. Panos had said he'd be able to tell me about the sponge history of the island, but our first meeting was simply to buy supplies from his tiny and densely stocked shop: olives, feta, olive oil, tahini, a few tomatoes and cucumbers, pickled peppers, a piece of *graviera*.

The next day we met for a longer time, with twenty-one-year-old Irini, a bright young woman who'd said she knew Mr. Petros personally and would be happy to translate our conversation. We'd found her working in the nearby store selling sponges and so-called traditional products. Like Panos, she was a migrant from Athens, in quest of a life that made more sense, though she'd be returning home at the end of the summer.

After the initial greetings and good wishes, I'd asked him about how Halki came to be as it is today. It was the same question that kept coming up on Symi. It's so beautiful, but everyone calls it a dry island: lots of rock, no fresh water, and nearly all the food comes in on the ferry. But it was not always like this. On the hills you can still see the old terraces where they used to plant crops and the stone walls that marked out fields.

"Can you tell us what happened?" I said.

He answered in an extended monologue to Irini from which one word sounded out repeatedly and emphatically in the flow of all the other words: "*Catastroika!*"

We were sitting on plastic chairs in the shade of a fig tree outside his grocery shop. When anyone came to buy something, he'd stop talking to go and attend to them. Behind us two women sat listening attentively outside their small *kafenion*. The afternoon was warm, the sea incandescent. People walked past eating fruity ice creams, and Petros was talking about the catastrophe.

On Halki the great catastrophe, Petros said, was when the sponge divers left for Tarpon Springs, Florida.

"That was when everything changed."

Still, the emigrants sent back money. They built a school, the mayor's house, the clock tower…and they sent home money for food.

"They used to feed the people," he said. "That was the biggest thing. They fed children at the school."

"He feels so proud of the island," Irini explained, "that the emigrants left and they still sent back money."

"I understand." I said. "It was a wonderful thing. It must have meant so much. And before this time, the fields were still fruitful? Would people still collect water during the winter to irrigate in the summer?"

Every house had a *sterna*, he explained. There were grapes, olives, wheat, cherry tomatoes…After the young men went away to America, there was nobody left to work the fields or take care of the flocks.

"The land is still good," he went on, "but now we have tourism. Nobody wants to go to the fields."

"Not that it's easy what we're doing here," Irini interjected. "We work hard. My ex-boyfriend works fifteen hours a day on another island."

"It's the owners that have it easy," Michael said.

It was a warm afternoon, and the conversation meandered

on for more than an hour. I'd come with questions about the sponge industry, but whatever Petros told us about the island, at the heart of his story was food and the memory of starvation. He had, after all, been a child during the German occupation. Again, he used the word: *catastroika*.

"He was three years old," Irini said. "But he remembers the war as if it was yesterday. The Germans were ruthless. They took everything. The Italians were better. They helped the poor people, gave them food."

It seemed fitting that after the trauma of those formative years, Petros now owned the island supermarket. The shop was one narrow room lined with shelves on which a meticulously arranged multitude of bottles and tins and packages was stacked all the way to the ceiling.

I told them what old Latari had said to me on Kalymnos, that after the war there were no more dogs and cats.

"Yes," Petros agreed, "the Germans ate the dogs and cats."

For a while we sat in silence, nothing to say.

Then he smiled, generously releasing us from the terror of those years. He began to tell a story that was chosen to illustrate the defining qualities of the island as it used to be. Before. Before the *catastroika*.

"You'll like this," Irini said, when she'd heard him out. "It's very poetic."

It happened years ago, she explained, maybe two hundred years. There was a very beautiful girl called Mario tou Mousi. One day she and the other young girls were playing music on Pondamos beach when pirates came. They all ran away, but the pirates managed to catch Mario. They caught her and they stole her. Maybe they sold her. For years when Halki people were traveling—because they always traveled—they would look for her in the ports. But they never found her.

Then one day, maybe ten or twenty years after Mario was taken, some Halki sponge divers were in a market in Libya. They were buying *psatha*. It's a woven fabric for the houses, Irini explained. For carpets, rugs. One of the women at the market recognized their speech.

"You see," Petros said, through Irini, "she knew they were from the island because the old Halki dialect is very, very distinct. Anyway, she approached them, and said, 'I'm from Halki.' The men said, 'We don't know you.' So, she said something to them to prove it... It's very difficult to translate."

At this point in the story, Irini and Petros took a while working it out. Finally, with his help she wrote down the words the woman spoke to prove she was from the island.

She said:

Ας είχα από την κράμπια κρύο νερό
Από την κάτω γη σταφύλι,
Κι από τους δυο λιαότες σκάρο.

> I wish I had fresh water from the cistern at Krambia
> Grapes from the Kato Ghi vineyards at Zies
> And parrotfish from Liaotes.[64]

As soon as they heard this, the sponge divers knew that the woman was indeed the long-lost Mario. So, they wrapped her up in a *psatha*, smuggled her out of Libya as a parcel, and sailed straight back to Halki, where she lived out the rest of her days.

Mario's story was a well-polished jewel of collective memory and longing. To pass the divers' test, she named three unmistakable elements of home, each harvested from a specific place on the island: fresh water, parrotfish, grapes. In naming them again, Petros was pointing out the staples of a life that

Halki no longer sustains. The place Mario remembered was fruitful.

I loved the story for the way it reset the old tale of abduction, rape, and human trafficking that people on the islands have probably been telling for as long as there have been stories. Pirates who steal young women. Gods who steal young women. Beautiful young women who are stolen away by powerful males in the face of whom they and their loved ones are defenseless. Often it happens at a moment when her attention is absorbed in play, or when beauty has distracted her from vigilance. She may be gathering narcissi like Persephone when Hades came by, or playing in a field of flowers like Thalia when Zeus swooped on her in the form of an eagle, or like Creusa picking saffron when Apollo grabbed her wrists, or playing the lyra and the laouto like Mario and her friends on Pondamos beach.[65]

The fact that the same scenario appears so often speaks of a world in which women's bodies are fair game. As Herodotus put it, "To abduct women is considered the action of scoundrels, but to worry about abducted women is the reaction of fools."[66] How so? Because it seems that women who are abducted want to be abducted. In other words, they're asking for it.

What's different then, in the story of Mario tou Mousi of Halki, is that after being sold and lost, she found her way home. The miracle is that she spoke, and that she was heard.

The telling of the tale had brought our conversation to an end. It was late and Petros needed his afternoon meal. But before we said goodbye, I said something about how the basics of life that Mario longed for—water, animal protein, fresh fruit and vegetables—are what he now provided for Halki through his shop. It was true enough, perhaps, but

my saying so was really an attempt to make things feel less painful. In fact, his purpose in telling the story had been the reverse. Petros knew more about the ecological and social realities of the place than I ever could, and his point was to make a comparison with the present situation on Halki, where the sponge days are over, the only industry left is tourism, and nearly all the food and drink consumed on the once self-sufficient island must now be bought and sold.

In response to my words, he smiled gently and said, "Everyone does the best they can. Every day. But there are always conditions..."

Then he told me about his son whose work is on the great ships that bring fuel to Greece.

"They destroy everything," he said. "Bring in toxic waste and fish that were not here before. These fish are dangerous to this environment. The ecosystem is affected. They eat other fish. Some of those fish ate sponges too."

"And your daughter?" I asked. Behind the shop counter I'd seen a photograph of a beautiful young woman.

He looked down, shook his head. "She was an oncologist, a surgeon. She died six months ago."

4.

The person selling tickets at the entrance of the Traditional House Museum seemed both young and old at the same time. She had dark hair and wore a black summer dress, and she was seated at a small table in the shade, crocheting tiny white doilies. She spoke no English, but her lively eyes made contact with me over her spectacles, and when you bought a ticket she gave you a little candy.

We were the only visitors. Inside the small house, a handwritten notice was tucked against two plates painted with bright-green foliage and crimson flowers. It read, in green ballpoint:

Dear Guests,

Welcome to Halki. We hope you like our house. Please make yourselves at home. To show you how people on Halki used to live, we have left all our old family possessions for you to see.

The invitation set the tone for an experience that was quite different from what you'd expect in a public museum. The place was personal and particular, an assemblage of one comfortably off family's things that, together, left a trace of the lives they'd lived in a particular home. Or at least, it was how they wished us to imagine them.

We wandered through the quiet rooms, savoring the memory of cheese making and wheat grinding and white embroideries, a tough but well-provisioned life before electricity and the synthetic sponge, a landscape of food and women's work in which wine and olive oil are stored in great vessels and the family dining table is a small wooden disk set low off the ground, just space enough for four adults to sit shoulder to shoulder on small stools, with children peeping over and reaching in. One small sign described the four main styles of Halki handwork—lace, crochet, cutwork, embroidery—while another noted that all the curtains and tablecloths had been made by Anthi.

Dark-eyed Anthi Fanarakis and her husband, Minas, gazed out seriously at us from an old photograph on a table in the midst of her home, which in some previously unimaginable world had become a museum housing the doll from her childhood (1950), her grandmother's white *kilota* (long underwear, 1900), her precious floral plates, and an entire realm of fine linens all white white white and spotless: the bridal sheets, the baby's crib, the fine cutwork, the lace. I wondered how Anthi herself would feel if she could know that we were walking through her mother's home and hers, glancing swiftly about, looking at her linens.

We stepped out into the midday glare, and I thanked the woman in black sitting at the entrance. She spoke no English, but she touched her heart. We smiled and lingered. I said, touching my heart too, that we found the house beautiful.

She pointed to herself and said, "Anthi."

"What?" I said. It seemed incredible. "You mean this is you, your house? You are Anthi?"

I'd simply assumed that the woman in the photographs was someone in the past and that the person selling tickets must be an employee of her descendants.

"*Ne.*"

"Wow."

Whatever complex of ecological and human relations had once sustained the lifestyle of the traditional house, that era was now over. There were no more harvests on the island of wheat or olives or grapes. No more sponges. Instead, the installation of the house itself had become a resource that drew some cash from the visits of people like us.

She held out one of the white crochet objects she'd been making.

"Souvenir," she said.

At first, I hesitated. Our house in Cape Town did not need little doilies, even special Halki ones to hang on the front door with a small ribbon. But the poignancy got to me. Our presence on the island was what made the act of memory a feasible project, even if barely. And it was also what sealed the fact that there was no going back. The entire purpose of gathering things together in the Traditional House Museum was to bring the past into focus in the face of a cloud of forgetting that seemed to have afflicted the island, except for some of the old people. Amid the storm of so-called progress, Anthi had brought her fine capacity for meticulous attention to the project of remembering. Skilled in the arts of home, she'd rebuilt her house in the imagination as an *ars memoria*. This is how it was, it said. This is how we lived. These are the curtains, the sheets, the baby's things, the tablecloths, the white, white, spotless white embroidered cutwork linens that

I spent my life making, the fine crochet work tacked along the edges of shelves.

"Souvenir," she said again, with a hopeful smile.

It must have been one of the few words we had in common: a trinket small enough to take home in your luggage, a holy badge that proves you've done the pilgrimage. But the piece of fine white crochet with a yellow ribbon she held in her hands that morning felt like more than that. Perhaps Anthi's doily was indeed an artifact of traditional craft transformed into an item for tourists in a globalized market, but its slender thread reached all the way back to another world: her world, and the hours of women's work, her work, that wove it together. Sitting across from her at the small table with its little cash register and bowl of candies that afternoon, I had the strongest feeling that the house and all the neatly labeled treasures of her former life were a flimsy signpost planted in the winds of forgetting. For if the angel of history can't make whole what has been smashed, her hands may still work a single thread of strong white cotton into tiny loops formed in concentric rounds: three flowers, three stars, three snowflakes. Souvenir, the snowflakes said. Remember.

I bought the doily, and it opened the gate of conversation. Anthi smiled broadly.

"*Skandalopetra?*" I asked, pointing back towards the house. I'd seen one propped up against the kitchen wall, a smooth white diving stone. Had the family been involved in sponge diving?

"*Ne,*" Anthi said, "*pappous.*"

Her grandfather. She and I mimed free diving, holding our breath, laughing, nodding, pretending to dive. Then I said *skafandro* and she nodded again. Had anyone in the family gone to Tarpon Springs? *Ochi.* No. Using Google Translate on my phone, I asked whether there was anyone at all left on the island who could remember stories from the sponge diving days. She shook her head and mimed death with eyes shut and head resting on her hands, palms together. They're all dead.

We were silent for a bit.

After a while Michael typed in some words on his phone and passed the translation to Anthi: *Aftó pou eínai ypérocho gia to spíti eínai óti eínai apó mia epochí prin apó ta soúper márke.* What's wonderful about the house is that it's from a time before supermarkets.

Anthi nodded wistfully, smiled. Then she and I began kneading imaginary dough.

5.

Petros tis Psarofagias, Petros Two, was four when Germany invaded Greece, and the chafing memory of his early years was of hunger. As a boy he dreamed of fish and a boat to catch them from.

We were sitting in the shade at a *kafenion*. Panos was genially translating everything, but the dream was important enough for Petros to tell it himself, holding me in his gray-eyed old man's gaze and the wide gesture of his hands and speaking the single English utterance of our conversation.

"I sleeping, very young," he said. "I think maybe I have a boat. A fish boat."

The dream of the fishing boat remained with him, he said, and years later when he returned to the island with a heap of drachmas from working at sea, he found his boat: *Maistros*, named for the northwest wind that brings the rain. She was strong in the water and loaded with nets. At first, his mother didn't want him to spend half his money, but then she took a kitchen sieve and made a prayer. She said, May my son bring home as much money as this sieve has holes.

And so it was. Thousands of bright fishes came home in the wonderful boat, and once before Easter he caught three tons.

"For twenty years," he said, laughing, "we never had nothing to eat."

Like Petros the grocer, he knew about starvation.

"The Italians were kind," he said. "They fed people. But when the Germans came, the people starved. Every day we lost five to ten people."

The truth of it was a child's recollection of daily devastation and mothers foraging for dandelions. I repeated Lataris's unforgettable memory about cats and dogs.

"Yes," he said, "the Germans were starving too. The cats and dogs, the Germans ate them."

"He believes the Germans lost the war because of starvation," Panos explained.

He was an empathetic translator. Gentle, a little wry, and sensitive to the old man's emotions of the story, which moved from laughter to tears and back, without pause.

Petros and Petros were the two elders Panos had suggested I speak to about sponges. Both saw the exodus to Tarpon Springs as the critical moment in the story, but both had also been powerfully impressed by the emigrants' generosity to the people back home. Petros tis Psarofagias told me about the church they'd built on the island, the clock tower, and especially the 1,001 checks the divers used to send back to their families.

"Every Friday they would send it," he said, his voice quavering with tears. "I feel proud of my island because...the Halki people in Florida did this. In the war it stopped, but then it began again. Every Friday, the checks. Every family was waiting for their check. They were waiting for flour to make bread."

"And in the old days, the island was fruitful?" I asked. As always, I was trying to make sense of the vineyards and orchards and fields of yesteryear.

Petros smiled and began remembering how it used to be. Some families owned a thousand or more sheep, he said, and every house had a *sterna* for rainwater.

"We're doing that again now in Cape Town," I said. "There was a terrible drought, and many people are collecting rainwater again. At our house we have a tank that's connected to the roof. We shower into a bucket and use the water to flush the toilet when it's absolutely necessary."

Petros laughed and said, "We didn't even have a toilet."

Then he explained that Halki had not always been a dry island. In May, he said, the island used to be completely green. You couldn't see any stones on the hills. The fields were watered with wells.

"And what changed?" I said.

"The youth are not interested, and the old people can't do it anymore."

"So, when did agriculture on the island start to decline?"

"Sixties, seventies, eighties..."

"Was that when tourists began to come?"

"Yes."

"Maybe they made a pact with the Devil?" Michael said to Panos and me. "Now everyone has Wi-Fi and you can buy Barilla pesto from the other Petros."

Panos smiled. "We used to have a *sterna*," he said. "For years we'd clean it out, keep it going. But you know how it is. We have desalination now. Everyone's turned their *sterna* into an extra room."

Throughout the conversation, Petros spoke from a deep sense of island pride. He told us that in ancient times Halki people were the first divers ever. The island also had the best celebrations when the sponge fleets came home. When I said that on Kalymnos we'd met the grandson of the diver who'd been eaten by a shark and survived, he claimed it for the island.

"No!" he said, emphatically. "That is a Halki story, an old story!"

"He says the Kalymnos people are liars," Panos explained. "It's the old rivalry between the islands."

Then Petros told us about the great sponge diver, from Halki of course, who was so good at diving that he only had to dive three times a year.

"Three times! He used to eat a chicken every day. People would bring him a male chicken every day to persuade him to go and dive again. But he didn't need to. He brought up so many sponges that he only had to dive three times."

By the time Petros was growing up, the peak of Halki's sponge heyday was over, but the leaving and returning of the remaining fleet were still the defining rhythms of island life. He told us about the special meal that was cooked before the boats departed, the three days' celebration when they returned, how the Halki celebrations were bigger and better than the ones on Symi, and how the divers didn't talk much during the feasting, to save time for drinking.

"You should have been here when they were putting the sponges out in the sun to dry!" he said with a faraway expression. "The bleaching place was called Hiona. It means snow."

Then he spoke about the great mounds of sponges coming home on the caïques, golden-brown at first, then pale as snow, gleaming.

"Do you remember the last sponge boat that sailed from Halki?" Michael asked Petros.

"It was his grandfather's boats," he said, pointing at Panos.

Panos was taken aback. He'd grown up in Athens. He hadn't known.

"*Mantoula* and *Kiki*," Petros went on. "Named after the sisters of his father. On Halki they were using the *skafandro* all the time until the end of sponge diving."

*Skafandro*. Just to name it was an invocation. Satan's Machine may be the shadow at the heart of the whole endeavor, but nobody seemed to be able to speak about it. His face became troubled, remembering.

"I know a lot of small poems," he said, beginning to cry a little. "What the mother used to say to her husband, her son...when he was leaving."

Then he told us a woman's wish. It was a poem not for her own man but for the one who helped him put on the *skafandro*, that irreplaceable comrade who held in his hands the lifeline back into the world.

"She would say, 'He must have the mind of the salmon and the wisdom of David,'" he said.

"That's beautiful," I said. "If you're a salmon, it means that even if you go far away, you'll know how to return."

Petros was choked up with tears. When I asked for more poems, he shook his head. The *skafandro* had a way of silencing things. There was nothing more to say.

Then I asked about his name.

"Petros says he doesn't want to be called by his surname," Panos had explained earlier. "He prefers his nickname, the name he inherited from his father. Psarofagia."

The old man smiled. The story of his name was one made

perfect with many tellings. "It was a special day to eat a special fish," he said. "It was the week before Easter, and on that day people had to eat *kolios*."

At this point, the two women who'd been sitting in the shade behind us throughout the conversation interrupted and said, no, it was a different fish. But Petros was settling into the tale and ignored them.

His father, he said, was up with the animals at the cave near the almond trees. It was the same place where the women and children were burned by pirates long ago. On that particular day it was raining hard, and it was too difficult to come back. It was the day for eating the special fish, but nobody brought him food. So, he made his own fish from cream!

Afterwards everyone called him Psarofagia, the Fish Eater. It became his name, and Petros inherited it. Panos wrote the name in my notebook: Petros tis Psarofagias.

## 6.

It was Sunday morning, and we were drinking orange juice under the awnings of the Apostolis café. Hundreds of tiny fish flowed through the clear blue harbor like clouds of migrating birds and the deep silence of the place was filled with the voices of pigeons, sparrows, and the singing of the priest, his ancient call answered by a chorus of young boys and the sound of bells.

After the service, Petros the shopkeeper came up to us, dressed as always in black. "*Kalimera*," he said with a large smile, followed by a single word: "Church." Then he bowed for a moment and walked over to open his shop.

After about a week, every walk involved greetings. The island was so small that anyone could tell we were visitors. But the social fabric was still intact enough for us to greet one another as we passed. *Kalimera. Kalispera. Kalinychta.* I see you. We make eye contact. We are human beings.

From the back of the café an elderly man had gestured to us to come and sit near him at a table out of the sun. He was doing his *kombolói*, flicking the dark-blue glass beads around and around as he gazed towards the sea in silence. Beside him was a younger man, also sitting quietly. It was something we saw often: people seated at a table together, looking out at the sea, no words spoken.

The proprietor of the café was a woman with eyes the color of water. I asked whether she knew anyone who could tell me about the sponge diving days.

"My father," she said, "Cheimonettos. He usually comes around ten."

The next day we returned to find the old man at an inner table with a bright pink oleander flower tucked behind his left ear.

He nodded at my greeting and, after some introductions, agreed to talk. Beside him were his son, Vasilis, and his daughter-in-law, Eléni. They offered to translate.

"My father was diving," Cheimonettos said through Vasilis. "He died when he was ninety-four, but until then he was diving. The money was good."

"Actually, no," Vasilis said to me. "His father was bedridden for the last ten years."

"My father did have problems with legs and eyes," the old man continued. "He lost one eye and one ear. One time near Suez, they thought he was dead. They put him back in the sea."

I remembered that this was one of the hopeful remedies for the bends—not always successful, but this time it was.

"When they came back," Cheimonettos said, "he was alive! It's very painful, blood in the legs." His face was grave. The *skafandro*. The excruciating pain.

"For every twenty men who set out in the sponge boats," he went on, "only ten or twelve returned. There were always more women on the island."

For Cheimonettos Cheimonettos—a rare name, as Vasilis explained, a name from *this* island—the stories of diving were part of his family inheritance. But over the years they seemed to have grown old, worn thin with time. More vivid were his own memories of goats and honey, and a room full of twelve sisters and brothers, all sleeping together.

He was born in 1939, and five of his siblings died as young children. One of them rolled on another in the night, stifling his sibling. In those days, he said, there was no doctor. The family would pay for school with goats and carpentry. They had bees. They ate honey. They fished. They didn't starve.

"But now," he said with a look of distaste, "there are too many sheep! They eat everything."

"We have eighteen thousand sheep on Halki," Vasilis said, as the conversation shifted to him. "They destroy everything!"

"And that's because of the EU subsidy?" I said.

"Yes. They pay for how many sheep and goats you have. It's crazy. An idiot government."

"It sounds like what happened with the sponge beds. Do you think we could compare the overgrazing of the island with overfishing of the sponges?"

"Oh, yes," he said. "If you cut the sponges the wrong way, they won't grow back."

Michael found the Greek translation for the phrase "short-term gain" on his phone: *vrachyprόthesmo kérdos*.

Vasilis nodded. "One man can destroy all the whole

earth!" he said. "They always want more. Now the fishermen catch very small fish and sell them for one euro. It's the same with tourism. Most people here who work with tourists, they just want to make money. Their level is zero. And the tourists, most of them too. They just want to eat, be in the sun…"

"I guess we're also tourists. But we're honored to meet the elders," I said. "And to meet you."

"No, you're not only a tourist. Our name for you is *periigitis*. It's a person who explores everything and communicates with local people."

"Thank you."

Google translated it as traveler. One who peregrinates, perhaps.

"And your father?" I asked. "Can you tell us about the lovely flower?"

Cheimonettos smiled and nodded as I pointed to the pink oleander tucked behind his ear.

"It's because he likes to enjoy," Vasilis explained. "He wants to celebrate. He is what we call *meraklis*: the one who is full of joy, who celebrates."

As we said goodbye, the old man put his arm around Michael.

"*Filia*," he said. "*Filia*."

The next day we drank coffee and homemade lemonade at the café and talked more to Cheimonettos's daughter, Pelagia.

"It means the sea," she explained about her name. "The *big* sea."

"How beautiful," I said.

"It's because of my eyes. Like yours. And my father's. We have the same eyes."

I looked into her eyes of the open sea: the blue, the deep,

the vast beyond. On this small island at the end of a lineage of sponge divers, her name still spoke the long knowing of that big sea, a child named for the pelagic deep, diving and swimming, her eyes.

"It really is a beautiful name," I said. She smiled.

Around ten, Cheimonettos arrived to sit at his table. He nodded to us and explained through Pelagia that he wanted to tell us about the bell tower of Agios Nikolaos.

Had we noticed what a high tower it is? From the top you can see the *castro* on the hill. In the old days, Cheimonettos explained, he and his family lived up in Chorio, but after the war the village was emptied and everyone moved down the hill. They built a new church for Agios Nikolaos. When the bell tower was finished, they put an icon of the saint in the church. But it disappeared! Why? They found that the icon made its way back up the hill to Chorio! This happened twice. It was a sign that the saint wanted to be able to see the *castro* in the original village from his new location at the port. So, they built the bell tower higher.

"It's the highest bell tower in the Dodecanese!" he said with pride.

This time the oleander flower in his ear was a deeper pink than the previous day's.

"He puts a flower every day," Pelagia said. "My father is the best man on the island. Some people look only money, no life."

7.

"I used to be the baby," Ioanna said.

We were sitting at Theodosia's café one afternoon, talking about the single baby on the island who was looked after by so many different people—various young women pushing her in the pram, old women cuddling, an old man and the baby laughing and clapping hands together under the vines—that we still didn't know who the actual parents were.

"Yes, that used to be me," Ioanna said, smiling. "I was the only baby, and everyone used to play with me."

She was a bright-eyed young person, recently out of school and working during the holiday in Theodosia's, her parents' patisserie café. It was a place with good coffee, cold drinks, ice creams, pastries, and a parrot that meowed like a cat. Ioanna was always happy to talk, and her English was good. But this time we were waiting for her elder sister Anna, who also worked there on different shifts.

Anna Livaniou had bright red hair and wore red lipstick, red-framed sunglasses, and a bold, in-your-face look that almost disguised the sensitivity of her expression, the kindness of her eyes. A couple of days before, I'd mentioned refugees, and suddenly she had a lot to tell me.

"Oh, it was very bad," she said. "Summer of 2015. We Greeks know what it is to be refugees. So of course we helped them. They are like us, you know. Like you and me."

It was the idea she kept coming back to when she joined us at the table that afternoon to talk some more. They are like us.

"We'd heard about the refugees," she said, "and most of what we'd heard were bad things. You know, disease. We were afraid. Then the first boat came. It was late afternoon, and the boat police heard that a boat had washed up on Alymnia. It's the little island over there.

"Nobody lives there, just stones. So friends and fishermen went to help. They found more than a hundred people on the boat. They'd tried to climb the mountain to see where they were, and they cut their feet. So all afternoon they were bringing them here to Halki. All night! They had blood on their feet and legs from the stones. The doctor came. The mayor. It was summer holidays, so he said they could stay at the school. Restaurants give them food, everything. Eggs. We do a lot of pasta. I think we take all the pasta from the shop."

The story was pouring out in a rush, the memory of it harsh and unforgettable.

"Next day, when everything is calm, we talk to the people. Most of them came from Syria. People became Facebook friends. We bring them sleeping bags, and at the school there was water, toilets. The police sorted out their papers. But the refugees didn't understand what's going on. They couldn't understand that they are illegal in our country."

"So they couldn't leave the school?" I said.

"Yes, they had to stay under police guard. Mostly we care about the children. The old women wanted to take the babies to their houses, but they weren't allowed to take them away from the school."

"And the boat they came on, was it one of those rubber dinghies?"

"It was a big old wooden boat. No captain. We believe they were sailing a few hours. The pirates abandoned the boat once they were in Greek waters. They told them one hour and you'll be in Athens. They gave them no water."

"And the pirates were...human traffickers?" I said.

The people we'd already spoken to on the islands believed that the refugee boats were being run by the Islamic State, extorting money from the fares to pay for their war.

"Yes," Anna said. "The people had to pay two thousand euros per person to go on the boat! Even the children!" She showed me pictures on her phone: adults, children, a few bags.

"And are you still in contact?"

"Yes. Quite a few went to Germany. One guy, he was a lawyer. He was lucky. He speaks good English."

"And that was just the beginning?"

"After that more boats would arrive every week or every two weeks. The shops and the restaurants...Everything we can do, we do. They are people like us, like you and me. Not poor people. One day you are having your life, and then it's all gone. It's hard to leave your house and your country, and you're going nowhere! With your baby!"

The way she described it, the experience had really opened her eyes. They were not refugees. They were people like us, like you and me. It was what she kept saying.

"You know, I'm thirty-two years old," she continued. "I don't know what war is. You can't imagine. I mean, it was surreal. These were people who had been in a real war, and the tourists were getting ice cream here at the café for their babies. Planning their holidays. It was crazy. The others had just survived. *From a rock!*"

Anna's imagery, like her red hair, was fierce. War and ice creams.

After a pause, she said, "In the end we couldn't make it. We couldn't do more. If you are three hundred people on the island, you can't feed them anymore. So we asked the tourists if they can help. Here, we don't have babies—well, there's one—so we asked if they can leave clothes. And they leave *everything* for the babies. Prams, clothes..."

"And now the refugees go to Rhodes instead?" I said.

"Yes, the EU set up a refugee hotspot in Rhodes. They say there are four million still waiting in the ports. But you know, we learned a lot from them."

"Like?"

"Drinking beer with lemon juice and salt. It's amazing, but it makes your belly big. And they had good makeup products."

It was a great moment. I'd anticipated some sort of lesson of endurance and courage, but what Anna remembered first was beer and makeup.

"And, you know," she added, as though it were obvious, "be strong."

Ioanna came by to replenish our drinks. It was midafternoon, and her father's parrot was especially active, striding about the café, saying hello, whistling, knocking, and most especially meowing.

"Why does he meow?" I said.

"He loves cats," she said simply. "Hates other birds."

Ioanna and Anna were young people with Facebook, Instagram, and WhatsApp on their phones, and they watched English-language series on the café screen during the winter. They had never known a war, and along with serving a menu that included green smoothies alongside baklava, they assumed a twenty-first century level of women's rights. But in Anna's stories, the sharp pressure of an entirely different world was always intimately present. Even as we gazed at the sparkling sea on that summer afternoon, you could feel it in the peripheral vision, as real as death.

"After the Big War," she went on, "the economy was very bad. Here in Halki before the eighties, it was a very poor island. We didn't have anything. Most of the families were separated, and the boys went off on the ships to America, Australia. My grandmother used to live up in Horio. They were eight children, and they had to give one child away to another family."

"Because they couldn't look after it?" I said.

"Yes. They were ten living in one room. My mother said the buildings were full of lice because of the war. By that time most of the healthy people were living here at Emborio."

Like everyone else, Anna described the Italian occupation positively in comparison with the terror that came next. They were nice, she said. They did a lot of building.

"And, you know, people say Italian and Greeks, they eat together. We eat the same food. Olives, that sort of thing. But not the Germans."

She pointed to a statue in the square outside Petros's shop. "That guy tried to hide people who were in the Resistance. He's an island hero. But did you know, there are still some people in Germany who believe that Auschwitz never happened? I went there, to Auschwitz, and still we met people who just didn't believe it."

Her own approach to the devastations of history was the opposite. The apocalypse can happen to anyone. Freedom is tenuous. When I asked about the sponge diving days, she spoke about women and economics and rights.

"Halki didn't have the great sponge wealth of Symi and Kalymnos," she said. "It was hard for the women. The men would die at sea and leave the wife to budget for the whole year. And the women of those days couldn't go out of the house! They had to stay inside. Make lace to trade with. Even in the eighties, my mother was the only woman who could go to the bar. She'd go with my father. They were communists—well, in Greece it's more socialism—and they used to like to drink, go to parties…"

Now it was different, of course. The EU had come to Greece.

"I believe that in the beginning the economy boomed, but it wasn't sustainable," I said.

"Yes. We are the lucky ones, because of island tourism. But we pay now, my generation, for that bubble that burst. Since 2000 it's been the third big war, an economy war. And it *is* a war. Everything the Germans say, we must do."

"You know," she said after a pause, "we lost. Some people recognize that and move on. You have to choose your path."

She put it ruefully and emphatically: while Germany may have been defeated in World War I and World War II, they had now won World War III.

"This is not democracy," she said. Then she added, "But this is *my* truth, you understand. My point of view."

Later when I told a Greek friend about the conversation, he said with a smile, "That is rare. Greeks know everything."

Anna's sense of relativism would have been unusual for anyone, but at the time I was focused on what she was saying about Greece and defeat. "I get what you mean when you say that Greece lost," I said. "But what you have here—it really is something very special."

"You mean, it's something that money can't buy?" she said.

"Yes."

"Oh, sure," she said. "But this is Halki. This is not Greece. We Greeks, we may be wise. And we like food...But we lost."

8.

Hiona. *Chióni*. Χιόνι. Snow. The mounds of bleached sponges used to gleam like snow. They would come in golden from the sea to be trampled and bleached, great mounds of snow laid out in the sun to dry. You should have seen them, Petros said.

The place where this happened, where the sponges were processed and stored, was called Hiona Vouvali. It was a large structure built at the far end of the bay and named for the big Kalymnian merchant Nikolaos Vouvalis and for the snow. With the sponge days long over, the building had become a hotel: large plate-glass doors, clean modern design, tanned tourists walking in and out, high-quality lounge beds overlooking the sea, a pile of German magazines in the reception area. Accommodating the needs of the business that had replaced it, the big sponge-processing warehouse was now transformed into a conference room.

At the entrance we met Yiannis Parlavantzas, the proprietor, a generous-minded Athenian in his fifties, who spent seven months of each year on the island. I had not arranged a meeting, but he was happy to sit and talk and called one of the waiters to bring us ouzo and olives.

"The place was owned by Vouvalis, wasn't it?" I said.

"Yes, that's right," he said.

Yiannis said the sponge trade used to bring so much money to the island that some people called Vouvalis a second god. He was rich, but he was generous.

"Well, he could afford to be," I said, thinking of his mansion on Kalymnos and the bronze sculpture on the dockside. "I mean, I keep thinking that people like him got rich while the men were dying at sea."

Yiannis nodded. "It is always like this," he said. "There are rich people and poor people. It's been like this for thousands of years. Life is not fair."

After a pause he added, "But death is fair."

He reached behind the counter for an old book about Halki sponges and started to read to us about the men leaving in April for the North African coast, the special prayers the families made back home when the weather was bad, the fires they lit when the boats were late returning.

"Oh, this is very difficult to translate," Yiannis said when he came to the song that was sung when a man died at sea. "It's very sad. It's talking to the man. It says, 'You made women wear black clothes. Is there water to make your lips not be thirsty?'" His voice quavered. The tears were close.

"That's very, very old," Michael said, "That the dead are thirsty, and you want to wet their lips. It's there in the Orpheus text, the oldest poem."

We sat together quietly without needing to say anything more. Then after a while one of the guests came to speak to Yiannis. An Austrian woman, very tanned, she had lost her room key. He got up to take care of things, and when he returned the moment had passed.

"You're very kind to everyone," I said.

Throughout the time he'd been talking to us he was gently tending to guests and staff, every few minutes.

"Thank you," he said, and smiled. "You have to think this: they are in my house."

"*Philoxenia?*" Michael said.

"Yes."

"And you!" he said, turning to me. "This is a beautiful meeting of people from overseas who are interested in the past and would like to be part of the present. It's touching me too. You see how I was moved by that story, that song. I didn't know that before, and it's from this conversation. Thank you."

Then he told us about his autistic son. "He taught us the most things we know. Compassion, patience...Would you like some more ouzo?" Michael's glass was empty.

"No, thank you. I've had just enough," Michael said.

"Good!" Yiannis said. "That is what we call *metron ariston*. It means knowing the limits to what you have. *Metron ariston*. Everything in moderation."

The phrase spoke precisely to what I'd been thinking about the sponge industry. I explained to Yiannis that I had come to understand the destruction of the Aegean sponge beds as a case study of unrestrained resource extraction: thoughtless, short-sighted, mine the seabed until it's all used up and destroy people's lives in the process. Part of my interest in the sponge story was that it was like a parable of our present condition as a species on this planet.

"I mean, we're in crisis," I said.

"Yes," he said, "I'm aware of that. You know, we humans are temporary here, like the dinosaurs. The planet doesn't mind, doesn't care if we survive. I think your sponge example is excellent."

"Of course," I said, "It's not that the sponge divers themselves were bad..."

"No. It was like, 'I have to put food on the table for my family.'"

"Right. And they'd been doing it for thousands of years. But once the technology got to a point where it gave them a whole new level of destruction, some people had the chance to become incredibly rich. For a while, anyway. It couldn't last. Anyhow, the way I see it, the devastation of the sponge ecosystem and the ruthlessness towards the divers is...like a microcosm of the whole thing. Our whole condition."

"Yes, perfect," Yiannis said. "Very good. You must write about it like that."

"And I could say *metron ariston*?"

"Yes, exactly."

We began talking about the future, and I told Yiannis the

fantasy I'd been having of a sort of green redemption for Halki. What if you could involve some of the most up-to-date green tech people to devise systems for solar and wind, harvest water again in the winter, renew the fields, and work together as a community to make the island both sustainable and productive? Halki is so tiny and was once so fruitful. Surely, surely, with the right combination of hope and daring and collective hard work it could become another kind of microcosm, a place that shows how human beings *can* live.

"Wonderful, yes," he said. "I agree! Come, I want to show you the *sterna*."

At the back of the hotel was a vast underground tank for water storage. It was now in disuse, but Yiannis told us about his plan to use it again for biological treatment of the hotel's waste.

"I want to use it for biological cleaning of the sewage. Then we'll put that into growing vegetables for the hotel. Tomatoes, cucumbers..."

"Wow. That's incredible," I said.

"But I think it will work!" he said. "It's what I want to do, in two or three years."

Then he said, "You know, Halki is a very special place. When tourism started up here, the island was very poor. The sponge fishing was over, and everyone saw it as a great opportunity. Easy money. Now some people have suggested building a big tourist marina. Chinese money."

"Oh, no!"

"Yes," he said. "They call it growth, but it's missing the point. The gem of Halki is what it is!"

## 9.

Everyone, everything faced the sea.

Before we left Cape Town, I wasn't sure that I'd be well enough to manage the trip, but Michael was insistent and once we were on the island, it filled me up with life. Each morning we watched the sun rising over the golden water, and then I swam out into the deep, rocked in the slow caress of small waves. I dived and looked up into the glimmering blue roof of the Aegean, swimming into the gentle glide of color from clear to turquoise to deep blue, the azure aqua cobalt ultramarine land of waters, an endlessness of sea and sky, a long unceasing rippling timeless place beyond words where floating diving gliding flowing bodies swim and sail.

All day the old men sat under the awnings of the *kafenia* gazing out beyond the harbor wall, sometimes talking a bit, sometimes playing with the baby. Petros sat on an upright chair outside his shop, sometimes saying a few words to a passerby, sometimes dozing. And each evening a burly, middle-aged man walked along the shore with an older man, holding his hand. Perhaps it was his father, thin and disabled in some way, gazing about and stumbling a bit. Where we come from he'd likely be in an institution, but here he was simply part of everyone's life, the younger man taking his hand, gently pulling him along for his daily walk beside the sea. The Black Sea, they call it, Mávri Thálassa, for the slate-dark color at that time in the afternoon.

On the last day before leaving for Symi, we took a bus filled with tourists and pilgrims up the steep climb to the bombed-out, abandoned Chorio where the fortress of the Knights stood like a child's paper cutout of a castle against the sky. Beneath it were the leavings of the huddled village, all broken walls now among olive and pepper trees, where islanders once took refuge from the pirates who steal young women away to Algeria, and where families and their lice lived crowded in a single room during the second big war. Beyond, the road tracked high into windswept reaches, a land of stone and forgotten cisterns where low walls marked out abandoned fields and vineyards, and sheep and goats bit the few small plants that remained. Higher yet, we reached the monastery of Agios Giannis Alargas, or John the Baptist, whose awful severed head lay bloodied on a painted platter above the portal. Inside the church was a model sponge caïque, for the saint was especially beloved of sponge divers. Golden beeswax tapers burned the small lights of our prayers.

Driving back, we took a long route home through desiccated mountain fields unfavored even by goats, a land where the wild thyme now grew free, a realm inhabited only by bees. High in those hairpin reaches of the island, vertiginous drop to the sea, the painted wooden beehives stood in quiet rows across the hillsides, blue as hope. The sun was setting as the sea came into view, and in the evening light through the bus windows, the thyme gleamed purple among the stones. The rows of sky-blue bee houses glowed like beacons.

# The House of Orfeas
SYMI, 2019

1.

The house was planted high above the Chorio on Symi, a long climb up through a labyrinth of twisting stone streets just wide enough for a laden donkey to pass through, and too far and bewildering for pirates to follow. On the first day I wondered how we'd ever find our way, but then the thread revealed itself in words and images. Story.

    Walk up the five hundred steps of the Kalistrata from Yialos to Chorio, then take a right at the faded butchery sign and begin the farther climb through an ancient realm of homes and ruins to where the great dog that looks like a golden wolf stands on a high parapet and frightens you each time with his bark, past the balcony with old tinsel that glistens in the sun, the particular broken walls overgrown with fig trees where the two white goats live, then up to the courtyard filled with sleepy hungry cats, onward up the stairs where we once saw a dead rat, and the step where three old men sit, past the hand-painted sign of the old supermarket that closed down during the Crisis and never reopened, the blue step beyond it, the empty shrine recently renovated with electric wires to light up some icon that is yet to be installed, the courtyard where three middle-aged women sit in the mornings and evenings with cushions or bright cloths hung up to dry, onward and upward to the white steps beside Stavros Church, past a recently painted villa on the left and on the right the gap-tooth open space of more buildings, abandoned or bombed and crumbled away where you might pause and look out at the sunset, onward past Ian and Lynn's house through a dark medieval alley of low stone arches and deep fig trees until you come at last to a sky blue wall, a deep blue door, the key turning in the lock.

We'd booked a stay in the house of Orfeas, he who visited death and returned. The tale he told when we met was of a sporting accident in which he'd nearly lost his leg. At the time it made him marvel at the preciousness of being alive, and how wondrous it would be simply to go for a walk in the forest.

It was before we'd left for Greece, and we were having tea in our living room in Cape Town. After I made the booking, it turned out that Orfeas was in the neighborhood at the time.

"That was quite an experience," I said about the accident. "Profound."

"Yes," he said, and laughed. "But I've forgotten that lesson now."

His house, like most of the high-quality stone structures on Symi, had been built with sponge money, a single small dwelling still standing intact and freshly painted in a neighborhood of ruins. Even the woodwork was still good. The tall bed platform was carved in curling leaf patterns, and someone had made by hand the old beams, the doors, the window frames, and the ornate *iconostasis*. From the front door you could look far down to Pedi and Yialos and across to Turkey. Watch both sunrise and sunset. Breathe the wide sky. And you could see the pirate ship coming from a long way off in untraceable vessels to plunder homes or steal maidens, the warships and warplanes appearing on the horizon bearing untold disasters, the sponge boats returning from the deep with their hoard of golden sponges, the cruise boats arriving during the season. Living and dying may be a terrifying mystery, but high in the beautiful house at the end of a maze of tiny streets, up there among the ruins of history, you felt safe.

And then at dawn and at dusk, a portal opened. The swallows swept through like dolphins, gliding and swooping at high speed among the broken houses, hunting. Each morning Michael made breakfast at sunrise as the fishing boats set out, insects tracking a small wake across a silver lake. In that gentleness before the day began, the island was asleep except for bakers and fishermen and the cocks crowing from Pedi to Yialos.

After breakfast we'd walk down the hundreds of steps to greet people at Yialos, to meet friends from last time and some new ones, and to swim. Then before the cruise boats arrived around eleven we'd return up the hill, sometimes stopping in Chorio for provisions or lingering for an orange juice or a coffee in that realm of human conversation situated midway between the hubbub of boats and people at Yialos and the remote refuge of the house. Peter Vidal lived there and we saw him quite often at the *kafenion*. He described how his work with refugees had changed its focus since our last visit. Next Stop Symi had evolved into an organization that could be used as a reliable transit for monies donated to support people in need. Then in 2019, when huge numbers of refugees arrived on Symi, the charity raised nearly 13,000 euros to provide breakfast and a bottle of water for them.

"We do what we think is right," he said simply. "We do what we can."

Back by midday at the house of Orfeas, the high solitude of the place was set between the limitlessness of sky and sea. The lanes that for centuries had been filled with the voices of human lives were silent, emptied out, the stonework broken apart, first by emigration and war and then by giant fig trees, with insects nesting in the crevices and goats hopping up to nibble the grass along the tops of crumbling walls. Farther up the hill was a steep reach of high rocks where the road snaked across the island to Panormitis. In the evenings we sat on the steps to eat bread and olives, wait for the last glow of sun, and watch the swallows turn to bats as the stars came out.

2.

One day Manuel appeared suddenly at the *kafenion* on his bike with the gift of a bottle of ouzo and a bag of ripe figs, the first of the season, just picked from his garden. Another time, in the early evening, we arranged to meet in the square and took him up through the labyrinth to the house for a light meal before dark. He brought sweet cakes and salt, and pictures of Tarpon Springs, Florida.

"What is it like there, Tarpon?" I asked.

"It's lovely. It's beautiful. Lots of people there from Halki, Symi, Kalymnos. You know, the Greeks lived on one side of the railroad tracks, the Blacks on the other side, and the whites on the outside. The whites, they had a feeling of superiority."

In the black-and-white or sepia photographs, men in old-fashioned hats and coats load mountains of sponges on a wagon, gather at the sponge market for the divine service on a Sunday, or fool around with giant sponges.

"You can see here that one of the sponge fishers is a Black man," Manuel said, pointing into a picture.

"They were integrated," he explained. "My uncle, he was one of the biggest exporters of sponges. One day, I was about eleven and helping at the sponge factory. A Black guy came in and he was speaking perfect Greek. You know, Greeks are really not racist. Unless they congregate."

We sat together, eating and telling stories as the day faded into night, and when Michael mentioned the squad of young men in uniform marching in formation that morning down near the monument in Yialos, it set the two older men talking about war. Manuel told about the man who stole half a loaf of bread from the Nazis during the Hunger, and how they beat his head in with rifle butts and then left him to live, mentally disabled for the rest of his life. And Michael told how his uncle Dave could not speak to a German for the rest of *his* life, having been marched through Poland as a prisoner when the Nazis were retreating from the Russians, and seen his comrades who were too weak to walk shot dead in front of him.

We sat together quietly for a while, watching the sea. No pirates or warships appeared on the horizon, and the thought that these days the marauders may be people of our own kind was too uncomfortable to dwell on. Instead, Manuel told us how his parents used to send back money from Florida whenever they could, and how there used to be wild cats on Symi. They were big golden cats with a bobtail, he said, but people set traps for them, and poison. So now you don't see them anymore.

"And you know," he continued, "my mother said there

was also a type of condor on the island. And in some parts of Italy, there are even griffins. I didn't believe it until I saw one. They're really huge. They can pick up a cow! Only about two hundred of them left now though."

3.

"It's like a human life," Michael said. "Distinct and recognizable for a while. And then it's gone."

He was once again painting tiny faces in black ink on the pebbles at Manuel's cove. The ink was soluble so they'd wash away with the next tide, but even my phone camera's software could tell they were people.

While he painted, I swam. I swam whenever I could. At the cove the little olive tree on the rock-rose hillside was laden with fruit, and the water shaded from clear to gold to turquoise to deeper and deeper blue. In the harbor the painted boats and buildings sent wide reaches of light into the water so that my eyes just above the surface were filled with the flow of boats and houses, swimming in the rippled paint gleaming red and gold and blue, the mirrored realm of hillside and sky and golden ripples. Over the hill at Pedi, where I swam off a little jetty, small boats moored along the edge and a berry-brown girl and boy in fresh white linen played at the edge, sorting pebbles. And at Saint Nikolaos, a walk away on a narrow path among rocks and oregano, a silver cloud of thousands of tiny fish flowed among the little waves.

Across the island in the sheltered bay at the Monastery of Panormitis, no swimming is allowed. But the luminous waters still enter the soul and the village bus leaves you there for hours with nothing much to do, so that even if you should arrive feeling rushed, the quietness of the place is likely to slow you down. Like Apollo, whose temple is said to have once been planted at the site, the Archangel Michael Panormitis heals people.

It was a bright day this time when we made the pilgrimage on hairpin roads through stony reaches and residual forests too remote for shipbuilding. I had been ill and was joyfully recovering, but each one of us, whatever our condition, makes the journey to Panormitis with a need or a joy or a fear or a gratitude, acknowledged or unacknowledged, little silver tags tied below the icon of the saint like ribbons on the branches of the ancient wishing tree that our family once visited on a hill in the southeast of Turkey, little boats and bottles that wash up from far islands, packed with prayers and sometimes oil lamps, propelled by faith and the Aegean winds, like refugees seeking asylum.

A woman swept the ground with a small grass broom and fervently kissed the finely wrought silver icon of Saint Michael. A young man wept on his knees before him. And Michael and I lit a clutch of tapers, golden beeswax, in the holy darkness of the sanctuary packed with Byzantine angels and saints.

Afterwards we drank orange juice under the tamarisk trees at the edge of the bay. As we sat there together, held in the sheltering arms of an endlessness of blue and the ceaseless waters lapping on the shore, the sparkling actuality of the place was like an invitation to let it all go. Release the fears and the judgments and the words, even the prayers.

4.

*I want you to be to this place.*

The emphatic WhatsApp message came in one evening from Yiannis Parlavantzas on Halki. He said he'd found the details of a diving museum on Kalymnos and felt strongly that I should visit. I'd not expected to see the Island of the Sponge Divers again this time, but his message was one of those injunctions I chose not to ignore. Take this path. So, I booked a ferry day trip, and we made the passage to Kalymnos, two hours each way.

Kostas was at his sponge barrow near the harbor, and he greeted us warmly. When I asked about Latari, he took out some neatly sliced rectangles of sponge that the old man had cut for him that very morning. Something specific and ancient to be used in church for the mass.

"Yes," he said. "He is very well."

"And Thodoris?" Michael asked the question with some anxiety. He had recently felt an absence whenever he thought of the gentle poet and somehow sensed that he was no longer alive.

"Yes," Kostas said gravely. "He has died. About two weeks ago. I didn't want to go to the church...I wanted to remember him as he was."

We shook our heads, silenced by the mystery. To be alive, and then to be dead.

"We don't know our expiry date," Kostas went on, shaking his head again. Then he brightened and said, "And that's good!"

We all smiled. Yes, indeed.

Michael said he wanted a couple of small fine sponges to use for watercolors. Kostas picked out several for him, but when Michael asked the price, he refused.

"No," he said insistently. "It's for you."

The visit ended with kisses.

"Enjoy your life," we said to each other, waving as we went down the street.

From the baker, I bought a bag of *paksimadi*, one of the

names for the hard-dried breads that the Kalymnian fleets used to take on the long journey.

Then at the hotel we found Henrik and sat together for a while in his shady courtyard. He was sad to hear about Thodoris and said he'd not seen him for some time. I told him the poet's parting words on our last visit, as I'd remembered them: "Life goes on. That is the mystery." Afterwards I realized that the word Thodoris had actually said was "beauty," not "mystery." But already it had changed in the memory.

"Yes, that's it," Henrik said. "And it *is* a mystery."

In our few minutes together before we set off for the museum that had brought us back to the island, he spoke about his life, how much he enjoyed the unpretentiousness of living on Kalymnos.

"You know," he said. "I have enough. For the hotel rent, for good food, for a happy life. I'm not interested anymore in buying another pair of shoes or changing the color of the sofa."

"Yes, exactly."

5.

The road wound through rocky hills to the coastal village of Vlihadia, a humble, untouristed place where people were swimming and playing in the sun at the edge of an azure sea. You could buy fruit and vegetables from an old van, and across the little road at the end of a stone walkway against the backdrop of a stony landscape stood the stone building of the Valsamides Sea World Museum. The walls of our destination were painted blue.

"I will tell you everything," the owner, Yiannis Valsamides, had said when I called from Symi, "and then you write it in your book."

We found Yiannis at his café, a powerfully built man with a strong gaze. Once he'd finished with the table he was serving, he took us over to the museum, leading us under an archway. Like many a gateway into another world, it looked quite unexceptional. Talking, we stepped through into an assemblage of seventeen thousand things.

"This is a one-man show," Yiannis explained. "Everything here was collected by one man. It was his hobby. He was diving for forty-eight years, so he probably spent more time under the sea than on land."

"Wow," I said.

"And this," he went on, pointing to the black diving suit hung up at the entrance, "is the suit he was wearing when he died."

"And who was he?" I asked, anticipating the answer.

"He is my father."

"I am sorry."

"He died underwater, so he was happy."

It's what we say to comfort ourselves when a person loses their life doing some other extreme sport. She would have wanted to go that way, we say when the woman who swims every morning is taken by a shark. He died doing what he loved, when the hang glider is broken in high turbulence.

"He was sixty-five," Yiannis said. "He died on the tenth of August, 2013."

It was six years later now, and the day still burned clear.

"And everything here was collected by him?" I asked. "It's completely amazing. What would you like to tell us about?"

He looked doubtful, gazing at the multitude.

"What things are special to you?" I asked. "Any special stories?"

"Everything is special. Everything has a special story."

It was the multiplicity that was the wonder, not particular objects. Still, Yiannis showed us an amphora, the sculpture of an Assyrian god, the largest sponge in the world, a massive shell from Malta...and waved his hand towards the masses of things brought back from the deep.

"This museum is to promote Kalymnian history," he said. "Kalymnos is the sponge divers' island. Since Homerus. The only history we have here is diving. The sea means Kalymnos, and Kalymnos means the sea. Kalymnians say the sea is our property."

I laughed and said, "That's not true."

"Yes, it is!" he said emphatically. "Because Kalymnians have died all over the world."

"Okay, yes, sure. I do understand that," I said. "It was very dangerous."

"And why did the sponge diving stop?" Michael asked.

"Two reasons," Yiannis said. "After Chernobyl, the industry was destroyed. And then, the mothers and families said please don't do it. Go and be a scientist. Doctors and lawyers. Now all the professors at the university in Athens are Kalymnians."

Like many people I'd met, he had an answer to the question that left little place for uncertainty or for the idea of overfishing. At the same time, his view of diving was not uncritical. Growing up with a diver in the family had made him keenly attuned to the obsession.

"He was crazy to dive," he said. "There's a saying on the island, *I sfoungári I tomári*. You can't translate it, but it means 'You can go for sponges and die, or you can be a normal man.'"

I remembered then that it was the title of the book about

sponge diving Latari had shown me on Kalymnos, on our previous visit. "Thank you. That puts it very clearly," I said.

I added that it reminded me of what I'd understood about the macho ethos among the sponge divers generally, and on Kalymnos especially. "You know, something like, 'It's dangerous, but I'm a strong man.'"

"Yes," he said, and nodded. "It is a madness."

Yiannis explained that his father was born just after the war, so when he was a child the sponge boats were still going out in great numbers. It made a big impression on him. All he ever wanted to do was dive.

"He became a maniac of the diving," he said. "Everything about the sea, my father did it. *Skafandro*, scuba, *skandalopetra*, free diving. All the systems. His life was the sea...he *was* the sea. One English magazine called my father Poseidon. He was so passionate. He was crazy for the sea."

Yiannis did not say directly what it meant to be the son of the god who dwells in the mind's seabed, lord of the watery deep and the tempests. He did not explain what it felt like to be the child of Poseidon, always left behind on dry land. But he'd made an entire museum to honor his father, and the grief was tangible.

"He didn't care about nothing," he said. "Only the sea."

Then he left us to wander among the collection of exhibits. Pearls, coins, fossil fish, hundreds of cowries of every size and hue, many species of other shells, desiccated crabs, dead starfish, sharks' teeth, sharks' heads, dried seahorses, turtles, turtle shells, ancient bowls marked with the traces of the sea, amphorae of every kind, bronze rings, sponges of every variety and size, shears for clipping sponges into saleable shapes, a rotting old canvas sponge-diving suit, a smooth *skandalopetra*, a sand glass for tracking the sponge diver's time underwater, a sponge boat lamp, a collection of about twenty compressed air tanks, harpoons for harvesting sponges in the old way, rusted anchors, a safe rusted closed, items of use in Orthodox worship, rusted chains and propellers, a drowned radio, photographs of divers and soldiers and sponge boats and villagers, a black-and-white picture of three tiny boys each holding a massive sponge on his head, an image of a mountain of sponges on the shore of Florida in 1918, rusted swords and flintlock pistols, airplane parts from shot-down German planes, rows of great cannonballs turned green from the sea, and exploded and unexploded bombs encrusted with the white calcareous structures of sea creatures.

"Everything from the sea is here," Yiannis said, gesturing to the multitude as he left us to return to the café.

No doubt about it, the place was magnificent. A wonder. Seventeen thousand things brought back to land by one man. Everything. The myriad things. When I'd asked about his father's day job, Yiannis said it was something to do with flour.

Now meandering among the vast assemblage, I tried to glimpse a hint of the joy of his real work, the ecstasy of the dive, descending through the portal of blue darkness into that other world, swimming almost weightless among the people of the sea, flying free in the land of water, returning over and over to the deepest deep. The memory of Lefteris—another god, if Katerina Mourati was to be believed—came back to me from Patmos, his smile as he shook his head, remembering his sponge diving days. That was really life, he told us, and when he stopped diving it was like an amputation.

Now the Sea World Museum was packed with Poseidon's findings, the map of a wide-ranging mind fascinated by every kind of sea plant and sea animal, and every random artifact of human culture that appears among them, especially the remains of sponge diving and war. Even for those of us who remain on dry land, the impulse is familiar. You travel to another realm and you want to bring things home. To share it, to tell the story. You want to say this is how it is there, look what I have seen! For Stavros Valsamides, the repetition of this quest seems to have become a defining purpose: to dive into the terrors and beauties beyond the reach of our sunlit world, to witness the miracle, to return home bearing the gifts of transformation, and then to dive again.

We were the only visitors, and we picked our way ponderously among the displays, taking notes, taking photographs. As Yiannis described it, the museum of his father's dives had been set up to provide information about the history of Kalymnos, and to promote a sense of wonder about the sea. Yet the overriding effect for me was a mixture of astonishment and weariness. It truly was extraordinary that a single brave and determined man had brought back from the deep such a multitude of things. Each one was the record of a moment of discovery and fascination. Each one, as his son said, was special. But the seventeen thousand things we saw were set in place like an array of butterflies in an eternal showcase, or an aging arrangement of stuffed animals with glass eyes and moth-eaten flanks, fairy gold that turns to dust when it's brought home to our world.

What was missing, of course—the essential element—was sea.

The walls were painted blue, and a few small aquarium tanks served as a reminder. But for most of it, the Sea World Museum was dry. Out of the deep and the dark, out of the watery tides and the ocean forests, one object after another had been brought into the light, placed on dry land, put into order. But the living smell of the salty deep that had called to the man who desired it more than anything was gone. The living mind of the sea had been disassembled. And the man himself, gone too.

What happens when a community of beings becomes a collection of things, when a wild world of interpenetrating lives is mined for its riches, when something is so desirable that we're compelled to plunder it, no matter the cost? And what is it that happens when a journey becomes a traveler's tale, fixed in place by our words? Perhaps the sadness I felt was for all of it. The father lost to the sea, the sea lost to plunder, the dark forests of Poseidon lost to light and organization, the breathing flow of the world lost to an assemblage of things.

By the end of the visit, as we peered out of the building towards the midday sun, facing the azure radiance beyond the beach like exhausted travelers, the Sea World Museum at our backs felt like more than simply some idiosyncratic collection of underwater treasures or a monument to one godlike man's obsession. There was something about the place that held a lens to the whole endeavor. The quest, the deep dive, the return, the treasures.

The visit was wondrous and rather uncomfortable, and I was grateful to Yiannis Parlavantzas for instructing me to make the pilgrimage. And then, at the threshold, stood the sculptures.

Near the museum entrance was a collection of bronze human figures, sensitively made, about half life-size. Their presence was so quiet that I'd walked past them when we arrived, eager for the main attraction. Now, as we were leaving, their silent power called for my attention: a gathering of sponge divers and the human world that enabled them. We turned back to look.

6.

"He's the most famous sculptor in Kalymnos," Yiannis Valsamides said, when we were finally leaving the museum and I told him how much I loved what we'd seen of the work.

"I can believe it," I said.

Each sculpture in the assemblage depicted some aspect of the Aegean in the forms of human life, almost all of them directly concerned with sponge diving. One good-looking young diver waits expectantly before a dive, helmet under his arm. Another has taken off the helmet and sits wearily smoking a cigarette, the first test that his lungs have survived the dive. A lone man harpoons sponges in the ancient way. A group of tired comrades sit together in a boat, their bodies speaking the intimacy of knees and boots and shoulders. Other divers tend the precious hoard of sponges, trimming, cleaning, packing, or stringing on a thread. A captain stands alone, gazing into the beyond with a face that looks familiar. On shore a group of powerful-looking men in suits gather to talk, while a diver walks painfully with a stick, his legs crippled by the bends, another plays an ancient instrument, and a woman dances.

In each of the works the body and its labor are intimately rendered, and while the sculptures are informative, even documentary, they are also full of heart. Most poignantly, and Yiannis drew our attention to this sculpture in particular, in *Marine Pietà* a diver cradles the still body of a young dolphin in his arms. The sculpture was made of bronze. It had never lived. It was inert. And yet in its stillness, something stirred.

The diver's face was filled with an extraordinary expression of tenderness.

"You must visit him," Yiannis told me, as we said our goodbyes. "His name is Sakellaris Koutouzis."

I felt the same way, but the ferry was about to leave and there would not be another for some days. So, once we were back on Symi, I tracked down the sculptor online and we arranged a video chat, something quite new to me.

Sakellaris was a man in his late sixties, with a gray mustache, serious eyes, and an expression that was at once genial and grave. Having seen his work, I did not find the wise sensitivity of the man himself surprising. Yet I could not have anticipated his warmth and openness.

"Art is a strange necessity of people," he began, apologizing for his English. "But what it offers is not a complete information or quantity. And the meaning depends on who is looking."

He explained that in his professional life he had been a mathematician, but when he'd turned fifty in 2000, he'd stopped teaching and begun sculpting. The works at the museum were part of a larger collection on sponge diving.

"So, you focused on the sponge divers because...?" I asked.

"I was born here on Kalymnos, and in my first years, even before electricity, life was lived much closer to nature," he said. "I had the feeling: I have met the last divers."

He said it emphatically, with a sort of wonder. I realized he was of exactly the same generation as the Sea World diver Stavros Valsamides, two boys who'd grown up in the enormous presence of the gods and taken different life paths in their response to them.

"Living underwater," Sakellaris went on, remembering, "they were almost like dolphins."

He told me how awed he'd felt by the divers when he was a child, by the difficulties they'd faced in their daily lives, and how hard they'd had to work to support their families.

"Some left the profession," he said, "but I don't know if they were happy. They were *proud* even when they were working so hard. A diver would know: I support families. That is something that doesn't exist today. Maybe they were poor, but they had pride."

The way Sakellaris described it, they were the last Greek heroes. Much has been told about the terrifyingly difficult life of the sponge diver, and I could see it in the faces of those I'd met. On Patmos, Lefteris the sponge diver had become somber when he'd talked about it. On Kalymnos, old man Latari had simply shaken his head. And even after the *skafandro* had become obsolete, it was a ruthless and dangerous life. Yet both men, aristocrats of the sponge boats, had a quiet grandeur in their walk that was discernible long into old age. And for all the exploitation and deprivation, the hunger and loneliness of six months at sea each year, the longing for women and children and home, the terrible sunburn, the tough captains, the profiteering merchants, the anxiety of sharks or death or disability—for all that, Lefteris remembered his life well. And now it was the memory of diving that kept him alive. Underwater, underworld. Diving deep and surfacing. Dying and returning. Over and over again.

"Nowadays people would run away from the sort of difficulties they faced," Sakellaris said. "But they were brave men."

Then he said it again, "I had the feeling that I have met the last sponge divers."

To make quite sure that I got what he meant, he told me a fable from a small village in India. For generations, he said, people from the village had been extending their capacity by diving for corals, pearls, sponges. Then one day the maharajah's daughter went swimming in the sea and was taken by a monster. Her distraught father asked everyone, "Who are the brave men?" It was, of course, one of the divers who swam out, and he found the maiden and rescued her. But then—and here the story takes a different turn from the magical ending you may have expected—once the diver had brought her safely to shore, the monster began pulling him back. "Don't forget my children," he called to the others, as he was taken out to sea.

"You see," Sakellaris said, "I think this story fits with all people living on islands, or on coastlines, all over the world, people who live this category of risk to bring something home for their families."

At the time it seemed an extraordinary context to be having a conversation about the tragic heroism of ordinary human lives and the capacity of art to evoke it. But even through this unfamiliar medium his intense conviction came through.

"And what about the men in suits?" I asked. "I can see why your work wants us to see the divers in this way. But what about the bosses, the merchants, the ones who made all the money? I was interested to see how you depicted them."

"Those are people like Aristotle Onassis, big international personalities, people who worked for profit, who chose this category of work to make their success. I put them together with the divers."

"But they didn't die or come home paralyzed."

"Yes. I could have done them fat, you know with big cigars...But no. I wanted to show them as people, just in a

different condition. I didn't want to do a whole class structure critique. I wanted them to be people."

"Thank you. I see."

The subtlety of his response was a gentle but firm corrective to my own version of the story. Where I may be likely to see stereotypes, he recognized human beings. And human beings are the focus of the whole collection. For although Sakellaris called it *Forms of the Aegean*, these forms do not appear in images of waves or sea creatures, but in the attentive representation of human people like Stavros Valsamides, the diver whose life *is* the sea. As his son had put it to us at the museum, the sea means Kalymnos and Kalymnos means the sea.

The single sculpture with a nonhuman person in it is *Marine Pietà*. I imagine that the sponge divers had often brought back wondrous tales about dolphins, their fine consciousness and their capacity for friendship. But Sakellaris's dolphin is not just a sentient being; it is a sacrificial one, and the work speaks back to Michelangelo and all the other pietàs.

"I wanted to depict the diver with a sensitive face," he said. "A polite, well-shaven, intellectual man. Someone who is feeling for the dolphin as he would for a member of his family."

"It's very moving," I said. "Beautiful."

"I wanted to give a message about pollution," he went on, "to say something about... the solidarity of mankind to other lives."

"Yes."

"We are facing important difficulties for the earth at present. And we are receiving important messages from Nature. Maybe it's too early—or too late. I don't know."

Returning afterwards to my notes, I could not help thinking of Amitav Ghosh, his work on climate change, and in particular *Gun Island*, which was published around the time of this conversation. In the novel, his character keeps receiving such messages. And while the experience is hugely unsettling to his rationalist skepticism, he slowly becomes more receptive to the sentience of the living world, and to the imagination as the gateway of its communication.

That afternoon with Sakellaris, a year before COVID was to make us wearily familiar with the technology of video meetings, it felt odd and somehow remarkable to be sitting in front of computer screens on our different islands after a siesta on a warm afternoon in midsummer, talking from the heart with a person you'd only just met about emergency calls from living nature. But the sculptures had opened the gate, and we'd simply stepped through.

"The way I see it," I said, "the ecological crisis of the Aegean is like a microcosm of the planetary crisis. And the sponge industry, well, the overfishing of the seabed, seems like an allegory of the whole problem."

"Exactly," he responded emphatically. "*Yperaliefsi.*"

"Which means?"

"Overfishing."

I told him then about the ouzo we'd shared with Yiannis Parlavantzas on Halki and the phrase he'd taught us. *Metron ariston.* All things in good measure.

"You think we can apply that to...to what has gone wrong?" I said.

He laughed heartily, and said, "There was no *metron* at all!"

"Right. On Symi someone told me how his father used to drag an iron bar behind the sponge boat, scraping up everything in its path."

"Yes!" Sakellaris said. "They destroy everything! All the life! They make the ocean floor like the road of an airport! But that iron bar, it's become illegal now. For the last decades it's not been permitted by the EU."

"I guess that's something."

I said that how wherever we'd been on the islands, I'd thought I was looking for the story of sponge diving, but in fact what I'd discovered, over and over, was something about the heart.

It was the same with his sculptures. The focus is the Aegean, seeing its forms through human beings' involvement in the sponge industry. But his real subject was surely the sympathetic imagination.

"You know, the way you see your subjects, and the way they relate to each other, it's very compassionate. It's almost as though what you're really depicting is the heart. Even the men in suits. You could have simply represented them as caricatures, but you're seeing them kindly. Even the bosses," I said.

Sakellaris smiled and nodded. "I agree with everything you say!" he said.

Then he told me about the sculpture of the man with a familiar face. "It's Odysseus Elytis. I called the sculpture *Oh Captain, My Captain*. You see, I want to bring poetry into my art. I find it interesting. In the Greek language, poetry and sculpture have a lot of connections. Well, music too, of course. So anyway, Elytis is the one driving the boat."

"The poet is driving the boat! Thank you. That's perfect."

After all, when Jason and the Argonauts must pass by the Sirens it's Orpheus whose music offers the way through.

It was enough. More than. We'd said everything that needed to be said. But before saying goodbye, I showed Sakellaris a painting that Michael had done after our last visit. It was a picture of another man who loved the music of words, the poet Thodoris.

"Oh, yes," Sakellaris said, looking closely at the image of his friend on his screen. "He was a very good guy, a good heart. You've got him there. All his kindness, his good heart."

7.

It was a Sunday morning when Michael called out to me. He had seen on his news feed that the man who wrote "The Girl from Ipanema," that quintessential song of a certain era, had just died. At that moment the bells began to ring, each church on the island calling with a different voice, each with a distinct tune and character of ringing in which the fine irregularities in the rhythm speak of a real human being tolling the bell, arm muscles pulling the ropes.

Looking out from the house of Orfeas, what you see is beautiful. The distant prospect draws the eye across the sea all the way to the place formerly known as Greece, as Manuel once called it with a wink, blue mountains layered one behind the other like fine tissue papers, boats setting out in the rosy-fingered morning, swallows diving and twittering in the early air and at dusk. You could also call it peaceful, a light breeze moving the leaves of the fig trees, pigeons calling, and six churches immediately in view. But one afternoon, as I'd walked back through the narrow lanes between stone buildings where old men sit together on a small step facing the path, or old women sit together, the beauty or peacefulness or picturesque qualities of the scene had simply slipped away and I'd been released for a moment from wanting to frame or document any version of Greece or island life, or even the beautiful. Instead, what had appeared was simply the tender, ruined, painful livingness of it all.

Now, on a Sunday morning that marked the death of a musician and the small continuity of his song, up there with all the bells ringing, our small world carefully tended among the houses abandoned during the Italian occupation, or bombed out during World War II, up in the craggy land of gray rocks, a few pine trees making it in the heat with only winter rain, up among the thyme and sage and oregano, now drying in midsummer, the houses in the valley below us terracotta and white and dusky yellow and a faded cerulean, fig trees growing through the windows of ruined *salas*, the arches broken and the windows filled up with stones and the hard green fruits turning purple in the heat, from up there the sea gleams blue, always blue—though Homer never called it that—and the sky is blue too, an infinity of blue, and it seems to me that the old gods of the place are possibly no other than ourselves, each one of us, children and overladen donkeys and broken stone walls and flaking paint and cat shit and cats and a smiling young woman in black talking on her phone and the golden dog on the parapet and the other dogs in chains, and the chair chained to the wall where one particular old man sits smoking in a present moment in which everything is interesting, everything is beautiful. Bees on the honey we left out for them, fig trees loud with cicadas, blue mountains, cerulean sky, azure sea, swallows that swoop and dive, and we humans who keep on ringing bells, lighting candles, making songs, making art, telling stories, cheating death, breathing deep, if only for this moment.

8.

"Something you may enjoy," Manuel wrote in a WhatsApp message to me a few days before we left Symi. "It's a sort of Greek rap."

The gift was the link to "Dirlada," a song recorded by Captain Pantelis Ginis and his crew in 1965. It was the same year that, as Google informed me, "The Girl from Ipanema" had won a Grammy for record of the year. "Dirlada" is a call-and-response with a catchy riff and rhythm that won't let you go once you've heard it. Spliced into the audio track on YouTube was some familiar-looking video footage of a sponge caïque at sea, a diver getting into a scuba suit, a diver harvesting sponges in dreamy blue waters, the sand glass on board, the rope connecting to his comrades, men cleaning the live black sponges on deck, divers eating a meal together from the same bowl at the end of the day, sponges strung on long threads, a view of Kalymnos harbor as the fleet returns, bells ringing and ringing as women come running out, laughing, tiny boys following in their own small gang, more cleaning of sponges on land, treading and sorting, strong muscles, strong men, packing the sponges in wooden crates, dancing.

I knew Sakellaris would remember the song, as would Russ Bernard whose main research on Kalymnos and with the sponge fleet was from just this time. So I emailed them both, and both responded at once. Sakellaris wrote back that "Dirlada" was an old Kalymnian folk song and sent me a copy of the sheet music. At sea, he said, it was sung by sponge divers during the long voyages, and on land in cheerful moments people would sing it again, with different lyrics each time.

Russ identified the footage as being from his film *Matadors of the Deep*.

"Nice to hear from you," he wrote. "Wow, listening to that song playing over scenes from the film I helped make... really took me back. Ginis took an old Kalymnian song and made up his own lyrics. Those lyrics are what everyone my age remembers."

The slightly bawdy lyrics that the recording set in place don't translate that well into English, but they speak of exhaustion, of the Poli, of women, of the lords' throats, of more women, of cutting violets...It was a song to raise the heart, to remind everyone on board of the women and sex and other good things that awaited them at the end of their labors, to offer a quick jeer to their mercantile masters, and to give everyone working on the caïque in terrible conditions the courage to continue. As the story goes, Captain Ginis composed "Dirlada" on board with one hand on the tiller, and the crew members would sing it and clap hands to hold a rhythm for the man turning the wheel of the air pump for the diver underwater.

After they recorded it in Athens the song went on to become a popular hit in Greece and elsewhere in Europe in the 1970s and was performed in several languages.

But "Dirlada" reaches far back into folk memory. I found a survey that said the song may have its origins in the forms and rhythms of North Africa, after centuries of contact between Kalymnos and the coast. Once it reached the island, generations of Kalymnians went on to sing some version of it as a work song to keep people going in the midst of hard labor.[67]

As Russ put it, the song takes you back. Whatever its exact origins, the tinny sounds playing on my phone were a trace of the life on deck and on the islands that reached into the past and continued into the memory of people who are now elders. More extraordinarily, even magically, it takes you back to the soundtrack of the sponge dive itself. This was the music on deck of those who were waiting for the diver to return: the clapping rhythm, the voices of comrades, the anxiety, the hope.

These things now seem irrecoverably lost, but for a few minutes the song returns you, even if you hadn't been there at the time, and even, paradoxically, in the very moment that the song itself is lost. Once Ginis Pantelis and his crew recorded "Dirlada," that particular version of it was set in place as the lyrics that everyone of a certain generation remembers. Perhaps by then the old songs, sung at festivals and danced in couples, were already slipping away, even as the long lineage of sponge divers was coming to the end of its run. Perhaps if the captain had not recorded it, the song would have disappeared along with the *skafandros* and the island gods. It's the perennial paradox of memory and recording and even all storytelling. The act of recording it marks the end of the utterance in which it was something less tangible and more alive. Yet if you do not fix it in place, it may well be lost entirely.

Playing the song repeatedly over the next few days, I came to imagine "Dirlada" as a kind of time capsule, a Proustian cake that when tasted floods the mind with the tune of things at that precise moment in the 1960s before it was all about to change. What came to mind for me was the meticulous list Russ had made in 1964 of the shops and craftspeople working on Kalymnos at the time, and for some reason I kept thinking in particular of the single shop of the kerchief maker. Each time as the song came to an end, I'd tap Repeat and listen again, hoping to catch a hint of it, a world in which there is time and place for grown men singing together while a comrade makes a risky dive, and for the occupation of kerchief maker.[68]

On our last afternoon on Symi we walked down to Yialos and found Dinos sitting on the harbor wall outside his shop, washing a crate of sponges in the sea. We'd come to say goodbye and to ask if he would listen to the song. He stopped his work and a broad smile opened his face as he nodded his head to the rhythm.

"Kalymnos," he said.

Later we bought a goat milk ice cream for ourselves and one for Panormitis the baker from Giorgios, a man about my age who looked like Cat Stevens. As we ate our ice cream, I played the song for him, and again the strange magic of the song produced that smile, a knowing smile full of memory and youth.

The next morning on the village bus down to Pedi for a last swim, I found Manuel's link and tapped Play once more. The only other passenger on board was a tiny elderly woman in a black dress in the seat in front of us. The instant the song began, she gave a start as if she'd been shocked, and the driver whipped his head around to say something to her. Then we all listened in silence as the bus drove down the hill to the sea. As the rollicking, irresistible tune played to its end, the woman in black took out a handkerchief to dab at her eyes.

9.

The blonde student beside me on the deck of the ferry to Rhodes was checking her phone when the young sailor approached her. He was athletically built, with smoldering dark good looks and a flash of smile against tanned skin. I watched as he handed her a piece of paper with three words written in English. "Angel. Beautiful baby."

She read it and looked up at him with a puzzled expression.

"It's you," he said. "You are so beautiful."

"Oh." She laughed, perhaps a little nervously.

"What are you doing tonight?" he said.

"Sleeping, I hope." She spoke with an English accent.

The situation was so stereotypical and the pickup line so absurd, even naive, that I was surprised when she agreed to meet him at her hotel after he'd knocked off from work at seven.

Then I remembered the *kamaki* and a description of an old style of sponge fishing. Instead of diving for sponge, two men would set off in a small boat, one sculling while the other scanned the seabed through a glass-bottomed bucket. Once he saw a likely sponge, he'd hook it with a trident attached to a long pole, tearing it out to bring to the surface. Sometimes the sponges were so mutilated by being torn from their roots that they were of little value or would not grow back. And even a skillfully hooked sponge was always damaged, with a hole penetrating right through. The word for the hook was *kamaki*, a name also used on the Aegean islands for Greek men who seduce foreign women with their charm during the season and boast about their conquests in the *kafenia* during the winter.[69]

The two young people beside me talked for a while, and then the good-looking sailor said he had to leave.

"When I am with you," he added, gazing at her with smoky eyes, "I can't control myself. I must go away now. I will see you later."

The English student smiled up at him. She was blonde and young and lean and lovely and she was on holiday in Greece.

# The Gate
## RHODES, 2019

1.

Through the Sea Gate on the little beach beyond the Knights' great fortress, the water was clear as living glass. I put down my bag, pulled off my shoes, rolled up my dress, waded in.

Afterwards we found a table on the roof of a taverna where the waiter poured an entire glass of ouzo and ice and a glass of water down my back. He was a thin man dressed in black, in his late seventies probably. When the tray slipped out of his hands, he was so mortified that he ran away.

After a few minutes he came back with a dry cloth, and said, wringing his hands with a tragic expression, "Oh, Madame! First time in my life!"

"It's really no problem at all. Really."

My dress was soaked. But it had been a hot day and I didn't mind. Still he went back to the kitchen looking horrified, and when a young waitress came to our table with more ouzo and a gift of olives, tomato, and feta, she told us sadly, "He's feeling very bad."

A little later the man returned. Shaking his head, he said to me, "I cry."

However much I tried to reassure him, it wasn't enough.

After he'd gone, we had the idea of asking Google Translate how to say "it is a libation." The word felt suitably Greek in an ancient sort of way, but the translation my cellphone suggested was "*eleftheria*," which we knew meant "liberation". That might have worked too, but instead I tried typing in the words, "it is a blessing." It came up with "*eínai mia evlogía*."

There was no way of being sure whether this was any better, but it was probably better than nothing. And I felt it too, a blessing. As we were leaving the taverna, I handed my phone to the old man.

He read the words slowly. Finally, he smiled. "Now I can work," he said.

2.

The next day at the airport boarding gate, a big young man in a police uniform pulled a couple out of the line ahead of us. The policeman was angry, adrenalized.

"This is not you!" he shouted, holding up the man's maroon passport in one hand and striking it repeatedly with the index finger of the other.

The man he was addressing was perhaps in his forties, with stress lines across his mouth and eyes, dark hair and olive skin. His partner said nothing but watched his face keenly, mouth a little open.

"*Sprechen Deutsch! Sprechen Deutsch!*" the young policeman shouted.

He was answered with silence.

The man in uniform shouted even more emphatically, pointing to the face on the *Reisepass*, "This is not you! This is not you!"

As our line moved on to board the plane, all we could see

was the policeman shouting and beating the passport, and the man saying nothing, mesmerized by the enormity of the moment. He looked like a cornered animal, dark eyes alert.

# PART THREE

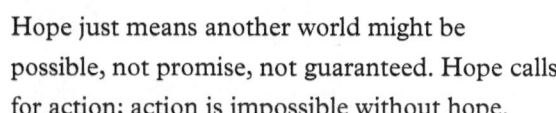

Hope just means another world might be possible, not promise, not guaranteed. Hope calls for action; action is impossible without hope.
—Rebecca Solnit, *Hope in the Dark: Untold Histories, Wild Possibilities*

# War
RHODES, 2022

I.

It was our first day back on Rhodes. This time I was well again, but everyone on the plane had been wearing surgical masks. After two and a half years of severe lockdowns and social distancing, Michael and I felt shy of other people. But as we set out into the streets of the Old Town again, the social anxiety that had become familiar since the beginning of the pandemic gently melted away. It was gloriously warm. Everyone was in colorful summer clothes. Hardly anyone was wearing a mask. For the first time, we took ours off in public. We walked through the stone gate to the sea.

Our previous trips to the islands felt like another era, as though the pandemic had erected a wall of mist separating Before and After. Looking back on that time, what I find most remarkable is how vague that deeply strange period of our lives has become in the memory.

The clearest image that returns to me from the mist, probably because it was our family's main contact with other human beings, is of a small ritual that began in our street on March 27, 2020, on the first night of the lockdown. Beginning on that day, like many people around the world in those early weeks, neighbors in our small cul-de-sac would come to our gates at an appointed time in the evening to ring bells, strike gongs, beat drums, shout and whoop. "Thank you, doctors and nurses and health-care workers!" we'd call out, adding in anyone in particular who came to mind. Over the months, the ritual grew. The meek elderly man across the road who turned out to have been a long-time drummer in a rock band set up his drum kit on the veranda and began to lead the music. A little girl danced on the wall, neighbors in the stone house leaned out of their windows to whoop and clap, others found bongos, Michael rang his Tibetan bell, I rang my finger cymbals, and sometimes a passerby paused to dance.

Perhaps we were the last people in the world still doing this every night. But it was a cheering thing, and our longing for human community had made us find it among the people we'd known by sight for years and hardly greeted. We learned one another's names. We sang happy birthday. We sent each other pictures of sunrises and of our first vaccinations. The evening band of drums and bells continued almost without a break for the next eighteen months, not because of any persistent belief or even solidarity but because we couldn't let go of this daily fragment of community.

Now back in Greece, it was not just the terrifying mist of COVID time that made things feel different. Our last visit to the islands was before the wildfires that had erupted when temperatures had risen to 47 degrees. It was before Putin's war in Ukraine. And it was before Erdoğan's recent threats. Young soldiers once again were being sent out to die. Bombs were shattering neighborhoods not far away. Millions more people had been displaced from their homes. Millions more had become refugees. And there was talk of yet another war on the horizon.

As we sat at the edge of the Ippokratous Square on our first day eating big ice creams, it was a relief to have lost touch with international news since leaving Cape Town. But soon enough the man inviting customers into the jewelry shop next door said hello, and when he learned Michael was a jeweler, he was keen to talk.

"Have you heard that Erdoğan now says he wants the islands?" he said.

The old antagonism with Turkey had just been wound up another notch. At a recent display of large-scale Turkish military drills near İzmir, the president had warned Greece not to arm the Aegean islands. Everyone had recognized this as a threat.

While Michael and the jeweler talked, I watched the other tourists wandering through or stopping for selfies in front of the fountain with its bronze statue of Athena's little owl. The shops now sold gelati, restaurant food, jewelry, T-shirts, leather, fridge magnets, and the atmosphere was infectiously relaxing and buoyant. Even so, when I tried to shut out the men's talk of war, the square where we were sitting was tracked through with ghosts from the last one.

My notebook recorded that there used to be a spice shop on the north side, owned by the Habib family. Elie Rahamin had the ribbon and button shop. The Yerushalmi and Hassan families and Sammy Notrica all sold textiles. Yosef Capeluto sold bottles, plates, pots, and pans. Rafael Franco had a cheese shop. Heskia Codron was the jeweler. Bension Levy was a photographer. The Modiano family sold postcards. Mussani Mizrahi and Yosef "Hai" Franco were the money changers. Behor Hasson was the shoemaker.[70]

It was a hot July day like this one. Stella Levi was twenty-one and her sister Renée was twenty-three. In Stella's heart was a dream of studying in Italy, her suitcase already packed and her life mapped out. Right up to that moment, she says, her face on my phone screen at once both sparkling and tragic, they believed that the persecutions could only happen far away. When the Nazi soldiers came for them, they were wearing cotton summer dresses and cork sandals. Stella's dress was white with green polka dots. I find these details unforgettable.

After the war, Stella and Renée were among the 151 Jews from Rhodes who survived the death camps. Their parents were among the many who did not.

The sisters made their way to America, but for the rest of their lives the vanished community of their youth and the terror of its devastation remained an open wound. I lost my home, my roots, my father's house, Stella explains on my phone screen to an audience of New Yorkers who all seem too young. Even now in her late nineties, the memory of that stolen life is as clear as yesterday, she says, as though the horror of its irreparable erasure had branded a clear space in the heart in which an entire world might be preserved whole.

2.

"We have a very old name," Kostantinos Dionysiu said. "The god of wine. From Kalymnos."

The present paterfamilias at the guesthouse where we were staying in Rhodes was telling me about his family. His father, Vasilis, was born in 1926, the same year as Renée Levy, and he grew up on the sponge boats after his own father was shot for being a communist and his mother died.

When the Germans occupied Rhodes in 1943, he happened to be on the island and with three other young men managed to slip away to Turkey. From there he made it to Cyprus, where he joined the British army. Because Vasilis was an orphan, Kostas explained, when he went to Alamein they put him in the artillery. As he mentioned this, the image came to mind of my own father: young Mick who faked the eye test in order to join up at seventeen, wrote terrifying poems about the Libyan Desert, and physically survived what he called the electric storm of Alamein but found himself afterwards in a hospital in Alexandria with a passage home for when he was mentally well enough to travel.

Vasilis also survived the war, and after years of fighting and finally the liberation of the Dodecanese, he was due to receive sixty gold coins to buy land and a house. But Greece was poor, Kostas said. No money. Everything was bombed. And anyway, all he wanted was to go back to sea. Like young Petros tis Psarofagias on Halki, he wanted a boat. It wasn't part of the plan, but his commanding officer somehow found a boat for him that would go with wind, and he returned to the only life he'd known before the war. Sailing, fishing, diving for sponges.

Yes, they were using the *skafandro*, Kostas said when I asked. And, yes, it was dangerous. He explained that in his great-grandfather's day, when he used to take three big caïques to the coast of Afriki from Kalymnos for six months each year, he was free diving for sponges with the *skandalopetra* and the main danger was sharks. Later, it became the diving suit itself.

"My father said it was like Skýlla and Cháryvdi."

Scylla and Charybdis. The ancient metaphor of two inescapable terrors sounded vividly right for the seafaring man.

"You mean it's a choice between two bad things?" I said.

"Yes. Like that."

"Okay, so you try to choose the less bad one."

When at last one day his boat was split apart in a great storm, Vasilis did come back to Rhodes, and there he met his wife. Now he was ready for a house, Kostas said, so the military bought him two Nissen huts. This is where Kostas himself was born, in 1957, and lived as a child, while his father went on to work on other men's boats.

He paused the conversation then to fetch something, a picture he'd done when he was a boy. After so many years, the paint was still bright and the brushwork preserved the vibrant clarity of the child.

For all the stories of heroism and the joy of diving, I'd come to see the sponge industry's slaughter of the seabed and its injustice to divers and their families as a kind of warfare. And in a sense it was. In his brutal collection of stories about sponge diving, *Oi Kolasmenoi tis Thalassas*, Giannis Mangklís describes the divers as the damned, people who become meat.[71] But the child's joyful painting of the defining Dionysiu family story brought a different tone to the narrative. A golden diver wearing the *skafandro* is harvesting an abundance of golden sponge while behind him a cheery caïque flies a snow-white sail and all about, filling up the scene, the sea and the sky are merged in an ecstatic daubing of royal-blue paint. Kostas pointed out to me two sharks, their sharp, bright teeth. But the pair were swimming safely away from the diver, out of the picture.

"For you," he said, handing the precious painting to me in its handmade wooden frame, its powerful innocence.

"Kostas! I couldn't. I just love it. It's really beautiful. But please keep it for the family. It's such a special thing."

"Okay," he said with a shrug. "For my grandchildren. If they're interested."

# Restoration
SYMI, 2022

1.

"I'm up at the graveyard, painting the walls."

Manuel's WhatsApp message when we arrived on Symi sounded like the opening line of a blues song.

"Well, we first met you with a paintbrush in hand," I reminded him.

"At least it'll be nice and clean when I'm laid to rest," he wrote. And then, "Actually, I'd rather them throw me in the sea. The fish need food also."

When the day's work was done, he met us for a walk up the mountain. Passing the newly painted white walls of the graveyard, he explained that it was there that his grandmother had taught illegal Greek lessons during the Italian occupation when the children weren't allowed to speak their own language at school. Along the way we picked sage and oregano, and he said that his grandmother knew all the herbs. She used to mash them together to make a curative poultice.

The path led high above the settlements of Yialos and Pedi, and the air was full of cicadas. Our destination was the monastery of Agia Marina, aka Saint Margaret, a beautiful and feisty maiden who before her final martyrdom endured numerous tortures for the purity of her faith, including an encounter with Satan who took the form of a dragon and swallowed her whole. But just like the shark who vomited up Latari's grandfather on account of the *skandalopetra* he was holding, the devil dragon spat Agia Marina out again because he was unable to stomach the cross in her hands. In the iconography she is depicted as a forceful young woman wielding a hammer over her head with which to smite a cringing devil.

"I'm coming up here to show you," Manuel said, as we reached the perennial spring at the site of her little church. "But it's also for me. It's the best water in the world. Lots of minerals. It comes from the Himalayas or the Alps or somewhere. Goes under the ocean and then comes out here."

We all drank the healing water and then collected some in bottles to take back. Outside the entrance to the church stood a massive cypress tree.

"You could build a ship from such a tree," Michael said.

Manuel said, "There are barn owls living in its branches."

2.

We had returned to the island so often in the imagination that I somehow expected it all to be just as we'd left it. In the years since our first visit, Symi had become for us a place in the mind, a touchstone of something extraordinary, and we were not disappointed.

The sea was still a glory of blue, the enfolding girdle of every hour. The painted harbor was still the most beautiful in all of Greece, and now that COVID restrictions had been lifted, the cruise boats and ferries once again brought in day-trippers and tourists like us to drive the island economy.

In the Chorio village people still greeted one another in the little streets, and many even remembered us. On the hills above the settlement, the terraces that once held vineyards were still empty of cultivation, and many kinds of food were still being shipped in. On the Kali Strata, a piece of lined paper covered entirely with a blue ballpoint scrawl of words and stick figures had once again been taped to one of the wide marble steps. In the wide sky the swallows returned as ever at dawn and dusk to hunt and swoop, while near the entrance to the *kafenion*, a canary in a tiny cage still twittered and fluffed its feathers, and in the tiny streets mules and donkeys waited stolidly as before to be loaded with rocks or water. At the garbage bins on our walk down to the harbor, a new generation of scraggly kittens skipped out with dirty faces from the piles of kitchen waste, and to the side of the bins in an enclosure attached to a large house, a big setter-type dog looked out at me when we walked past each morning through the bright green bars of his cage.

Yet while the ruined buildings around the house of Orfeas were still ruined, and the fig trees growing through the rooms were taller now, several of the structures down in Yialos were being renovated or restored. In a street above Dinos the Original Sponge Shop an old house roof was being replaced, and we watched with some alarm as three men, macho as divers and seemingly as unconcerned for safety, loaded uncovered asbestos sheets into a truck. Inside, the sponge shop hadn't changed much, but Dinos had handed over the business to his children. Kiriakos was a schoolteacher who worked there during the summer, while his brother and sister had both returned to the island with economics degrees to run the place full-time. As before, we bought homemade goat milk ice creams from Georgios, but his neighbor, the tender-hearted baker Panormitis, had left for Rhodes and the tiny bakery had been taken over and transformed into something more upmarket. Near the harbor bridge the hand-painted sign for Stavros's stall was the same as it had been, and the place was hung with bunches of oregano and rosemary and garlic, but Stavros had officially retired and passed it all on to his son Dimitris. Still, he was up each morning at dawn, walking the hills to pick fresh herbs, and most days we found them talking together at the stall.

"He goes to university," Stavros said of Dimitris, "and then he comes back here to sell herbs!"

There was pleasure and humor in his voice, and I noticed that father and son had the same ironic eyes.

I asked Dimitris what he had studied and he said, "History. Five years of history." Looking out pensively at the late-morning tourist traffic, he added, "Nobody even grows tomatoes. The tomatoes come from Nisyros. Imagine Symi without cars or bikes."

I wanted to buy some mountain tea from them and a big bag of oregano, but Stavros refused to let me pay. He explained that since he gathers the herbs on the hill, they don't cost him anything.

"But this is your work," I tried to insist.

"It's okay," he said, with a nod of his head towards the flock of day-trippers that had just arrived on the island. "They're coming."

In the afternoon when we walked down the steep hill to Manuel's cove, the midsummer rock roses had all set seed. The purple thyme was still in flower but fading. The little olive tree was laden with fruit. We picked sage. And the water, the water... Something about the particular shading of the water at the cove, from clear at the shore to gold to greenish-blue to a deep azure, had as before the unerring capacity to fill me with joy and a sense of infinitude. Swimming, I met garfish, flocks of silvers, brightly colored wrasse, myriads of tiny ones.

On the beach, Michael had found just one limpet shell and painted a human face on it to last until the next tide.

"It's like a desert," he said as I got out of the water. "Our False Bay coast is a rainforest. Remember those Minoan vases? That's how it used to be here, just teeming with life."

He was thinking of the glorious multitude of octopuses and dolphins and seaweeds and sponges that stream across the surface of vases in the marine style from the late Minoan.

"Well..." I said.

It's what someone back home is always likely to tell me when I say how much I love the Aegean. Oh, but the Med is dead, they say. My reply is that it's not. The sea may be sparse and much depleted, yes. But it is not dead. Not yet.

Still, returning to that luminous brilliance at the cove, I could not forget Eleni Voultsiadou's work on extinction. The families of corals, the many kinds of dolphin, the whales, the porpoises, the loggerhead turtles, the sharks, the oysters, the scallops, and the monk seals basking on the shores in the old stories and the rippling octopuses on the vases kept crowding into the mind, along with the myriad communities of sponge, at least two hundred species in the Aegean.[72]

On the Mediterranean bath sponge, *Spongia officinalis*, once delivered to the Topkapi Palace in their thousands each year and now on the brink of extinction, marine scientists Roberto Pronzato and Renata Manconi wrote in 2020, "It seems impossible to imagine that such an important historical, cultural and biological heritage as that of the bath sponge can be permanently lost due to human carelessness. Tens of millions of specimens of *S. officinalis* have usefully served humanity since the appearance of the first Mediterranean civilisations. Tens of thousands of fishermen have risked and lost their lives to take possession of this legendary marine Golden Fleece. Now this may all come to an end." The word the authors used reminded me of Petros speaking about the emigration of the divers from Halki: "This," they wrote, "could be considered the beginning of a final catastrophe."[73]

"If they'd just leave it alone, it would all come back."

"Yes! Like the strip of no-man's-land between the two Koreas. It all came back. Even tigers."

"No *man's* land is the point, I guess," Michael said.

Later, as we were walking home in the dusk, the elder Panormitis whom we'd first met at the sponge shop made an appearance on his way for a swim. He was almost unrecognizable.

"You're looking ten years younger!" I said. "Maybe more!"

He laughed and explained that after a health crisis he'd stopped smoking, stopped working, and started walking every day, doing gymnasium, and swimming 320 days of the year. It was a delight to see. The rest of us had all grown older, but this man, named for the archangel who slays the dragon and heals people, and who had rescued his father from the brink of death in a storm, had become younger, lighter, fitter, stronger. He was no longer working indoors in the sponge shop all day, and he was smiling.

3.

"The purpose of restoration is to bring it back," he said. "But the aim is not to freeze the structure in some idea of the past. The house is a house, not a museum. If it's alive, it changes. It continues to have a story. Buildings continue to have a story."

Dimitris Zographos had arrived for our meeting on a turquoise bicycle with a wicker pannier, wearing a sky-blue linen shirt and floppy white linen pants. He had gentle brown eyes and a compelling voice, and he was explaining how he'd created the exquisite 1900 Hotel from one of the old sponge mansions. Since he was an architect, much of his work on the island involved restoration, but this upmarket place was not just any mansion. It was the house of Evgenia Mastoridis, the first person in the Aegean to dive underwater wearing the *skafandro*.

As the story goes, Fotis Mastoridis fell in love first with her sister, whom he'd met when his ship had stopped at Lemnos to load goods. A few months later when he returned to marry her, she had died from an illness. Undeterred, he asked Evgenia in her place, and she accepted on the condition that one of her brothers accompany her to live on Symi. Beyond this gossip fragment of being her husband's second choice and the historically memorable moment of the *skafandro*, I'd been able to find nothing more about Evgenia's life. So, when the hotel came up in an online search, I was keen to visit it.

"And this is the house they built?" I asked Dimitris. "Evgenia and Fotis and their family?"

"Well, it's what we believe. We like to believe that it's the Mastoridis house."

"Perhaps it's all we have, the stories of things. This world our mind makes up."

"Yes. I think so."

As Dimitris led us through the rooms you could see that his restoration of the neoclassical building we like to believe was the Mastoridis house involved an ongoing negotiation between historical accuracy and imaginative truth. He showed us how the walls were painted in darkish greens, grays, and blues that recalled the original colors and created cool spaces in the heat. At the same time the effect was intentionally lyrical, drawing the gaze outward to the view of harbor and sea framed by the great windows so that the darkness of the interiors made the picture of the outside world gleam more brilliantly.

"We try not to touch it," he said. "The interventions we make—you know, turning the kitchen into another bedroom, that sort of thing—they're what is called diversifiable. You can easily put things back to how they were before. The concept of the hotel is that you're living in a house, a generous house with large rooms but not very many of them."

Now that the main project of materializing that concept was complete, the ongoing daily work of restoration—of keeping the house and the story of the house alive—involved a continuous activity of tending and curation. The spacious rooms built with sponge money were meticulously inhabited by perfect white double beds, a well-lit bowl of nectarines and plums placed under a glass dome on a carved table, and trompe l'oeil ceilings painted with creamy angels and leaves and magical beasts against a gray-blue sky. Although Dimitris kept speaking to us during the tour, his attention was continually focused on the details of this meticulous installation: remove a long-stemmed freesia or a lily that was just beginning to look tired, straighten a bathmat when a foot had scuffed it, keep things in place and immaculately fresh.

"And the Mastoridis family?" I asked. "What can the house tell us about them?"

"Look, they were nouveau riche," he said. "You can see where the house is placed, a bit forward at the edge of the sea, facing all the other houses, and a bit of a different style. I think it was sort of in your face to the wealthy people of Symi."

His own family would have been some of those people. His grandmother was the daughter of a sponge merchant from the Petridis family, a powerful lineage whose patriarch, Nikitas, arrived on the island from Istanbul in the mid-nineteenth century and went on to have seven sons. As Dimitris spoke about them, I realized he was the first person we'd met in the sponge story who was descended from this social class.

"These people," he said of them, "they were basically trading. That's how they became so wealthy."

"Like the Chatziagapitos family with that *sala* on the hill?"

"Yes, just like that," he said. "My grandmother's mother was a Chatziagapitos. I have the family ring. It's a seal with Hermes on it, protector of merchants."

It was intriguing that the old god was still around, but Dimitris was deep in the family narrative, speaking about his ancestors with a mixture of pride and irony.

"My grandmother married my grandfather Zographos who was the son of a captain. They loved being posh. You know, everything tailored, English tea at the windmills, that sort of thing. Of course there are also some dark stories. Which I love. It's said the family found some antiquities that they sold. That's apparently where the first wealth came from. And they did very well. But as soon as they realized things were going down on the island, they left. Didn't come back."

Dimitris himself had grown up in Athens and studied in New York.

"And you came here because?" I said.

"A parachuting accident," he said. "The parachute didn't open. I fell on rocks. I should have died, but I lived. With a broken back. In fact, today is the thirty-first anniversary. I'll tell you that story next time."

Our conversation had gone on longer than expected, and in a few minutes Dimitris needed to welcome some new guests to the hotel.

"Come and see me again," he said. "In my office. It's across the harbor."

4.

High on the hill we were living once again among the ruins. In the mornings the world is as still as a sleeping child. Afternoons hot as a stove. The fig tree grows through broken houses, and the bells from churches across the island call and call to each other in different voices. All day the cicadas sing their everlasting song, and at dawn and dusk the swallows track through.

I'd learned that when Italy took over the Dodecanese in 1912 during the Italo-Turkish War, it was not only the wealthy who fled. After the occupation, the concessions and liberties that Symi had enjoyed under the Ottomans came to an end, and the effect on people's lives was more terrifying than anything Metrophanes Kalafatas had described in the catalog of social upheavals listed in his long poem just nine years before. The coast of the Turkish mainland, so close to the island that a strong swimmer could make it across, had always been part of the island's economic and social reach. But this lifeline was now cut: no more logging of trees from the mainland to build the legendary fast boats in the Harani shipyard that had once sent ships to Agamemnon's fleet, no more farming and grazing in the fields of Anatolia. On top of this, Italy barred the Dodecanese fleets from fishing for sponges off the coast of Libya, at least for a time.[74] While

Satan's Machine had made it possible to descend to depths never before reached, the Aegean seabed was still being fished out of sponge, and the annual journeys to the North African coast had become a crucial engine of economic growth for the islands. The result of these converging factors was a swift descent into hunger, even starvation. And, for everyone who could make it, exodus.

I'd heard pieces of the story before, what Petros the shopkeeper had called the *catastroika*, but it became clearer when Robert Dalziel, an English architect friend of Dimitris whom we visited in his house overlooking Yialos, showed me a population graph of Symi. By 1912, with the boom that had followed the arrival of the *skafandro* in 1863, the eight thousand human inhabitants counted in 1850 had expanded to more than twenty-two thousand. This was the so-called golden age of sponge fishing, when five hundred new boats set off from the island each year, when divers ostentatiously rolled up bank notes to smoke and their wives wore silks, when hundreds of men were killed or paralyzed and the living beings of the seabed were raked and ravaged deeper and deeper for more and ever more, and when Dimitris's family, as he told us, built twenty mansions on the island in twenty years. And then came the crash. The population graph plummets from twenty-two thousand in 1912 when Italy occupied the island to a mere seven thousand ten years later.[75]

When they made it out of Greece, the diaspora of traders, fortune hunters, and refugees spread out across the world. From the sponge islands, many of these were the ones who emigrated to the west coast of Florida, specifically Tarpon Springs. Whole sponging crews and with them emissaries of the great merchants were all drawn to the Gulf of Mexico by the seemingly inexhaustible bounty of sponge. Perhaps they

## Restoration

meant to come home someday. But when they sold the roof tiles, the doors, and the windows to help pay for the sea passage and blocked up the openings in the walls with rocks, the houses lost their souls and began to fall apart.

First the paints peel off the old walls in layers, the whites and the blues and sometimes a creamy yellow. Then plaster turns mottled in shades of gray, like lichens. In time that layer falls off too in flat flakes, revealing stone upon stone, each stone of the wall placed by human thought and hand, the old mortar like swallows' mud, hard but impermanent. Between the stones the small seeds take root and grow, find moisture and shelter, a rocky crevice on the hillside. Roof beams long gone, the top of the walls fill with grasses that blow in the wind and flower, and an entire population of burrowing and crawling beings find habitation among them. Often a lizard rests quietly in the sun, breathing fast, and sometimes the goats pass through nibbling on the tops of walls. In what was once kitchen or bedroom, a single speck of fig seed germinates to a great tree. And though a century ago someone filled in the windows to hold up the structure, when the wooden lintel goes, the cracks reach upward and the chunks of stone begin to fall.

If it is to be alive, if it is to have a story, the house must be constantly renewed, Dimitris said. But up on the hill the wild grows freely into broken rooms, supplanting our human stories with the narratives of other lives. Through the gateways of the empty doorframes the sea sounds a far gong of blue.

Whether you call it ruin or restoration, and regardless of whether you care or even notice, all day and all night the fine bones and veins of the world are growing and dying and giving birth, quietly inhabiting the small streets built among houses constructed of mountain stone where children once laughed and darted, old men sat on the step in the evenings, smoking or talking or simply sitting, and where in the afternoons everyone stayed indoors if they could, sleeping or dozing or making love. Now the nightjar finds a place on the ground to rest during the day, and at dawn and dusk the swallows come hunting.

"They seem like a continuity," Michael said, "and they are. But the individual birds fall from the sky and are replaced by their children. It's seamless. The generations roll over."

"Perhaps you could call it change," I said. "Say change rather than death?"

I was thinking of Renata, our host on Rhodes whom we'd finally met during a brief visit to Nisyros where she gave us tea and cherries and spoke about the hopes for a better life for the Pakistani migrants she worked with, and about her mother who'd lived with her until her nineties, and who had recently died in her arms.

"I don't even let myself feel sad about it," Renata said. "It's normal. It's right."

Then she told us about the wedding that was taking place that night. "The whole island is invited, everyone! You must go. Go to the wedding and dance."

We went to the wedding with our neighbor Maria, and the celebrations were astonishing. Great platters of food and drink were continually being brought to long tables on the village square, the solemn man we knew from selling tickets for the volcanic swimming pool was playing the bouzouki in a little group of men while a woman sang, and the place was packed with dancing that continued until dawn, everyone dancing the ancient steps with arms around each other's shoulders, old men in white shirts and a red scarf and the

# Restoration

smiling bride in her sparkling white dress leading the snaking chain while tiny girls in pink satin watched it all until they fell asleep.

Yes, you could call it change—the dying mother, the glowing bride, the pink satin girls—yet still, how to imagine it for more than a moment, the fact of our death? Or the decay of our house, its uncountable stories? Or to know that our days are like the grass that grows along the top of a ruined wall, our treasured edifices crumbled to dust? The pictures of Dinos in his sponge shop show a man in the strength of life, tanned and smiling, but now his young people tend the sponges and the tourists, and Stavros too claims to have retired. Meanwhile, up on the hill, the long song of the cicadas continues all afternoon, and the tiny wild figs on the great tree start green, turn purple, and then drop. Far below, the silent ships sail on, and above us a single swallow's dancing flight dives and soars in the gentle light, scissoring the air.

Perhaps the windy days incline the mind to contemplation, but the broken structures around the house of Orfeas are simply houses, not temples, each once distinct and precious, the stone-built shelter for ordinary lives. Across the valley each morning the first rooster sings his ancestral song to the dawn and then the next takes it up, and the next, and the next. In the afternoon the winds blow the grass seeds all over the island. Far below, the wide blue reaches into infinity: *pelagia*, the deep, plundered and pillaged.

Once seen, the mystery comes to reside with you, glimpsed for an instant and then forgotten. And sometimes the lightness too finds some habitation in the heart. The simplicity, the release.

5.

"I adore it when the swallows come," Dimitris said. "They fly into the house in the spring, and I let them stay for a while. But once they really start building their nests they're dropping mud everywhere, so I have to close the doors."

We were sitting in his office overlooking the harbor, a generous space artfully cluttered with myriad things and sedimented with layers and layers of ancestry. The furniture had a worn stylishness, and he told us that the leather chairs were designed by his uncle and the sofa was designed by his father, while he himself had designed the big desk. It was stacked with orderly heaps of papers, drawings, pictures, postcards, and a big piece of driftwood that he'd transformed into a sculpture with the most minimal intervention. On the walls hung gold-framed engravings, a little metal shrine, carved wooden panels from some old building. The low table at our knees was filled with smooth stones, more driftwood, an ancient coffee pot, the sculpture of a bird, and a mass of indoor plants in terra-cotta pots.

Dimitris passed me a framed photograph of one woman and thirteen men in suits who'd arranged themselves with the skeletons of many kinds of sea sponge set out around them like hunting trophies. A sign at their backs announces the General Sponge Fishing Co Ltd, and the members of the Symi branch address the viewer with settled assurance. Near the center is great-grandfather Panagiotis Petridis, a man whose stocky build, chubby cheeks, and pleasant expression reminded me of Dimitris.

"He was the third generation of the Petridis family, very wealthy and powerful on the island," he said. "They built the clock tower, the school, and the little bridge at the port."

"He looks like you!" I said.

"They say I look even more like his father, Michael."

As he showed us more photographs of his ancestors, the ambivalence they evoked in me brought to mind pictures from the same era of my own revered grandparents and great-grandparents. They too were at once similarly implicated in activities and values we now reject—the colonial project, in their case—and at the same time they were human beings doing what they could to make sense of the mystery of living and dying. I realized that Dimitris's forebears were among the merchants against whom Kalafatas had directed his tirade in the poem "Winter Dream." Yet in the pleasure of meeting him now and hearing their stories, and recognizing his features in faces of people whose portraits had been tenderly preserved for more than a century, it was no longer possible simply to dismiss them.

"And when was the picture taken?" I asked, returning to the group photograph of the sponge traders.

"It must have been the early twentieth century. Before the Italians in 1912."

"Yes, definitely before," I said.

It was one of those images that invokes an entire ethos on the brink of change. Written in English, the sign above their heads speaks the international reach of their trade: London, Paris, Symi. In retrospect, the confidently forward-looking gaze of the sponge traders seems almost innocent. Even the two little boys who've sneaked into the frame to the right are outside their range of sight.

"What a moment," I said. "They just don't know what's coming."

Now, more than a century later, the sun was streaming through the big doors and windows from the sea, while across the bay stood the Mastoridis house. It was a spatial arrangement that made it possible for Dimitris to commute easily across Yialos on his colorful bicycle between two modes of being. On one side of the harbor stood the fastidiously maintained rooms of the 1900 Hotel, and a short cycle away and facing it across the water was the layered and thoughtfully cluttered ecosystem where he lived and worked. Like his ancestors, the hotel he'd created liked to be posh. But his home office was the lively space that made the imaginative work of restoration possible.

Perhaps it was also an assertion of bohemian freedoms in the face of power and ostentatious wealth. When he was a young man, Dimitris said, he would move between New York City, where he was studying architecture, and the island of Symi, where he made a living from diving.

"I used to fish for octopus," he said. "To sell."

"You know that *My Octopus Teacher* was filmed near where we live?" I said.

The Oscar-winning documentary had appeared since our previous visit, and while it was very popular, marine scientists in our part of the world were often uncomfortable with the way it depicted the man's relationship with the octopus. I mentioned the film because the footage showed what a rich ecosystem is still flourishing off our Cape coast. But Dimitris's response had the some of the same defensiveness we encountered whenever the topic of the film came up on the octopus-eating islands. Everyone had seen it, and it seemed to leave them somewhat uncomfortable.

"I was fishing to survive," Dimitris said. "I must have killed thousands of octopus. I didn't want to depend on my father."

It felt like a confession of sorts. But then he changed tack and showed us a photograph of his old diver friend Manolis.

"My good friend. He's no longer alive. You know, he told me once how he and some others robbed my grandfather's house. He said, 'We took the chairs,' and he showed me how they put hoods over my grandparents. Then he said, 'I have the chairs at my house. You can come and get them.' I never did."

We all laughed.

"And you came here from the parachuting accident after growing up in Athens?" I said.

"I was a skydiver and a sea diver. And I had this problem. Fear. I didn't have it. Now I'm not like that anymore, but when I was young I didn't feel fear. When the accident happened, when the parachute didn't open thirty-one years ago, I shouldn't have lived. But I did. With a lot of injuries. My doctor said find a quiet island and stay as long as you can. So I looked at several and ended up on Symi. Architects had said it was beautiful, and I remembered coming here as a child of thirteen. It was like a dream.

"So I'd shuttle between here and New York," he went on. "And then at some point... Oh, my mother died. And my father jumped off a building. And lived."

"My goodness."

"Yes, it's in the family. There's a story that one of my ancestors jumped off one of these Yialos balconies with an umbrella as parachute. He wanted to get into the sea. Afterwards they called him the Comet. As my father said to me once, it seems we're not going to die from falling.

"Anyway," Dimitris said. "By 2005 it was enough. I came here to live."

"And the rest of your family?" I said.

"When I came back to Symi they gave me the Chatziagapitos ring. But there's a sad story there too. At a point someone was doing a genealogical tree. When I mentioned online that I was on Symi, the reaction was really intense: 'Why are you in that place among those savages?'

"I mean," he went on fiercely, "when everyone else left, the so-called savages were the ones who stayed! They kept it going. All that time, they were holding the Greek flag."

Throughout this visit and the previous one, a low-level restlessness was the indication that Dimitris was in severe and constant physical pain. He explained that the old parachuting injuries to his back had become almost unbearable, and he'd soon be taking time off to get an assessment for surgery. Still, it was a miracle he was alive at all.

"And since I came here I've restored many houses." As he said it, it felt as though in doing so he was in some sense putting himself together too, though this was not said.

"You know I do what I do for the buildings themselves," he went on. "It's decent work, and it's brought a lot of money to the island. But now the circle has closed, the circle of being. I have roots here. I don't have to run away anymore."

As we said goodbye, he hugged us both warmly and I said something about staying in touch.

"Anything," he said with a sweet smile. "If the connection is there, it's there from the beginning. If not, there's nothing."

6.

Each time we walked down to the sea past the garbage bins, I greeted the big setter dog in his green cage where he lay among his own shit. He wasn't the first caged dog I'd seen on Symi, but his eyes looked into mine with such longing that, even though it was a cliché—well-meaning foreign visitor arrives on an island and chastises the locals about their treatment of animals—I felt compelled to do something. I started talking about him to people, and everyone seemed to agree—it's wrong to keep a dog in a cage, but there's very little one can do about it.

One expat friend who wanted to remain anonymous said, "The police here are so intertwined with local families that unless they receive a complaint they will not get involved. As long as it's being fed regularly and exercised, that's fine by the law. And if you're talking about the dog by the bins, I've seen it being taken out for walks."

"That's a relief," I said.

"And you know," he said, "what's important is that the standard of care on the island generally has improved dramatically in the last few years."

It was all good to hear. But still!

At the beginning of our visit the dog was friendly, standing up to wag, and I felt a little comforted. Whatever treatment he had received from human beings, he seemed to have retained the hope that *Homo sapiens* are potentially kind. But during our time on Symi, he gradually became less and less responsive. I'd stop and say hello, but he was too listless to respond.

I emailed the Symi Animal Welfare people, and they wrote back:

> Unfortunately there is very little we can do. Previously in past years we have attempted to reason with owners who keep dogs in such poor conditions but we have had no positive results. The police are not interested...and many owners don't care enough for their animals...It's an educational issue...Yes, the Greek law has changed. And

the local authorities should act on such information from tourists/visitors and from concerned residents but they do not. We are very sad to hear about the dog and if you make a complaint to the police...then pls let us know.

It was the day before we were to leave. This time when we walked past the bins again, the dog looked at me but wouldn't even lift his head.

I wanted to go to the police, although Michael said we had no standing to issue a complaint. Then, on our way down to Yialos, we stopped somewhere for breakfast and the proprietor, whom we knew to be a kind person, asked why I was crying into my fruit salad. I told him the story, and he seemed a little hopeful until he saw the photo I'd taken.

"Oh, no," he said with finality. "That is a hunting dog. He is working. Nothing the police will do."

"Working!" I couldn't believe it.

The word acknowledged the dog's agency and sentience, a working being like us, while at the same time condemning him to a life of solitary confinement.

"But that dog is a slave!" I said.

Looking back, I wonder now why I didn't push through and make a complaint. I suppose it was despair and lack of courage. Everyone said it was hopeless, and I didn't want to become entangled in island politics on our last day. Instead from the breakfast table I messaged my oldest friend, Allison, who was living in rural France. She messaged back, saying it sounded all too familiar—Don't Touch Our Traditions:

—*Apparently they starve them to get the blood lust.*

—*I feel as though I should do something but perhaps need to be told that I can't,* I wrote.

—*That's what I was thinking,* she wrote back. *You've done*

*what you can. Raising awareness is important. But we Miss Fixits can go too far and just invoke animosity. Horrible dilemma.*
—*Well, at least I can write about him.*

Over the course of our visits I'd come to imagine that when humans and their dogs first came to the Aegean islands, the land must have been deeply forested and inhabited by many beings. But it was only after meeting the hunting dog lying alone in his terrible cage that I made the effort to find out more. Who was there before?

Elephants. Pygmy elephants. In an extraordinary map of the region, the paleoarchaeologist Marco Masseti shows each of the islands where the Middle and Upper Pleistocene remains of elephants have been found. So many elephants! Not on Symi, as far as we know, but their traces in the region give a glimpse of the complex ecosystems of living beings that would have dwelled there in the pre-Neolithic period when the first humans arrived in their small boats. Masseti's book sets out a detailed picture of the terrestrial mammals of the Ionian and Aegean islands and imagines the primal lands once covered in jungles of evergreen oaks.[76]

These days the endemic ancient ones are long gone, along with the pygmy hippopotami of Crete. But Masseti's study records the fading presence of furred and pawed beings who were still living on some of the islands within human memory.[77] Golden jackal, red fox, weasel, stone marten, badger, otter, African wildcat, wild boar, fallow deer, wild goat, hedgehog, shrew, rabbit, hare, vole, hamster, mouse, rat, and very occasionally even leopard. On Symi, by contrast, although the resident populations of reptiles and amphibians have not been much affected by human intervention, and although Michael and I did photograph someone on the mountain above Nimborio in 2017 who looked very much like a wildcat, when researchers recently analyzed kestrel pellets and mammal carcasses to make a list of the island's remaining mammal fauna, they could find only the remains of shrews, field mice, house mice, rats, and one mole carcass.[78]

What could "recovery of the islands" mean, Masseti asks, in terms of conservation and management? Towards the end of the book, he reflects on how few other regions of the planet have been maltreated by humans as much as the Mediterranean and says that what remains offers only "the vaguest impression of what the ancient natural riches, vegetable lushness and primeval faunal luxuriance of the region may have been." In a phrase that has remained with me ever since I read it, he writes that much of the islands' environment has been "reduced to little more than a mineral skeleton."[79] Like Eleni Voultsiadou's work on marine extinctions, his meticulous study is a calm lament in the face of the war against Earth, what sociologist Jacklyn Cock has called the war against ourselves: this present war that is our own, our people, all of us.[80]

Hunting! It's what our kind have done since the beginning. But now the hills where the hungry setter dog must leave his cage to hunt are dry and stony, ravaged by goats. Is there anything left up there to kill?

# Change
## HALKI, 2022

1.

Panos was standing on the harbor wall when our ferry came in to Halki. He looked the same but different. Probably it was the new beard, a little grizzled. He smiled broadly and as he opened his arms for a hug I realized how few hugs we'd given and received since March 2020.

"It's never locked," he said, as he gave us the keys to his house. "In all the years, there's never been an incident."

The house was spacious and familiar. The sea was blue-green and silver and black. It was midsummer. In the evenings the children of the island gathered at the port, darting like swallows.

Still, in the three years since our last visit, the world had changed. And on Halki itself, the elders whom I'd felt so honored to meet, the island's last living memory of the sponge days, were passing on. Panos told us that Petros tis Psarofagias, the Fish Eater, had become old and confused. Cheimonettos, the *meraklis*, who used to place a bright-pink oleander flower behind his ear each morning, was now bedridden and no longer speaking, fed with a spoon by his womenfolk. And a few months back we'd received the sad news that Petros the shopkeeper, who told me the story of Mario tou Mousi, had passed away. Meanwhile Ioanna, whose parents owned Theodisia's patisserie and who used to be the single baby on Halki, seemed suddenly to have grown up. Like her older sister Anna, she was now a strong and beautiful young woman who was used to holding her own point of view.

"How *are* you?" she asked warmly, when we met again.

Pausing to talk at our table, she told us how after starting out doing computer science on Crete she'd realized it was not for her. She wanted to work with her hands. So, she went to Rhodes and completed a baking degree. "But when I was at school there, I just wanted to come back here. Too many cars, people…"

"I can understand," I said. "I think Halki is heaven."

"Oh yes," she said matter-of-factly. "It is. It's paradise."

It was early evening, and the children of the island had come out to walk and run and talk and play on the central square of the port across from the café, there at the threshold where the boats arrive bearing cargo from the world beyond: a fridge, a family member, a vanload of garlic and ceramic pots and house plants, boxes of fresh fruit and vegetables, crates of medical supplies or tools, tourists in the summer, and sometimes refugees. No island is an island, but what a place for a childhood or even a life. No wonder Ioanna had come back.

"And it's wonderful to know that it's going to be an eco-island," I said. "Greening…"

"I think it already is!"

It was one of the reasons we'd returned to Greece: news of an extraordinary new vision, and the will to implement it.

"We become eco-friendly now," she explained, "because it will be easier for us. We are trying to be independent."

2.

In late 2021 our friend the hotel manager Yiannis Parlavantzas had written to me about the greening project. He said that under a new mayor, Halki had just been proclaimed the first GR-eco Island as part of a national initiative of the Greek government. The aim was to transform Greek islands into models of green economy, energy autonomy, digital innovation, and ecological sustainability, and Halki was the first.[81] The man to speak to was Vasilis Roussakis.

It was a vision that sounded uncannily close to what Yiannis and I had allowed ourselves to imagine for the island on our last visit. After such a short while the actualization of this dream seemed almost incredible, an extraordinary attempt to turn history around. But we are living in extraordinary times. Since our first visit to the islands in 2017, awareness of the global environmental catastrophe had increased to the point at which anyone in the world with access to mass media could know about the climate crisis, and initiatives from activists, communities, scientists, and even some governments had escalated dramatically. As New Orleans climate activist and writer Mary Annaïse Heglar put it in 2023, "Climate is no longer niche. It's mainstream. It's about time."[82] So while the war against the earth and all beings continues unabated, the end of fossil fuels is now in sight and a variety of renewable energy solutions are being developed at a rate that would have seemed unbelievable just a few years ago.[83]

Walking up the steep reach of freshly painted white stairs to the municipal center for a meeting with the deputy mayor, I remembered Kostas Dionysiu telling me on Rhodes,

"People say these big roads and buildings were built by the Italians. But you know, they were built by Greek hands." It was a building designed to make you feel that something triumphal was about to happen. Perhaps, impossibly, this time it was.

At the threshold of the boardroom we met Vasilis Roussakis, a middle-aged, bearded man with a penetrating gaze and a ready smile, who led us in and introduced Vasilis Chantziaras, the head of the island's energy community project, a man of the same generation who was also smiling warmly. The four of us sat down at the big, polished table, and Vasilis Roussakis asked the people working across the room to quieten down.

"We started thinking about this in 2020," he said, "and now slowly, slowly, things are changing. We want the island to be energy independent."

It was the same word Ioanna had used: independent. The plan was to reduce Halki's $CO_2$ footprint by 40 percent by 2030 and to reach net-zero $CO_2$ emissions by 2050. It sounded remarkable, but the figures were close to what the recent UN Intergovernmental Panel on Climate Change report set as the minimal requirement for avoiding catastrophic levels of global warming. So far, Vasilis said, they'd built a 1-megawatt solar park. It would cover the needs of the island, he said, and the extra would go to Rhodes.

"But, you see, we didn't want to commercialize it," the other Vasilis said about the solar park. "This would make us lose our focus. So we set up the energy community."

"It's the first energy community in Greece," Vasilis Roussakis said. "People assisted."

"Yes, they saw that...We were working towards energy democracy on the island," Vasilis Chantziaras said.

"Energy democracy!" I said. "That's a great term. Can you explain?"

"Everyone should have access to energy," Vasilis Chantziaras said. "It's not a product."

"It's a right?" Michael suggested.

"Yes," he agreed. "It's a right! Like the air and the water. We want to give people free energy, clean energy. They don't need to put solar panels on their roofs. They can get it from the solar park."

It was already sounding remarkable, both the extent of the installation itself and the intention that accompanied it.

"I have to admit," Vasilis Roussakis said, "that it was funded. Big companies in the renewable energy sector. There *are* financing options available."

"Yes," Vasilis Chantziaras said. "The only thing that needs to be done is the decision to move forward."

In the face of the global environmental catastrophe, hope often seems naive and difficult to trust. But I knew that to buy into despair was to give victory to the destroyers, and I was grateful for the clarity of their resolve. Sometimes one or two people are all it takes to catalyze change. I thought of fifteen-year-old Greta Thunberg's lone protest on Fridays outside the Swedish Parliament in August 2018, which set off a global movement of millions. And the rainforest that returned with all of its springs and animals to Sebastiao Salgado's ravaged and denuded ancestral land in Brazil after his wife, Leila, said let's rebuild paradise.[84]

"What people don't realize," Vasilis Roussakis said, "is that the environmental crisis is already costing them a lot. We need to show that this is costing money already."

"Sure," Michael said. "And how do you raise this awareness? At the school?"

"Yes. We established a tech lab on the island. You know, the kids realize more than the adults."

Vasilis Chantziaras agreed. "We sometimes think the kids don't know so much about this, or care. But they do."

"Oh, yes," I said. "And internationally, the youth movement has been a powerful organizer. Any kid with a cellphone could tap into what's been happening."

"Anyway, this is a start," Vasilis Roussakis said. "We need to keep taking other steps, taking it forward."

"It really sounds so positive," I said. "And although you said it was going slowly, you've done a lot in a short time. I wonder now about other aspects. Water, waste, the land..."

"Yes, energy is our first step," he said. "Water and waste are next. We need a holistic solution. Desalination has already been happening for some years. Now we're fixing the sewerage waste system so as to purify the water for irrigation."

I could see that garbage recycling on the island still had a long way to go, but the intention was at least a start.

"And what about the *sternas* on Halki from the old days?" I said.

"Yes, but people don't want the *sterna* anymore," he said.

"Put a tourist in the room under the house?" Michael asked.

"Exactly. When I was a child and we used to come from Athens, my grandmother would say 'Slow down with the water! It's coming from the *sterna*. It must last until the winter!' But we don't think like that anymore. People want to have water. Scarcity changes your mindset, and we don't have that awareness anymore."

Talking about irrigation brought up the question of agriculture that had been traveling with me since our first visit to Symi. "So what about the old terraces, the *terazza*?" I asked.

"The elders have told me that the island used to be more fruitful. You can see it even high up on the mountains, everything terraced and marked out with stone walls."

"Now there's nothing growing up there," Vasilis Roussakis said.

"Just bees," I said.

"Yes. Just bees."

It was a poignant moment, the image of the bees in their sky-blue hives continuing to make honey in the stony mountains.

"You see," he went on, "the *needs* bring the result. So before, when they couldn't get tomatoes from the supermarket they had to grow them. They also knew how to collect the water up in the mountains. Because otherwise, no water. Now youngsters don't want to be part of agricultural renewal. They want to make it easy. They're globalized. I think we must start by growing things in places where it's easier to grow something."

"Sure," I said. "And I realize it's complex. Farming is very hard work. And none of the four of us sitting here is choosing to do this sort of work for our livelihood. So it's of course not simple to just say start growing food again, even if there is enough water."

"Yes exactly. Get it from the supermarket," Vasilis Roussakis said.

"But..." I didn't want to let the idea go. "It's still what's needed, isn't it? One thought that comes to me is something our friend Renata said about the refugees she was working with, helping them get papers. She said many of the people come from Pakistan and have the skills for agricultural work. Her feeling was that these are the skills and labor that Greece needs."

When we'd visited her on Nisyros, Renata had also compared the current waves of migrants and refugees with the earlier generations of Greeks who'd emigrated around the world. Some of them have nothing and are driven by actual hunger and devastation, while others are in search of a better life.

"But of course," I said, "I appreciate...that's raising other issues."

"Yes, that's of course another issue," Vasilis Roussakis said. "Another big problem is people's difficulty to accept strangers."

"In spite of *philoxenia* or xenophilia."

"Yes."

I understood that not long after our previous visit in 2019, there'd begun to be pushback from some of the Aegean islands when the little boats had landed. And on Symi the mayor had successfully appealed for some five hundred refugees and migrants to be transferred to the mainland, arguing that the island was not equipped to deal with them. Meanwhile the unimaginable suffering of the millions of people displaced by war from their homes in the region continues as I write. I wonder what happened to the desperate couple who had somehow reached the boarding gate at Rhodes airport with their forged passports on our last visit, the terrifying policeman shouting at them to speak German.

"Maybe we can find something in the middle," Vasilis Chantziaras said. "Bring in some people who want to work the land, and also get young people involved. Use contemporary smart technology. We don't need to always use the old ways. In the village, in Chorio, I'm hoping that we can do something to work the land again using modern methods."

"Agriculture needs to be smart and cool," Michael agreed.

"Yes! It needs creativity and people working together," Vasilis Chantziaras said.

"And what about waste?" I asked. "I realize I interrupted you earlier to talk about agriculture when you first mentioned water and waste."

"We've started a procedure of recycling: paper, glass, plastic, metal," Vasilis Roussakis said. "It's new. It's very difficult to ask people to do something else. It needs time and education."

"Yes!" Vasilis Chantziaras said. "Let's find a solution."

From what we'd seen of the garbage on the island, it was clear that recycling was not yet working. But the energy and focus of the two men was exhilarating. Having been involved for years with the environmental movement, I knew how easy it is to give in to a feeling of futility.

"It's inspiring to talk to you both," I said, "because you have a fine sense of the problems involved, but it doesn't make you give up. You seem determined to make it work."

"It's a matter of attitude," Vasilis Roussakis said. "There are always problems."

"Action is interconnectedness!" Vasilis Chantziaras said.

"And what makes you do it?" I asked. "What inspires you?"

"Love for the island," Vasilis Roussakis said simply.

Once again, a conversation had brought us back to it: the heart at the heart of it.

"Wanting to make things for the kids," he went on. "To make them love the island. It's very important to keep the youngsters here. For them to continue. People think that living on a small island, you're disconnected. But we need to show them that living here, we can be part of the world."

"Great," I said. "And your dream for Halki? What do you hope for?"

Vasilis Roussakis paused for a moment and then said, "A sustainable island in all means."

"Halki presents a manageable scale," Michael said. "It's possible to do this here."

"Yes, exactly."

"In contemporary terms," Michael went on. "We can't go back to the past."

"Though we can *learn* from the past," Vasilis Chantziaras put in.

"Yes, absolutely," Michael said.

I had two last questions, things I hoped to find while we were on the island. The first was from the story that Petros the shopkeeper had told me on our previous visit. I explained that he'd used it to say something in a poetic language about the life of Halki in the past, its ecological and social dynamics. When neither the deputy mayor nor the head of the energy community seemed to know the story, I told it to them. Mario tou Mousi is stolen away by pirates, and to convince the sponge divers in Libya that she really is from Halki she names three places: Krambia for fresh water, Zies for grapes, and Liaotes for parrotfish.

I said, "I've been thinking I'd love to visit these places and see what's become of them. In memory of Petros, I suppose, what he wanted to show me. I think he wanted me to imagine the island as it used to be before modernity. I feel if we could see what it's like there now, visit each of the places, it could give a picture of how the island has changed. And maybe an idea of what it could become in the future."

Vasilis Roussakis explained that Zies lay just over the hill on the way to the solar park. It would be no problem to get there. He'd show us. In fact, he'd make a time to take us to see the solar park and show us on the way. As for Krambia and Liaotes, we'd need a map. He directed one of his assistants to give us a good one.

"And the other question?" he said.

"It's about the sponge boat reenactment you did earlier in the year, the boats leaving the island in the spring," I said.

"Yes, we wanted to show how they were doing it in the past, the day the boats leave the port. We had two boats from Kalymnos and the rest from here. People came from all around to see. They loved it."

"And did they sing the old songs? 'For you I am wearing the *skafandro*… For you I am wearing the iron shoes.'"

"Yes, they sang these songs."

"And 'Dirlada'?"

"Yes, that too. It was a very emotional procedure."

"It sounds amazing," I said. "But okay, my question. At the time, Yiannis from the hotel sent me a video clip, and when I look closely, I can see that the diver wearing the *skafandro* is a woman! Is that so?"

Vasilis nodded.

"That seems very significant," I said. "I mean, they were all men!"

A special sort of smile crossed his face: "It was the first woman to dive in it since 1863."

"Evgenia Mastoridis. The men wouldn't put it on. So that was a deliberate choice?"

"Oh, yes. We wanted it to be a woman. She's a professional diver from Kalymnos."

"Wow," I said. "I'd love to meet her."

My plan had been to visit Kalymnos again to meet the

sculptor Sakellaris in person and visit our other friends, but the ferry schedules had changed, so it was difficult to travel there from Symi. Any meeting with the diver would have to be online.

"I can put you in touch," he said. "I'll get someone to send you her details."

I began to gather my notes together, but then Vasilis Chantziaras, who had been quiet for a while, said he had two questions he wanted to ask us. "First," he said, "could you tell us what it is that you love about Halki? What is it that makes it different?"

"What a question," I said. "Well, the beauty. On so many levels. The sea, the buildings, the little lanes—the scale of the place that is small enough to walk everywhere, to meet people, to know them. I love people's warmth that's so full of heart. And you know, I love being able to return to conversations that we began three years ago. And now, meeting you both, I love your vision."

Michael said, "It's a microcosm. And it's all connected, just two hundred and forty people. People know each other. And they talk to us. You don't have to go very far on Halki to step into something intimate."

"Good. And what do you think we need to avoid?" Vasilis Chantziaras said, his voice serious. "What should we watch out for?"

I thought for a while. It was another huge question, and surely they would know the answer much better than we did.

"Okay," I said. "From my point of view, the particular place I'm coming from, perhaps one can draw some analogy from the sponge history. I see it as an object lesson. When I talk with the older people on the sponge islands—not so much young people, but elders—when I talk to them about what went wrong with the sponge industry, almost nobody wants to say that it was overfishing. But it was. And it seems to me that this gives us a metaphor. Of the whole disaster. A microcosm.

"I think the story of it, which is such a key part of the island's own story, shows us clearly what must be avoided. They took too many sponges. They were only interested in short-term gain. They didn't care enough about the divers and their families. And they didn't recognize that the marine ecosystem is a whole world of living beings. So, people's lives were destroyed. Much of the seabed was destroyed. For a short while some people got very rich. Halki itself became very rich. And then it crashed. Even if people had not left for Tarpon Springs with the Italian occupation and the synthetic sponge hadn't been invented midcentury, it could not have lasted much longer. Within a few decades it was basically all over.

"Anyway, perhaps this is something you could work with. The sponge history as an example of how not to go. You want to develop, yes, but as Yiannis said to me three years ago, the gem of Halki is what it is. So, not too much."

"Very good. Yes," Vasilis Chantziaras said.

Michael had been quiet. Then, recalling the phrase we had learned from Yiannis on our previous stay, he said, "I feel that *pan metron ariston* is your salvation."

"And that is so Greek," I added. "I mean, this is Greece! You have all the resources you need to draw on. The science, the philosophy, the art, the history, the literature…"

"But sometimes we forget," Vasilis Roussakis said.

"From what I can see," Michael said, "there's been a great emphasis on science on these islands. Sending young people away to university to study science. That's a great resource."

"But I think maybe it's gone a bit too far," Vasilis Chantziaras said. "Too much emphasis on STEM. We also need..." He paused, looking for the word.

"The humanities," I said.

"Yes, the humanities. We need the art and the literature."

"I guess that's where I come from," I said. "But you know I often feel that we in the humanities could pay more attention to what's being done in the sciences. Environmental sciences, especially."

"They need each other," Vasilis said.

"Yes, they really do. I think," I said, "in our response to the environmental crisis, the humanities can give us values, help us understand what it is we really value. And of course, educate the imagination. Without which, no vision."

"They need each other," he said again, "the science and the humanities."

"There you go," Michael said. "It's *metron ariston* again."

3.

We recognized the baker from last time, a dark-eyed, bearded young man built like a Greek hero, but we couldn't remember his name.

"I'm Menelaus," he said.

"Oh, so you're in *Iliáda*," Michael said.

"I play in *Odýsseia* as well as *Iliáda*."

"Yes!" Michael said.

"And my wife is Eleni," the baker said.

"Perfect. We're staying in Villa Polyxeni. She was the brother of Hector."

"Yes. I'll keep two *kouloures* for you for tomorrow."

The next morning, we fetched the *kouloures* to take with us over the little hill to Pondamos beach. It was lovely for swimming, and it was also the place where Mario tou Mousi and the other young women were playing their musical instruments when the pirates had come and carried her off.

A few months earlier I'd seen some dispute on Facebook about sun beds that made it sound as though Pondamos had been entirely taken over by loungers and umbrellas. But while there were ranks of them just like the ones we'd seen on every other so-called organized beach in Greece, they were set out on a separate flat area, a little above where the tide could reach, and occupied by people tanning. The beach itself where the young women once made music seemed undisturbed.

We sat down under a tamarisk tree to enjoy the azure glory of sea. Right there was a mass of small plastics just lying around in the sand. Blues, greens, yellows, reds—I arranged them in a rainbow spectrum. There were more blues than anything else: bottle caps, labels, unidentified strips. And many nurdles. Cute-sounding and about the size of a lentil, nurdles are the building blocks for all our plastic stuff, microplastic pellets that spill into the oceans in the trillions every year and soak up toxic chemicals. Too often the nurdles are mistaken for fish eggs and swallowed by sea creatures who then feel full when they're not and become starved or poisoned.[85]

I left the shade of the tree and glided into the water. It was clear and warm, a dream of sea, and I swam out to the white yacht moored in the blue, swam with the little silver fish, played in the water like the other human beings who'd also come to play. I dived and swam again.

In the old days it was pirates who came to snatch away young women from this shore. But no pirates had been seen for years and the people on the white yacht looked harmless enough. Still, the island seemed more permeable than ever, porous as the honeycomb body of a *kapadiko* sponge. Swimming out and back, I thought of the invading microplastics and of Vasilis and Vasilis, their visionary labors. What could they ever do to stem the tide of colorful detritus that washes in from the world?

4.

Back on shore we ate the *kouloures* baked by Menelaus, and while Michael painted faces on pebbles that would wash away with the next tide, I spread out the map to look for Mario tou Mousi's places. It was one of those waterproof, rip-proof, plasticized hiking maps that are the result of extraordinarily meticulous fieldwork. There were photos and notes, and a legend explained in four languages the signs for roads, a variety of paths, and the icons used for sites of cultural, topographical, and other interest. My purpose in acquiring it had simply been to locate Krabia for fresh water, Zies for grapes, and Liaotes for parrotfish. But as I pored over the map, it began to reveal itself. It was both the picture of an island intricately tracked with generations of human habitation and an image of the mapmakers' attentiveness.

Zies was easy to find, the vestiges of an agricultural area not far from Emborio on the way to Kania beach. We'd walked through it on our previous visit, and Vasilis Roussakis had said he'd take us there on the way to see the solar park. But the other two sites were not obvious, and the people at the municipality hadn't known them either. So, to find them I had to slow down and look at everything.

The icon for a cistern was a tiny blue square, and there were many scattered across the island. But in one high region in particular, the old farming lands of Kila, Kipos, and Koka,

I counted one well and ten cisterns along the footpath. One of them was marked Krabia.

"Look, I've found it!" I said to Michael, who was still painting stones. "The place where Mario's sweet water came from. It's high up on the other side of the island, but the land used to be cultivated and there are lots of old *sternas* up there."

"Great! And could we get there?" Michael said.

"In this heat you'd need a car to take you as far as the road goes, and then it's walking. The cisterns and fields are all from a time when you went everywhere on foot. Or donkey."

It was strangely touching to find it on the map, the source of the fresh water that the stolen woman longed for from her servitude in North Africa, and to trace with my finger the ancient paths she must have walked maybe two centuries ago, tracking along the edge of a cultivated basin through a remote, high, rocky region that was once familiar and inhabited and dense with stories. Beyond the cistern at Krabia the path passes three Byzantine churches, a winepress, and the remains of settlements, and then descends 100 meters through a realm of caves and intermittent streams to reach the cave known as Kamenos Spilios where, in one of the island's most enduring memories of trauma, the women and children of Halki took refuge from the Venetian admiral Francesco Morosini in the seventeenth century. It's said that Morosini was so enraged with the Halkiots for warning the Ottomans that his fleet was heading towards Rhodes that he ordered his soldiers to pursue the women and children and to light great bonfires at the base of the cave with wood from the nearby almond grove. Every single woman and child was suffocated. Now the Burned Cave is a destination for visiting hikers and the site of a tale people tell. But until quite recently the place itself and the footpath to reach it had been intimately woven into the islanders' known world. It was there that Petros tis Psarofagia the elder got his name when he'd made a fish from cream.

After I found Krabia I tracked around the rocky coastline of the map, reading name after name of inlet and beach. The entire human population of Halki is now a fraction of what it was, and all living at Emborio. And as Marco Masseti said of the Aegean islands generally, over thousands of years of anthropogenic impact, the island's ecosystem has been reduced to a mineral skeleton of what it once was. But the map records a relation to place where every cove and beach was once named and each of the dotted blue lines that runs to the sea was a known watercourse. Lothi, Garopnichtis, Sarakiniko, Ichalous, Pachis, Limnes, Giali, Piaghia... Moving west around the perimeter to the Kefali peninsula, I found at last Liaotes, where the parrotfish came from. It was the farthest reach of the island from the present settlement at Emborio, a rocky bay on the east coast in a region of ancient agricultural settlements. The mapmakers note that the nearby Byzantine chapel was built on the remains of an ancient temple and record the presence of huts, dry stone walls, a tower, an ancient oil press, two regions designated by the words "Alimounda" (almonds) and "Kritharia" (barley), and farther south a cave formerly used for making cheese.

"You see what she's doing, Mario tou Mousi," Michael said when I showed him the place. "It's not just about fresh water and so on. By naming those specific locations, she's saying to the sponge divers: I know my whole island. I know it from east to west, from the coast to the mountains."

"Okay, right," I said. "So, it's a whole livelihood of sustainable agriculture that she's calling up, but it wasn't just that. Her words prove to the divers that it's home. She's covered the entire territory in those three lines."

While Michael wandered off to place his painted pebbles, I walked down to the beach for one more swim. The map had invoked a bittersweet taste of nostalgia for a lost world of windmills and oil presses, and an island densely alive with an interwoven mesh of human paths felted into the land. At the same time it brought the unsettling recognition that it was precisely this occupation by *Homo sapiens* and their goats and fields and stories and names for everything that had displaced the original inhabitants.

I slipped into the blue, blue sea where Mario's story begins, where all our stories begin.

"I was sponge," writes the philosopher Baptiste Morizot, pondering our descendance from the primal Porifera.[86] "I am Water," says the slogan of the ocean conservation organization close to where we live in Cape Town. They take youth from underresourced coastal communities, lend them wetsuits and snorkels, and invite them to open their eyes underwater and see.

I dived and swam. The water at Pondamos was clear as glass.

5.

Dressed in blue jeans and a T-shirt, and with a spring in his step, the deputy mayor was all set for an excursion. He stopped the electric van on the side of the road to pluck a sprig of sage and gave it to me with a smile.

"*Faskómilo*," he said.

"Thank you," I said. "We'll use it in our supper."

"And this is Zies, the old agricultural area."

"Where the sweet grapes came from," I said.

"Yes."

On the side of the van were the words "Energy Community of Halki," and since our last visit to the island the old road to Kania Beach had been rebuilt. We passed a graveyard of rusting cars that Vasilis said they'd collected from all around to sell for scrap metal. As we drove through Zies, there were no vineyards left that I could see, but some olive trees were still alive and stone walls outlined the agricultural boundaries.

A little farther away on the hillside above Kania Beach, an open rocky area where nothing seemed likely to grow, we came to the solar park: a massive assemblage of twenty-five hundred panels designed to produce 1 megawatt of electricity, enough to power the whole island and export some to Rhodes.

"We began building in July 2021," he said, "and by November it was done."

"It's amazing," I said. "Really impressive."

As we stood in the baking midsummer heat, the sense of it was self-evident. Hope requires action, so farm the sunlight.

Vasilis explained that people paid a onetime fee to join the energy community. This in a sense gave them a share of the solar park. Some had asked why it couldn't be free, but the thing must be maintained, so there had to be some initial cost. Soon it should all come online.

"The power company is just dealing with the logistics," he said. "It's a new thing: iconic net metering. But soon they should see a 70 to 80 percent reduction of their electricity bill."

"Wonderful. That's the ordinary consumers," I said.

"Yes."

"Once that first bill comes in for the people who are on

the system, word will get out and other people will want to join too."

"Exactly. We hope so," he said.

"And how long have you been on the island?" I knew he'd been educated in the United States and had recently come from Athens to take up the post.

"Two and half years now. But when I was a child we used to come in the holidays to stay with my grandmother. My grandfather was a sponge diver."

"With the *skafandro*?"

"Yes. And like the others, he went to Tarpon Springs. Became part of the expat community, sent money back for the clock tower, all of that."

"It's good to see the clock working again now," Michael said. "Last time we visited it was broken."

"Yes," Vasilis said, and smiled. "When my grandfather was very old he came back to Halki. Anyway, my mother would send us from Athens to my grandmother, and we used to play on the island, just like these children do now."

"We love watching them. They're so free. And Vasilis, you're doing all this for them, aren't you?"

"Oh, yes. I'm not doing it for myself."

A generation ago, the sponge divers seemed to be the last Greek heroes. It brought a nice karmic turn to the story of overfishing and exploitation for the grandson of a *skafandro* diver to be speaking to us about smart green tech and his labors for sustainable renewal.

As we stood together under the twenty-first-century shade of a large bank of solar panels, I remembered Metrophanes Kalafatas and his desperate rage against the Machine. In the poem, when he presciently sees the true uncommodifiable wealth of Symi being eroded by modernity, the only positive way forward he can imagine is back: to go back to the mythic past, to the age of sail and the purity of naked diving. But Halki's green vision for a wholesome eco-social order involved solutions that were definitively technological and cutting-edge. This change since our previous visit was almost bewildering, but then Halki's turnaround was one instance of people waking up to the reality of the climate crisis. It's the scientific consensus that what happens in our present decade will be decisive for the future of all beings. We are on the brink. But the story is not over. Not yet. It's not too late to come back.

As Joëlle Gergis, one of the lead authors of the Intergovernmental Panel on Climate Change report, has written, this realization, that the 2020s will be remembered as the decade that determined the fate of humanity, can electrify the present moment in a way that brings meaning and purpose to our lives.[87] Having met the deputy mayor and the head of Halki's energy community, I had no doubt that this was their experience. Still, I wondered to what extent the community of the island had taken possession of the vision. Until that happened, it felt precarious.

I asked Vasilis about broader participation in the project and he said, "Yes, it's a problem. We need more people to be involved."

"Maybe they will be when the electricity comes online?" I said.

"We hope so," he said.

We spoke then about the goats who were meandering on the hill, their ancient continuity, and the EU subsidy that encourages people to have too many. Michael mentioned the Sahara, that it's thought by some to have been a human-made desert, with lush grasslands stripped out by crop-growing

humans and their livestock, which set off an environmental cascade. What would happen if goats were removed from the equation? Would it all come back? Vasilis said he thought it unlikely that they'd get people to control or reduce their goats. Mostly though, they were owned by older people, and perhaps in the end the goats would die out. It sounded dubious, but what else?

"And other animals?" I asked.

I didn't think to mention it at the time, but I knew that on all the islands we'd visited in the region, Halki included, people still poisoned cats. Why, I don't know. Our friends on Patmos were continually doing their best to rescue them, and visitors on social media expressed their outrage.

Instead, I said, "I've found that on the islands, the beauty just opens your heart. So, it means I feel everything more intensely, the pain as well as the joy, and especially the pain of animals. Seeing animals being treated cruelly in the old ways. Dogs tied up or in a cage, that sort of thing. It's terrible."

"Exactly, yes," Vasilis said. "Here on Halki it's getting a bit better. The police came to undo the chains of the dogs. And for the cats there are programs for vaccination and sterilization."

As he spoke about the dogs, he gave a strong tug around his own neck, releasing with both hands an imaginary chain.

## 6.

In the afternoons we often found ourselves talking to Ioanna at her parents' restaurant. Once the single baby of the island, recently a child, she now looked into the future with the bright gaze of a young adult. I wanted to hear more about her vision, so one day we arranged to have coffee together.

"I would love to open up the old paths," she said, her dark eyes warm with love of the island. "And roads to all the beaches that you can now only get to by boat."

I had told her that Mr. Giannis, who did the boat trips, had quoted me 200 euros to take us to Liaotes when I found it for him on the map. It was fair enough for a long trip that nobody else was interested in doing but still too much for us to pay. And for Krabia you'd need a car, which we didn't have. Ioanna seemed not to have heard the Mario tou Mousi story before, so I told it to her. Like everyone else I'd spoken to, when I mentioned Liaotes and Krabia, she looked at me blankly. It was disappointing but quite telling. Two places that were once defining landmarks of the island had slipped into forgetting and were no longer really accessible, at least not to locals. It gave a hint of the extent of the task of restoration. If the sites of fresh water and parrotfish were lost even to memory, what would it take to bring them back in actuality?

Still, Ioanna's idea of rediscovering the paths was great.

"It can happen!" I said, and told her how Despoina Vakratsi had researched the ancient networks of paths on Patmos and was getting local women together to walk them again. "You could do it here too."

Then Ioanna told me the story of what had brought her back to her beloved island: not grapes and sweet water and fish but a yearning that sounded just as strong.

"When I got into the computer science program," she said, "everyone was very proud of me. Except for me! Then at the university they kept telling us we were so lucky. The place was one of the best in the country and they had collaboration with lots of big companies. Anyway, there were three options—networks, hardware, and software—and I was figuring it all out on my own, living on my own. But then a friend of mine there had olive trees. And you know, working with land and with animals, it's more productive than working in an office. Better for our mental health. It's not *me* that's saying it. It's scientists that are saying it."

"Yes," I said.

"So I decided it was not for me. I wanted to do the same as my mum. Work with my hands."

"Right."

"And I knew that I wanted to live *here*. After I'd done my baking degree in Rhodes, I came back here. Rhodes is too crowded. People did not say good morning or hi. Here everybody says good morning."

"It may sound like a small thing," I said, "but it's actually very significant."

I thought of our evening ritual of bells and drums at home during the pandemic, how it changed our relationships, and I told Ioanna about a particular neighborhood in San José, Costa Rica, that my son had read about when studying economics. Once people agreed to set aside five minutes every morning to greet their neighbors, instituting what they called *El ley del saludo*, "The Law of the Greeting," it catalyzed a whole chain of social transformation and neighborhood solidarity.[88]

"Yes! Imagine you've lived here for eighteen years," she said. "This is the only thing I know."

Across from us the priest was at his usual table with an espresso, smoking and playing backgammon. This time his little granddaughter Anna sat beside him with a milkshake. She was a decisive-looking child, maybe eight years old, with glossy dark hair cut in a bob and thoughtful dark eyes. We knew her from her distinctive stride as she walked up and down the harbor. I smiled at her grandfather, and he nodded a greeting.

"So, Ioanna, what is your dream for the island?"

She paused. Then she began to describe a vision.

"In my imagination, I want Halki to be independent. I want to bring the whole island back to life as it was before, with four thousand people living here. People must be able to live and feed themselves from the island. So we need technology for energy and building and so on. In my grandmother's time they used to filter the water to get the insects out. Now in our generation we have the technology to filter the water in a new way."

Her eyes were bright and focused, as serious and hopeful as it was possible to be.

"But you know," she went on, "it's hard to convince people of my age to leave the big cities. We crave the money."

"You have something here that is beyond the money," Michael said.

"Oh, yes," she said.

I mentioned the island's sponge industry. Even if the remaining Aegean sponges were to regrow in their multitudes, that particular era, with its particular obsession, was over. And now that the old ones who witnessed it were slipping away, the living memory was becoming a story we tell. A metaphor, even a parable, a tale of heroism and suffering and profit and short-term gain.

"Yes," Ioanna said firmly, "Because there were no limits. So many people were killed in the diving. As humans we ask for more and more every time. We don't have limits. We don't understand the relationships we have with our friends and family. We put money first."

"But, Ioanna, you yourself have such a strong sense of what is valuable," I said.

"Well, it's not just from growing up on the island. It's also from my family. If someone is in need, I must help him, even if I don't know him. The Christ will come in earth as the stranger who is in need."

I was reminded of what her sister Anna had said about helping the refugees.

"If we help a stranger it makes a paradise in our life," Michael said, and made the ancient gesture of the kneeling supplicant, which he knew from reading the *Iliad*. "We must recognize the stranger who asks."

"Yes." Ioanna spoke with fierce simplicity and the certainty of youth. "And if we translate it into nowadays, it might be an old lady who needs help. You see, my mother, she told us we don't have to follow traditions, but we must have respect."

I said, "I remember Anna saying that your mother was

the only one of her generation who was allowed to go out at night."

"Oh, yes!" Ioanna said. "I'm not used to what a submissive woman looks like.

"But you see," she went on, "We grew up with this mindset: do what you like with your lives, with love and respect. Whoever we meet. We have it as a rule. My father grew up in a small community in Rhodes with the belief that people are all equal. He had an ethnically diverse friend group. Then when I started going to school here fifteen years ago, there were Albanians as well as Greeks and we were all equal."

She paused and then said again, "We *are* all equal!"

7.

"If that happens," Yiannis said, "I'll stay here and get a gun!"

It was late afternoon, and we were sitting with our gentle Athenian friend on the veranda of his hotel at the edge of the sea, talking once again about war. He felt disbelief at the idea that one could, in 2022, think of invading and conquering another country. As Panos had said a few days before, "We Greeks, we're not interested in conquest. Maybe in the past, but not anymore. Turkey, they still have this idea of taking other people's country." Like everyone else, both men were concerned by Erdoğan's threats. Perhaps they'd blockade the island.

Just then we saw the gray form of a big ship gliding into the bay. Yiannis leapt up.

"What's happening?" I said.

"A military boat! I must get my flag!"

He came out again quickly, carrying a huge Greek flag on a long pole. "They're doing a patrol in the Aegean, to keep us feeling safe."

He stood at the edge of the sea and began to wave the flag at the boat, over and under in a figure of infinity. Guests flowed out of the doors and windows to watch.

"We will not give them an *inch*!" Yiannis shouted to the sea. "This is our *home*! Greeks have been here for over two thousand five hundred years!"

Then he took out a little horn and honked it at the ship, waving the flag all the time. The ship responded with a long, loud *boop*. He waved and waved until the ship did a big slow turn and sailed out of the bay. I felt the tears welling up in my throat.

"What is it about a flag?" I asked him afterwards. "I mean, I'm not Greek, and I don't particularly like flags. But it made me feel so emotional."

"Well, if you overdo it you become a nationalist," he said firmly. "I am not a nationalist. I don't believe in a Big Greece. It's human beings not nations."

"Absolutely."

I told him how we'd kept coming back to the idea he'd explained to us three years before: *metron ariston*. It was so clear and direct, and made such good sense at many levels.

He smiled and nodded. "And, you know, you don't have to care if it will succeed. If you plant the seed of *metron ariston*, it's not sure if it grows. But you try."

Just beyond the railing, the color of the sea was beginning to change as the long day slipped away. I said it was time for us to go, but Yiannis wanted us to watch the dance of light on the water.

"Please stay," he said. "I want you to see a unique dance on the surface of the sea. After the sun goes down."

So, we stayed and talked some more. Families, children, the Halki greening project.

# Change

Like just about everyone we'd met, Panos included, Yiannis doubted whether anyone with political power could ever really act with integrity. Also, he was concerned about waste. Recycling wasn't happening and the garbage was piling up in the bins. On the island of Tilos they'd got it right, a zero-waste program. But not on Halki. Still, he was keen to hear what happened in our conversations with Vasilis. After all, it was he who had suggested I meet him. And yes, he'd paid his deposit for the solar park and was waiting to see how things turned out.

We shared stories about his children and ours, his autistic son, whom he called "my prince," and his daughter, who would be arriving soon to help in the hotel. At some point I mentioned in passing that our twins were vegan.

"You see!" he said. "One day the world will become better. Sometimes we are predicting wars and so on. But if you look back over the last fifty years, you can see that some things are becoming better."

"Yes."

I thought of Ioanna's firm love of Halki and the forty children in the island school for whom the green dream was being actualized, and the millions of young people around the world who had mobilized to take action in response to the war against the earth, and my mind filled with the immensity of it all. The warships and the heartbreak and the open heart.

"We don't always have to go back to the past for glory," Yiannis went on. "Glory to the human beings! Not to the Greeks. I love this country, and I want to be able to have this kind of beautiful experience with other human beings."

We sat quietly then, watching the sea together in the changing light until the sun dipped behind the hill. You *can* be attached to the sea, Eleftheria had said to me at the beginning of the journey, because it is always changing.

"Look!" Yiannis said, pointing at the water. "They call this bay the Black Sea, Mávri Thálassa, because of the way the sea changes when the sun sets. But I do not see it as black. I see it as silver. Look! When I watch it sometimes, my mind is going quiet. It's a very beautiful dance."

8.

"I hear you're going to have souvlaki with Panos," Menelaus the baker said.

"Yes, tonight," I said.

"But you're vegetarian."

"We're having halloumi."

It was our last full day on Halki, and for all my carpe diem, the day, the moment, the breath itself was irretrievably slipping away, as though we were bodysurfing on the edge of change. Nothing to do but walk and swim and say goodbyes and try to let it all go.

In the late afternoon we'd just ordered an ouzo when one of the waiters came up to our table with an empty tray. He smiled.

"Vasilis!" I said to the deputy mayor. "What are you doing here?"

"Just helping out my friend Maria at the taverna," he said.

We laughed and chatted for a while, and then he said, "Have you met the mayor? He's sitting over there."

"We haven't. Shall we come over?"

"No, he's lazy," Vasilis said, and laughed. "He can come here."

So, the mayor, Angelos Fragakis, came to our table to talk.

"You'll be surprised," he said with a smile when I asked

what he was doing before he came to Halki. "I was a policeman in Athens."

"We're inspired by the greening work you're doing on the island," I said.

"Well, it's a team," he said. And then, "It's very difficult."

"I'm sure. But the island is small enough to make it work."

"Yes!" He smiled. "And now what is there that we can do for *you*?"

I told him how Mario tou Mousi's story had made me wonder about Krabia and Liaotes, and that I'd found them on the map but not managed to visit.

"Oh, I've been on a walk up to Agios Georgios," he said. "We saw many *sternas* up there. I know someone who would know."

"Thank you! But next time. We're leaving tomorrow."

"Okay, good. You know, I actually spoke with the woman who made that map. She told me that Halki is the real Apocalypsi. She said there's something holy happening here."

"I think she's right."

After a while, when the mayor had gone back to his table, the deputy mayor came over to clear away our glasses.

"Vasilis," I said, "I've been wondering. The beauty. Do you still see the beauty that we see, now that you're living and working here all the time?"

It was the same question I'd asked Manuel on Symi during our first visit.

"I see the beauty," he said.

It was that particular moment of dusk when the children of the island begin to gather at the port, and the sea turns silver, the beautiful dance.

"I see the beauty," he repeated, "and I'm glad that things are changing in a good way."

Later we met Panos for souvlaki at another taverna along the harbor wall. While we talked and ate, in the wide space of the port where the world comes and goes, the congregation of children discussed the urgencies of their lives and played games in the gathering dark, darting like swallows.

"As long as they can swim," Panos said, "you don't have to worry about anything."

The safety and familiarity of it all filled me with longing.

"And the children of the Albanian workers?" I asked, remembering what Ioanna had said about the school. "Are they integrated with the others?"

"Oh, yes! If they're living here, then yes," he said. "Completely integrated. And about different sexualities on the island, the gay and so on, there's also no problem at all."

At the end of our meal he excused himself from walking with us past all the tavernas along the harbor wall. He said he'd be taking a back way to the place where he was staying for the summer.

"But why?" I said.

"If I go the usual route I'll have to speak to everyone, and it will take all night."

We laughed and hugged goodbye, and he walked into the dark.

On the way back to his house we passed young Anna striding purposefully along the harbor wall, arms swinging.

# The Diver
RHODES, 2022

The first person in Greece to breathe underwater was a woman. She brought back a stone from fifteen meters deep and went on to live in a grand house at the edge of the harbor.

After Evgenia Mastoridis, the sponge divers who followed her into the *skafandro* were all men. It was they alone who were the gods, who lived the hellishly tough lives on board and dived on empty stomachs into paradise, the foolhardy heroes who died or were paralyzed, who in the pay of more powerful men brought back golden mounds of treasure from the seabed and for a brief while, if they survived, were fabulously rich, returning with carpets and embroidered shoes and cigars and stories of friendly dolphins and sentient sharks, and who, when the glorious Aegean was nearly all fished out, left for Florida with their families to do it all again, and in the end, if they were lucky, came home at last to the islands to grow old and sit gazing at the living mind of the sea from under the awnings of the harbor *kafenia*. However remarkable the island women undoubtedly were, stories of the sponge ripple out from the lives of men. So, when I zoomed in on the photo of the diver who had taken part in the reenactment of the sponge fleet's departure from Halki in 2022, and saw that it was a woman, I had to meet her.

Michael and I were back in Rhodes on the way home, staying once again in the house of Kostas with his childhood painting of the sponge boat and the sharks. Our online conversation was scheduled for midafternoon, but the diver messaged to say, sorry, she was still on the boat.

Later, after she'd emerged from the deep and had had time to eat and rest, she appeared on my screen: Zinovia Erga, marine scientist, professional diver, scuba instructor, Kalymnian. She was warm and focused, a young woman with long dark hair, relaxed strong limbs, the trace of the sea still about her, and an eye that held your gaze. It was the sort of face you want to see smile because it's tough and clear and no bullshit, and when she smiles it radiates.

"I was excited to see it was a woman who put on the *skafandro* again," I said. "I mean, after Evgenia Mastoridis, the sponge diving was such a macho thing."

"Oh, it was super macho! The scuba world too. Scuba was associated with the military," Zinovia said.

"I didn't realize that, but it makes sense."

Macho and war may have been an inevitable part of the story for generations, but for Zinovia, diving was the primal joy of being an island child.

"Here on Kalymnos, I grew up swimming," she said. "I would free dive. Then my first scuba dive was when I was nine. I grew up loving Cousteau."

She went on to study marine sciences and oceanography in Marseilles and became a scuba instructor, a commercial diver, and an underwater technician doing impact assessments. Then, in 2019, after about twenty years, she returned to Kalymnos.

# The Diver

"I rediscovered my island," she said.

"Just before COVID," I said.

"Oh, yes! I was so glad to be here during that time. We were hiking, rock climbing, diving, everything."

Once back on Kalymnos, Zinovia helped revive an association of women divers.

"It's quite unique," she said. "We do various events, underwater cleanups, that sort of thing. In late 2021 we were invited by the Halki municipality to do a cleanup at the port. It was mostly glass bottles, beer bottles, tires...not so much plastic, surprisingly. Then in May 2022 we were invited again. We thought it would be another cleanup, but it was a cultural event. They wanted to find a woman diver capable to put on the *skafandro*, in honor of Evgenia Mastoridis. The event brought the three islands together in some way: Kalymnos, Symi, Halki, connecting through our common culture."

"And how did it feel?" I said.

"Super heavy! Maybe eighty kilograms. It really took me to the limits of my physical strength. Underwater, it's nothing. Like a dry suit. But walking down the port...It was really difficult."

"Amazing. And they were singing the old songs." I thought of the traces of song and poetry I'd been given by some of the older people.

"Yes. It was theater. Very emotional. The ceremony of dressing of a diver...It was a sacred moment because they were never sure if they'd return."

She paused. Then she said with some deliberation, "I really felt when they closed me into the helmet that I was carrying with me thousands of lives."

Her sensitivity was palpable. Even in the telling, it sounded momentous.

"Then once I was underwater, it was super fun! My vision was quite restricted—the traditional helmets have a really small window, kind of tunnel vision—but I stayed down longer than expected, maybe fifteen minutes. My safety diver was also a woman, in scuba, so as not to be alone."

"And what about the air pump? Did you do it in the old way?" I thought of the comrades on deck pumping the air, and the sand glass timing when to come up.

"No, my business partner devised another method. Air banks from the scuba tank, connecting to the helmet. So it was a constant pressure."

"Okay, so that would already make it safer than how they used to do it," I said.

"Right," she said. "But you know in other parts of the world they were using the same deep sea diving suit at the time, but without the same fatalities."

"And here?"

"They just didn't use the dive tables."

"From what I've gathered, the divers were in a sort of trap. They might never come home, so they wanted their wages in advance. But then to earn back the money, they had to dive longer and more often and go down deeper than was safe. On top of that they seem to have been caught in some sort of fearless death-defying idea of masculinity that pushed them to take risks."

She nodded wryly. "Kalymnian people, we grew up with the sea. We are not afraid of the sea. Sometimes they can get arrogant."

"And many of them were so young."

"Yes. We see it now too. If someone is very aquatic, they feel so confident. They don't think they need to follow the rules. Like, you know, maintain your air correctly."

"And you?" I said. "You're very aquatic, but you seem pretty sensible."

Zinovia's presence on social media was of a highly competent professional in love with the sea. The images she posted of gliding weightless in an ecstatic blue realm of dolphins and nudibranchs and lyrical colors sit alongside others in which she's sorting garbage collected from the seabed, diving into wrecks, discussing energy solutions and overconsumption, or guiding people on dives that they describe afterwards as having been an experience of paradise.

"Well, when I was younger..." Her voice trailed off. "There are times when you think, how lucky I am to still be alive."

"I'm glad you are."

We spoke then about her experience as a marine biologist. She knew of Eleni Voultsiadou's research, of course, and her writing on extinctions in the Mediterranean. When I said I felt that the sponge industry could offer a metaphor for the broader ecological and social crisis, I heard for the first time about *Oi Kolasmenoi tis Thalassas*, a book that made a strong impression on her when she was young and was to help shape my sense of the divers' lives.

"It was written in the forties or fifties, and he describes the sponge industry in very dark and harsh terms," she said. "The author is Giánnis Mangklís. A bit Kazantzakis. He says the divers are like meat for the industry. I read it when I was thirteen, and I thought, and this is what we're proud of?"

"Meat! That's an extraordinary image." I resolved to track it down and get help with the translation.

Meanwhile I wondered aloud what Evgenia would have felt if she could have known the extent of what was coming.

"Yes," Zinovia said. "But it also brought wealth and development to the islands. The sponge industry was a huge motor of our economy. So it's a two-edged sword. And people like Vouvalis, he built things for the community. He did also give some back."

"Sure. And the divers themselves, it wasn't all suffering. One man I met told me that it's his memories of diving, of being underwater, that now keep him alive. Still, the level that Vouvalis and his family were living at—all those chandeliers— it was such conspicuous consumption. But, of course, it's easy for someone like me to come in from the outside and oversimplify. When I asked Sakellaris Koutouzis about his sculptures of the sponge merchants, he told me it was a deliberate choice not to caricature them simply as ruthless fat men with big cigars."

"He would do that, yes. I know Sakellaris well. He says something very interesting about the imprint of the sea on human character. He says we seem to bring back from the sea a capacity for making clear decisions. A certain firmness."

It was a quality I could recognize in Zinovia herself. She told me that when she returned to Kalymnos for a visit a few years back, she saw the island in a new way, the overfishing and the pollution, microplastics in particular. She realized that if she came home, she might be able to do something about it.

I asked whether the fact that she was a local person made it any easier. She'd returned with knowledge from elsewhere, but people knew her.

"Yes," she said. "I've worked with kids, and tried to work with fishermen. It is easier if they know you. You know the codes of communication.

"I do care about tradition," she went on, "but it must be sustainable. We can have a traditional life by doing other things. We don't have to overfish in the old way. So education is important. You have to artificially create an event, like the sponge boat event on Halki, and this can then start a discussion."

"And I guess the education can take many forms. You've seen *My Octopus Teacher*? It was filmed not far from where we live," I said.

"Yes, I've seen it many times. Look!" She showed me the great rippling tattoo whose tentacles flowed across her left arm and into her body, a glorious octopus inscribed not on the clay of a Minoan vessel but in living flesh. "The film has had a huge impact in the sensibilization of people."

"That's good to hear, especially from you as a marine scientist. And I like that word, sensibilization."

"But for environmental change," she went on, "political solutions are needed."

"Sure. You've seen what they're doing on Halki?"

"It's amazing," she said. "When I visited the island in 2010 I was very negatively impressed. Guard dogs chained up, and so on. But what's been done in such a short time is a very positive change. I felt jealous!"

"I think it's wonderful. But you know, just about every Greek person we've spoken to just can't seem to believe in leaders, or that real change is possible. Understandably, I guess, given the history. People lived so many centuries under occupying powers. And if you add to that the extent of the global crisis, it's all just so huge..."

"Well," she said firmly, "we must have hope."

Then she told me about the work she and a friend were doing, making a practical start on an ecological assessment of the Kalymnian region. "You see, some environmental damage is irreversible." She spoke simply and with a certain authority. "But the system is resilient. Much can be recovered."

After all I'd read and thought about sponge diving and ecocide, the grief at so much loss and devastation, the anxiety about the world our children will inherit, the magnetic tug of despair, Zinovia's calm words came as a tipping point of relief. If we'd been in the same physical space, I'd have bowed or given her a hug.

Instead, sitting in front of my screen in our bedroom in Rhodes, I took a deep breath and exhaled, and in that moment the quintessential joy of swimming in the lyrical waters of the islands was met with an image of the living tides of that sea thriving again with diverse families of cetaceans and corals and seaweeds and fish, octopuses playing, turtles diving, monk seals basking on the shores, the shores free of plastics, the hills reforested, terraces replanted, and all two hundred kinds of Aegean sponges alive in many colors, breathing in and breathing out. All of our relations, everyone breathing.

"We need research and environmental education," Zinovia said, with the clarity and decisiveness of one whom the Aegean has schooled since early childhood. "We need to create critical thinking. So far, my friend and I have done some workshops, and we're writing papers for the general reader. We are like ants. We're doing something small. But we need to keep our optimism up. Otherwise…"

She smiled.

# Epilogue ◈ The Sponge

Soon after Michael and I returned from Greece the first time, the cosmologist Richard Gott gave a presentation at the Royal Institution about the architecture of the universe.

In the beginning, he explained, in the very first miniscule fractions of a moment of the beginning of everything, the condition of What Is revealed itself in fluctuations. In that very beginning, these patterns of fluctuation manifested in regions of high density and low density, presence and absence. And immediately after that first cataclysm of being where it all began, everything started expanding outward at a fantastic rate that has continued ever since without a pause, birthing myriads of galaxies that reach across the void like incandescent filaments.[89]

How to imagine such a thing, a universe? Gott says the sparkling foam of galaxies has a topology structured like a marine sponge.

If you poured concrete into a sponge, he explains, it would fill all the air passages. And if you then took acid and dissolved away the poor sponge—he calls it that—what you would have left would again be the concrete model of a sponge. By this analogy, the great clusters of galaxies in the cosmic web are connected by filaments to make one connected whole that is like the high-density part of the sponge. The low-density spaces in the body of the universe, the complementary region of the body of sponge, are also all one thing.

Perhaps when Gott, an elderly man in a blue jacket and tie with a playful smile, looks into deep space through the maze of his intricate calculations, he sees a map of deep time in which the beginning is always now. The universe expands forever, he says, but the architecture of the ever-expanding web of galaxies and stars and worlds and worlds within worlds, this everything in which we reside, still bears the very same spongelike pattern that began as vacuum fluctuations in the first moments of its conception: presence and absence, being and nonbeing.

For a marine sponge in the Aegean, this ancient porosity is how it breathes the sea. All day and all night, the ancestral Porifera are breathing in water and breathing it out. Sponges are made of sea, of everything, filtering, filtering.

# Postscript

When we visited the islands in summer 2025, Vasilis Roussakis said that nearly everyone on Halki had signed up to the energy community and was receiving free electricity. A second desalination plant was being installed, and the water was safe to drink, tested monthly. The municipality now brings a vet from Rhodes once a month to do sterilizations and vaccinations, and the feral cats seem to be in much better condition than before. A biological water treatment facility is being built to process wastewater for agriculture. Garbage and recycling remain a big challenge for Halki and the other small islands, in part since the government requires all recycling to be sent to Rhodes. The inspiring zero-waste program on Tilos was initiated by a substantial private investment.

Slowly, slowly, things are changing, Vasilis said. But he emphasized that to make the small islands sustainable for future generations, the most important thing is to educate young people: to volunteer, to participate, to organize. May the happy children playing at the port in the evenings be empowered to take charge of their future.

# CAST OF CHARACTERS

Because of the informality of the situation, we knew some people only by their first name, and this is how I describe them in the book. Later inquiries have turned up some, but not all, of the surnames. While every effort has been made to contact each one of the people whose words I quote, some have been impossible to reach. I trust that my goodwill is apparent.

**Allison**—Allison Bruce, my friend since we were five

**Angelos Fragakis**—the mayor of Halki

**Anna**—Anna Livaniou, a restaurateur on Halki

**Anna**—a child living on Halki

**Anthi Fanarakis**—owner of the Traditional House Museum on Halki

**Aphrodite**—Aphrodite Papachatzis, proprietor of a sponge factory on Kalymnos

**Ari Sitas**—a poet and sociologist based in Cape Town

**Ariadne Vakratsi**—the proprietor of a clothing store on Patmos

**Chatziagapitos Chatzioannou**—a sponge trader on Symi during the late eighteenth and early nineteenth centuries

**Chatzidoukissa Chatziagapitos**—a sponge trader on Symi during the late eighteenth century

**Cheimonettos**—Cheimonettos Cheimonettos, an elder on Halki

**Costas Joakimidis**—a friend of Ari Sitas living in Athens

**Despoina Vakratsi**—a writer living on Patmos

**Dimitris Zographos**—an architect on Symi

**Dimitris**—Dimitris Orfanos, inheritor of his father's herb stall on Symi

**Dinos**—Dinos Lamprou, a sponge dealer on Symi

**Eleftheria Binikou**—the residence manager of the International Writers and Translators' Center of Rhodes

**Eléni**—Eléni Roumelióti, a teacher and the daughter-in-law of Cheimonettos on Halki

**Eleni Voultsiadou**—an Aegean sponge biologist

**Evgenia Mastoridis**—the first person in the Aegean to wear the *skafandro*, 1863

**Fotis Mastoridis**—the man who introduced the *skafandro* to Symi in 1863

**Giannis**—a boatman on Halki

**Giorgios**—a maker of goat milk ice cream on Symi

**Henrik**—Henrik Wetter, our Danish host at the Hotel Apxontiko on Kalymnos

# Cast of Characters

**Herbert** (not his real name)—a senior official at the heart of the EU in Brussels

**Ioanna Livaniou**—a restaurateur on Halki

**Irene**—the mother of Panormitis, a baker on Symi

**Irini**—Irini Ioakimoglou, a shop assistant on Halki

**Katerina Mourati**—an artist living on Patmos

**Kiriakos**—Kiriakos Lamprou (the elder), the founder of Dinos the Original Sponge Shop on Symi

**Kiriakos**—Kiriakos Lamprou, a teacher and sponge dealer on Symi

**Kostantinos Dionysiu**—the paterfamilias at Kristina's Rooms on Rhodes

**Kostas Zembillas**—a sponge dealer on Kalymnos

**Latari**—an elder on Kalymnos whose grandfather was swallowed by a shark and lived

**Lefteris**—Lefteris Kamitsis, a carpenter and retired sponge diver on Patmos

**Manuel**—Manuel Kyriakakis, our first friend on Symi

**Maria**—our neighbor on Nisyros

**Mario tou Mousi**—a character in Halki folklore

**Menelaus**—Menelaus Sfiriou, a baker on Halki

**Metrophanes Kalafatas**—Metrophanes I. Kalafatas, a school principal and author of the 1903 epic poem "Winter Dream"

**Michael Wessels**—my friend and colleague at the University of the Western Cape

**Michael**—Michael Cope, my husband

**Mick**—Michael Martin, my father

**Nicholas Vouvalis**—a sponge merchant on Kalymnos in the late nineteenth and early twentieth centuries

**Nika**—a restaurateur on Kalymnos

**Nikos Vassilaris**—a goldsmith on Rhodes

**Orfeas**—our host on Symi

**Panagiotis Petridis**—a sponge merchant on Symi in the late nineteenth and early twentieth centuries

**Panormitis**—a baker on Symi

**Panormitis**—Panormitis Kapsis, a sponge dealer on Symi

**Panos**—Panos Vali, our host on Halki

**Pelagia**—Pelagia Cheimonettos, a restaurateur on Halki

**Peter Vidal**—cofounder of the charity Next Stop Symi, living on Symi

**Petros**—Petros Antonoglou, a shopkeeper on Halki

**Petros tis Psarofagias**—a fisherman and elder on Halki

**Renata Papakosta**—our host on Rhodes who lives on Nisyros

**Renée Levi**—one of the few Jews from Rhodes who survived the Holocaust

**Robert Dalziel**—an English architect friend of Dimitris Zographos on Symi

**Russell Bernard**—a North American cultural anthropologist

**Sakellaris Koutouzis**—a sculptor on Kalymnos

**Sarandis**—Sarandis Giannaros, a ship's engineer and musician on Patmos

**Sky**—Sky Cope, my son

**Sofia (not her real name)**—a museum assistant on Symi

# Cast of Characters

**Sophie**—Sophie Cope, my daughter

**Stavros**—Stavros Orfanos, an herb seller and environmentalist on Symi

**Stavros Valsamides**—a diver whose diving finds stocked the Valsamides Sea World Museum on Kalymnos

**Stella Levi**—one of the few Jews from Rhodes who survived the Holocaust

**Thodoris Eleftheriou**—a poet on Kalymnos

**Vasilis**—Vasilis Cheimonettos, the son of Cheimonettos on Halki

**Vasilis Chantziaras**—the president of the energy community on Halki

**Vasilis Dionysiu**—a sponge diver from Kalymnos who lived on Rhodes

**Vasilis Roussakis**—the deputy mayor of Halki

**Vassilis Stavropoulos**—Gary Snyder's Greek translator

**Wendy**—Wendy Wilcox, the cofounder of the charity Solidarity Symi on Symi

**Yiannis Parlavantzas**—the proprietor of the Hotel Aretanassa on Halki

**Yiannis Valsamides**—the owner of the Valsamides Sea World Museum on Kalymnos

**Zinovia Erga**—a marine scientist, professional diver, and scuba instructor on Kalymnos

**Zoí**—a restaurateur on Symi

# APPENDIX

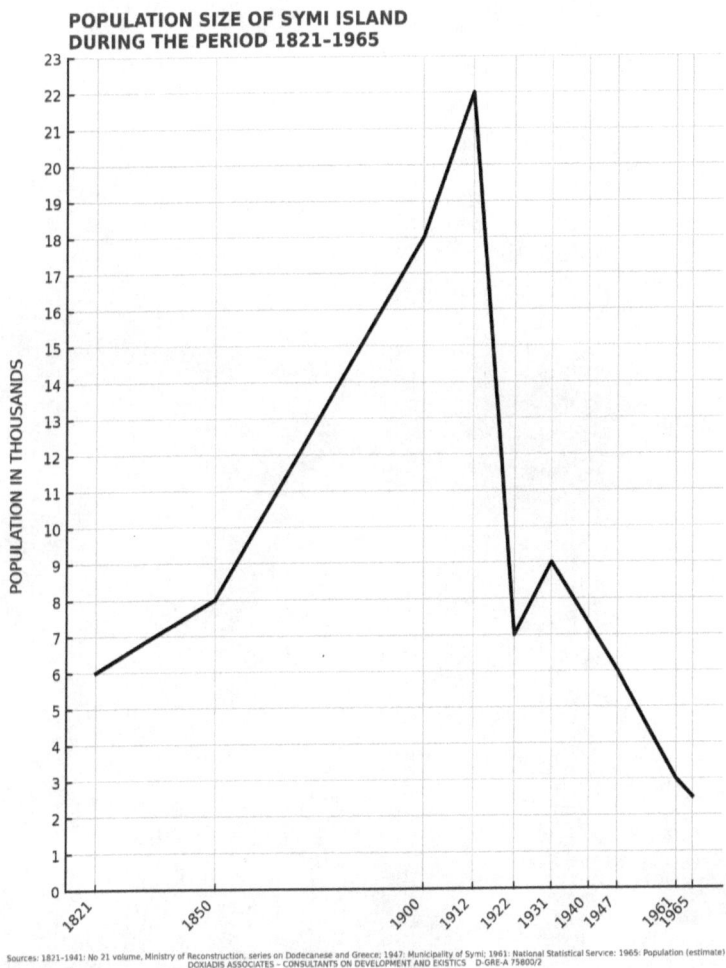

From Constantinos A. Doxiadis, *Development of the Island of Symi, Greece* (Doxiades Associates, 1966), 5.

# GRATITUDE

*On the Sponge Islands* is the fruit of so many people's involvement. I'm grateful to each one of you, to the myriad beings of sea and land and sky that inhabit the glory of the Dodecanese, and to the late Michael Wessels for imagining the journey before it happened.

The openheartedness and insight I experienced in Greece while working on this project have been extraordinary. I'm reluctant to single out anyone for particular mention, but four special guides require special thanks: Manuel Kyriakakis, for appearing on our first morning on Symi and inviting us into the island; Yiannis Parlavantzas, for *metron ariston*; Vasilis Roussakis, for the actualized vision of green renewal; and Zinovia Erga, for the living ocean. Dear friends, you manifested just when you were needed, and the book could not have been written without you.

Beyond this, a multitude of people generously became part of the story. On Rhodes, thank you to Eleftheria Binikou for saying that the sea is not a thing, Kostantinos Dionysiu for the painting of the sponge boat you did as a child, and Nikos Vassilaris for holding your ancestors' lineage of jewelers. On

Symi, thank you to Dimitris Orfanos for asking me to imagine Symi without cars or bikes, Dimitris Zographos for the intricate work of restoration, the late Dinos Lamprou for sharing an apple with us, Giannis for boat trips, Giorgios for goat milk ice-cream, Kiriakos Lamprou for continuing the family trade in sponges, Orfeas for the house with a blue door, Panormitis Kapsis for taking up swimming and gymnasium late in life, the late Panormitis the baker and his mother, Irini, for fresh *kouloures*, Sofia for guiding us through the mansion, Peter Vidal for collecting vanloads of clothes for refugees, Robert Dalziel for the history of the Italian occupation, Stavros Orfanos for walking the hills at dawn, the late Wendy Wilcox for compassion, and Zoí for your grandmother's dolmades. On Kalymnos, thank you to Aphrodite Papachatzis for strength, Henrik Wetter for stories of kindness, the late Kostas Zembillas for the love of the sea and sponges, Latari the pilot for the grace of a straight back and a daily walk along the harbor, Nika the restaurateur for a perfect meal on Mother's Day, Sakellaris Koutouzis for the sensitivity of your hands, the late Thodoris Eleftheriou for poetry, and Yiannis Valsamides for being the custodian of your father's treasure. On Patmos, thank you to Ariadne Vakratsi for inviting us to get lost, Despoina Vakratsi for the old paths of the island, Herbert for surviving the thunderbolt, Katerina Mourati for the networks, Lefteris Kamitsis for your great heart, and Sarandis Giannaros for music. On Halki, thank you to Angelos Fragakis for your love of the island, Anna Livaniou for saying that the refugees were people like us, Anthi Fanarakis for safeguarding the memories, the late Cheimonettos Cheimonettos for a bright pink flower tucked behind the ear each morning, Eléni Roumelióti for taking care of family and literature, Ioanna Livaniou for the certainty of youth, Irini Ioakimoglou for your tender friendship with Mr. Petros, Menelaus Sfiriou for knowing that we were vegetarians, Panos Vali for a perfect view of the sunrise, Pelagia Cheimonettos for the color of your eyes, the late Petros Antonoglou for your wisdom and humanity, Petros tis Psarofagias for the stories of fish, Vasilis Chantziaras for saying we need art and literature, and Vasilis Cheimonettos for *periigitis*. On Nisyros, thank you to Maria for companionship and *dolmadakia*, and to Renata Papakosta for saying go to the wedding and dance. And from Athens, thank you to Vassilis Stavropoulos for the message of spring. Among so many others, these images return.

During the research process, I also had invaluable support from scholars, writers, and translators. Thank you to Michael Kalafatas for writing the book without which this one could not have happened, and for permission to quote from your grandfather's poem, to Eleni Voultsiadou and Russ Bernard for generously sharing your important work, to Emilio Rodríguez-Álvarez for your attentive reading of the manuscript and your help with the archaeology of sponge diving, to the anonymous second reviewer for your thoughtful comments on the text, to Eleftheria Binikou for translating Petros Antonoglou's story into Greek so that his widow could read it, to Ari Sitas for the English translation of Thodoris Eleftheriou's poem "ΠΟΪΝΓΚ..." so that I could read it, to Ari Sitas and Costas Joakimidis for kindly collaborating on tracking down a copy of *Oi Kolasmenoi tis Thalassas* for me, to Costas Joakimidis for your helpful notes on this extraordinary book, and to Allison Bruce for talking about dogs.

In working on the manuscript, I was sustained by the encouragement of all the friends, colleagues, and students who enjoyed the island stories. I'm particularly grateful to my writer comrades Meg Vandermerwe, Kobus Moolman,

Mike Nicol, and Barbara Ras, each of whose perfectly timed enthusiasm for the book gave me the courage I needed at that moment.

Thank you to the University of the Western Cape and the National Research Foundation for their financial support of my research, and to my colleagues in the English department who did my teaching when I needed to take leave.

In making this story into a book, thank you to Tom Payton for saying yes to the manuscript with such warmth, to Steffanie Mortis Stevens and Sarah Nawrocki for your caring attention to so very many details, to everyone else at Trinity University Press who has made it happen, and to Jeremy Boraine and the team at Jonathan Ball Publishers for wonderfully making possible a South African edition. Thank you Angela Voges for your extraordinary care and sensitivity as an editor, and thank you Andrew Putter for a fabulous cover.

Finally, I'm grateful to my family for their unrelenting support and love. Thank you to Sophie Cope for your astute and affirming reading of an earlier version of the text, to Sky Cope for tech help and good humor, and to Michael Cope for being my first reader and my fellow *periigitis*, at every level, at every step of the way.

# NOTES

1. One instance of this story, well known on Symi where a statue of Evgenia Mastoridis was recently erected, is told by Giorgos Zachariadis, one of her relations. Giorgos Zachariadis, "The Diving Suit" in *The Voice of Greece*, February 27, 2024. https://vog.ert.gr/article/The-Ship-s-Log-Feb-27-2024-The-Diving-Bell/?lang=en.

2. This simple definition is from Karl Burkart, cofounder and deputy director of the organization One Earth, in "What is a bioregion?" *One Earth*, July 26, 2024. www.oneearth.org/what-is-a-bioregion/.

3. In 1939 the *Rim*, carrying six hundred people mostly from Eastern Europe, stopped at Rhodes, where another two hundred people went on board, and finally made it to Palestine. Then in 1940, more than five hundred Jews also bound for Palestine were rescued when their ship, the *Pentcho*, caught fire and sank. This story is told by Michael Frank in *One Hundred Sundays* (Souvenir Press, 2023), 87–90.

4. The first systematic study of free divers in antiquity is "Scyllias: Diving in Antiquity," a brief but wide-ranging article; Frank Frost concludes his detailed discussion of the evidence with the comment that "the divers of antiquity, as this survey shows, were skillful, courageous, and inured to hardship" (185). Frank J. Frost, "Scyllias: Diving in Antiquity," *Greece & Rome, Second Series* 15, no. 2 (1968) 180–85, www.jstor.org/stable/642431.

On the ancient names of sponge divers, see the survey by eminent spongiologist Eleni Voultsiadou, "Sponges: an historical survey of their knowledge in Greek Antiquity," *Journal of the Marine Biological Association of the United Kingdom* 87, no. 6 (2007): 757–63, DOI:10.1017/S0025315407057773. The mention of the sponge diver's prayer to "the blessed gods" is from second-century AD Greco-Roman poet Oppian's *Halieutica (Fishing Matters)*, which includes the earliest known account of what he calls "the task of the Sponge-cutters" (Book 5: 612–74). I found his description of the moment of the dive particularly evocative: "Standing upon the prow he scans the waves of the sea, pondering his heavy task and the infinite water. His comrades incite and stir him to his work with encouraging words, even as a man skilled in foot-racing when he stands upon his mark. But when he takes heart of courage, he leaps into the eddying waves and as he springs the force of the heavy grey lead drags him down" (Book 5: 639). Oppian, *Halieutica (or Fishing)*, trans. Alexander William Mair (William Mair Loeb Classical Library, 1928), https://topostext.org/work/524#5.612.

5. In an email regarding his work in the archaeology of free diving, Emilio Rodríguez-Álvarez discussed his as-yet-unpublished research into the fascinating possibility that women in ancient Greece may also have been free divers. Emilio Rodríguez-Álvarez, personal communication to author, March 12, 2025. Regarding free diving more generally, his article "The Archaeology of Freediving: A Foundational Study" explores the presence of divers in the archaeological records of the Mediterranean basin. Writing against the grain of previous scholarship that has tended to interpret references to diving in the archaeological record in symbolic or even mystical terms, this study proposes to "read" and thereby increase the visibility of underwater free divers in this material. Emilio Rodríguez-Álvarez, "The Archaeology of Freediving: A Foundational Study," *Studia Historica Historia Antigua* 41, e31300 (2023): 1–37, https://doi.org/10.14201/shha31300.

6. Natsume Sōseki, *Kusamakura*, trans. Meredith McKinney (Penguin Classics, 2008), 66.

7. David McCullough, quoted in Michael N. Kalafatas, *The Bellstone: The Greek Sponge Divers of the Aegean* (Brandeis University Press, 2003), 15.

8. These statistics are from Evdokia Olympitou, "The Introduction of Maritime Technology in Greek Fisheries: Diving Suites [sic] in Sponge Fishing in the Aegean," in *Greek Maritime History: From the Periphery to the Centre*, eds. Katerina Galani and Alexandra Papadopoulou (Brill, 2022),

240. DOI: https://doi.org/10.1163/9789004467729_011. Olympitou is here quoting from publications by Kyriakos Hatzidakis (1982) and Charles Flegel (1896).

9. Voultsiadou, "Sponges," 1762.

10. Voultsiadou, "Sponges," 1761.

11. M. S. M. Takrouri, "Historical essay: An Arabic surgeon, Ibn al Quff's (1232–1286) account on surgical pain relief," *Anesthesia Essays and Researches* 4, no. 1 (2010): 4–18, doi: 10.4103/0259-1162.69298.

12. Roberto Pronzato and Renata Manconi include a discussion of the soporific sponge in "Mediterranean commercial sponges: Over 5000 years of natural history and cultural heritage," *Marine Ecology* 29 (2008): 146–66, https://doi.org/10.1111/j.1439-0485.2008.00235.x.

13. Kalafatas, *Bellstone*, 169.

14. Kalafatas, *Bellstone*, 170.

15. Kalafatas, *Bellstone*, 177.

16. Kalafatas, *Bellstone*, 176–77.

17. See Autumn Stanley, *Mothers and Daughters of Invention: Notes for a Revised History of Technology* (Rutgers University Press, 1992), 260. This is also discussed in Kalafatas, *Bellstone*, 181.

18. See "The Soap Revolution, Mass Marketing, and the Rise of Advertising" in Howard Bloom's polemical *The Genius of the Beast: A Radical Re-Vision of Capitalism* (Prometheus Books, 2009), 379–82.

19. An advertisement for Pears Soap in the October 1899 issue of *McClure's Magazine* reads: "The first step towards lightening The White Man's Burden is through teaching the virtues of cleanliness. Pears Soap is a potent factor in brightening the dark corners of the earth as civilization advances, while amongst the cultured of all nations it holds the highest place—it is the ideal toilet soap." Among many others who have cited it, Ana Popović discusses this advertisement in "Late Victorian Scientific Racism and British Civilizing Mission in Pears' Soap Ads," *Pulse: The Journal of Science and Culture* 1 (2015): 99–112.

20. Kalafatas, *Bellstone*, 35.

21. Kalafatas, *Bellstone*, 246.

22. "This is how one pictures the angel of history. His face is turned toward the past. Where we perceive a chain of events, he sees one single catastrophe which keeps piling wreckage and hurls it in front of his feet.

The angel would like to stay, awaken the dead, and make whole what has been smashed. But a storm is blowing in from Paradise; it has got caught in his wings with such a violence that the angel can no longer close them. The storm irresistibly propels him into the future to which his back is turned, while the pile of debris before him grows skyward. This storm is what we call progress." Walter Benjamin, "Theses on the Philosophy of History," in *Illuminations: Essays and Reflections*, trans. Harry Zohn (Schocken Books, 1968), 257.

23. The story is titled "Eternally Grateful" in Kritikos Sarantis, *Moments of Silence: Real Stories from the Life of the Sponge Divers*, trans. Joanna Ioannido (YMOS Publications, 2007), 6–34.

24. Kostas Farmakidis and Agapi Karakatsani, *The Chatziagapitos "Sala" on Symi* (Electra Press, 1993).

25. I am grateful to Farmakidis and Karakatsani for their thoughtful reading of the space.

26. The building collapsed in 1940, and the family gave it to the state. In 1971 it was placed under a preservation order, and subsequently restored. Farmakidis and Karakstani, *Chatziagapitos "Sala" on Symi*, 12.

27. Farmakidis and Karakatsani, *Chatziagapitos "Sala" on Symi*, 11 and 54.

28. Farmakidis and Karakatsani, *Chatziagapitos "Sala" on Symi*, 64.

29. Kalafatas, *Bellstone*, 21.

30. Kalafatas, *Bellstone*, 165.

31. In Emily Wilson's marvelous translation of the *Iliad*, Nireus of Syme, who led three ships, was "the most handsome of the Greeks / who came to Troy, except for the great Achilles. / But he was weak and few troops came with him." Homer, *Iliad*, trans. Emily Wilson (W. W. Norton, 2023), Book 2: 671–76.

32. H. Russell Bernard, "Kalymnos: The Island of the Sponge Fishermen," *Annals of the New York Academy of Sciences*, 268, no. 1 (1976): 291–307.

33. The full name of the documentary by Bengt Börjeson and H. Russell Bernard is *Aegean Sponge Divers: Matadors of the Deep* (University of California, Berkeley, 1969).

34. Bernard, *Kalymnos*, 303.

35. This is discussed in H. Russell Bernard's article "Kalymnian Sponge Diving," *Human Biology* 39, no. 2 (1967): 103–30. He notes that after World War II "the casualty rate has generally decreased over pre-war years," but the statistics remain very serious (120).
36. Bernard, "Kalymnian Sponge Diving," 122.
37. Bernard, "Kalymnian Sponge Diving," 126.
38. Bernard, "Kalymnian Sponge Diving," 129.
39. This comment and the description of the *anathema*, the ritual curse, is from Kalafatas, *Bellstone*, 53.
40. H. Russell Bernard, "Kalymnos: The Island of the Sponge Fishermen," *Annals of the New York Academy of Sciences* 268 (1976): 304.
41. Vassilis Vassiliadis, *The Sponge Diver's Dance* (2003). https://vimeo.com/48480128.
42. For more on Vouvalis, see Kalafatas, *Bellstone*, 44–45.
43. Voultsiadou, "Sponges," 1759.
44. Faith Warn, *Bitter Sea: The Real Story of Greek Sponge Diving* (Guardian Angel Press, 2000).
45. Mukul Devichand, "Alan Kurdi's aunt: 'My dead nephew's picture saved thousands of lives,'" BBC News, January 2, 2016. www.bbc.com/news/blogs-trending-35116022.
46. Lesley Stahl, "What the Last Nuremberg Prosecutor Alive Wants the World to Know," *60 Minutes*, CBS News, May 7, 2017, www.cbsnews.com/news/what-the-last-nuremberg-prosecutor-alive-wants-the-world-to-know/.
47. Giánnis Mangklís, *Oi Kolasmenoi tis Thalassas* (Dorikos, 1986).
48. From a collection of photos and diary entries titled, "Food supplies reach the Dodecanese Islands," accessed April 30, 2025, www.johnhearfield.com/Bob/Dodecanese/Starvation.htm. For an account of what they ate, see Philip Chrysopoulos, "What Starving Greeks Ate During the Nazi Occupation," *Greek Reporter*, August 6, 2022, https://greekreporter.com/2022/08/06/what-starving-greeks-ate-during-the-german-occupation/.
49. Kalafatas was given this description of White Island in 1997 by many people who remembered it (*Bellstone*, 26–27).
50. Kalafatas, *Bellstone*, 245.
51. My thanks to Emilio Rodríguez-Álvarez for pointing out the connection between women divers and the *Pinna nobilis*, and for sharing this

link on the subject: "The Sea Silk Project," accessed April 30, 2025, www .seasilkproject.com/.

52. From Ari Sitas's translation of Thodoris Eleftheriou's poem "ΠΟΪΝΓΚ..." ("ppoink...") in Φεύγω...(Iolkos Publications, 2016): 11–25.

53. Eleftheriou, Φεύγω, 24.

54. Haeckel also promulgated a problematic version of social Darwinism, but still. On his relation to ecology, see Frank N. Egerton, "History of Ecological Sciences, Part 47: Ernst Haeckel's Ecology," in *Bulletin of the Ecological Society of America* 94, no. 3 (2013): 222–44, https://esajournals .onlinelibrary.wiley.com/doi/10.1890/0012-9623-94.3.222.

55. Despoina Vakratsi, *Footpaths of Patmos* (Anavasi Editions, 2014).

56. Eleni Voultsiadou, Vasilis Gerovasileiou, and Thanos Dailianis, "Extinction trends of marine species and populations in the Aegean Sea and adjacent ecoregions," *CIESM Workshop Monographs* 45 (2012): 59–74.

57. Voultsiadou et al., "Extinction trends," 67.

58. Voultsiadou et al., "Extinction trends," 69.

59. Voultsiadou et al., "Extinction trends," 69.

60. Voultsiadou et al., "Extinction trends," 69.

61. See for example the analysis in Emma Cebrian, Maria Jesus Uriz, Joaquim Garrabou, and Enric Ballesteros, "Sponge Mass Mortalities in a Warming Mediterranean Sea: Are Cyanobacteria-Harboring Species Worse Off?" *PLoS One* 6, no. 6: e20211, https://doi.org/10.1371/journal .pone.0020211.

62. For an extensive annotated bibliography of the debate that began in 2014 about the links between the Syrian civil war and climate change, see *The Syrian Climate-Migration-Conflict Nexus: An Annotated Bibliography*, by Gianna Angermayr, Pinar Dinc, and Lina Eklund (Centre for Advanced Middle Eastern Studies, Lund University, 2022). www.cmes.lu .se/sites/cmes.lu.se/files/2022-03/Syrian%20Climate-Migration-Conflict %20Nexus.pdf.

63. Voultsiadou et al., "Extinction trends," 73.

64. After hearing the story from Petros, I found it again in Panos's house in Vangelis Eliadis's lyrical text that accompanies photographs of the island by Manuels Talianis in *Chalki Island* (Topio Publications, 2003). In this version, Mario appears in Algiers, and we are told very specifically that she was smuggled aboard "the sponge-fishing vessel of Kapetan-Skoutas,

which had been sent by the wealthy Diakolios of Chalki to Benghazi for sponges" (14).

65. Roberto Calasso writes on the trope of young women being abducted by the gods, often when picking flowers, that "again and again such scenes were to prove irresistible to the gods." Roberto Calasso, *The Marriage of Cadmus and Harmony*, trans. Tim Parks (Penguin, 2019), 3.

66. Herodotus, *Historiae*, I, 4, 2, quoted in Calasso, *Marriage of Cadmus and Harmony*, 7.

67. Interestingly, in another version from the island that probably predates that of the sponge captain and his crew, "Dirlada" is a satirical women's song about husbands, and making food, and doing the laundry, and not being a slave. For an excellent survey of what's known about the song in its many versions, see "Ντιρλαντά / Ntirlanta / Dirlada / Dirlanda (1965)," in *Joop's Musical Flowers*, February 11, 2016, http://jopiepopie.blogspot.com/2016/02/dirlada-ntirlanta-dirlanda-1965.html.

68. Bernard, *Kalymnos*, 303.

69. Thanks to Kalafatas for this metaphor (*Bellstone*, 125–6).

70. This information is recorded on the Rhodes Jewish Museum website: www.rhodesjewishmuseum.org/juderia/.

71. Giánnis Mangklís, *Oi Kolasmenoi tis Thalassas* (1986). When I first heard it, the analogy of meat, of people who are treated like animals, brought to mind Elizabeth Costello's searing argument in J. M. Coetzee's *The Lives of Animals* (Princeton University Press, 1999). Here, the speaker invokes readers' responses to the Third Reich to shine a light on the ongoing holocaust of factory farming. "Let me say it openly: we are surrounded by an enterprise of degradation, cruelty and killings which rivals anything that the Third Reich was capable of, indeed dwarfs it, in that ours is an enterprise without end," she says contentiously (65). Sponges were not, of course, factory farmed, and the relative sentience of these meekest of our animal ancestors is arguably less significant than that of cows or chickens. But it is possible to see the devastation of the sponge beds and the associated ruthless disregard for divers' lives as another kind of holocaust.

72. Eleni Voultsiadou refers to the presence of two hundred species of demosponges in the Aegean. Eleni Voultsiadou, "Sponge diversity in the Aegean Sea: Check list and new information," *Italian Journal of Zoology* 72 (2005): 53–64.

73. "An irreversible depletion of the bath sponge banks of the Mediterranean Sea, due to the combined effects of overfishing and disease, has brought several populations to the brink of extinction since the mid-1980s. The recovery of affected populations has been long and difficult, despite the sponge's extraordinary regenerative capability due to the perennial morphogenesis of the sponge body. *S. officinalis* has undergone a major population decline. Since 1999 the situation has evolved dramatically for *S. officinalis*, and some of the few populations for which ascertained historical data are available are definitely extinct in the Mediterranean. This could be considered the beginning of a final catastrophe" (1). Roberto Pronzato and Renata Manconi, "On the current status of *Spongia officinalis* (the sponge by definition), and implications for conservation: A review" (2020), https://www.semanticscholar.org/paper/On-the-current-status-of-Spongia-officinalis-(the-A-Manconi/f84d86dca79de9e54beab1ecaf011c55add5a8da.

74. Thanks to Michael Kalafatas for some of the source of this account. He describes Anatolia as the lifeline for the island (*Bellstone*, 133–35).

75. This graph is included in the appendix. A century later, the population of the island is now around 2,600.

76. A map showing the islands where Middle and Upper Pleistocene remains of a genus of pygmy elephants have been found appears in Marco Masseti, *Atlas of the Terrestrial Mammals of the Ionian and Aegean Islands* (De Gruyter, 2012), 15.

77. Masseti, *Atlas of the Terrestrial Mammals*, 31–177.

78. Armando Nappi, Francesco Maria Angelici, Cristina Cattaneo, and Mauro Grano, "An introduction to mammal fauna of Symi island (Dodecanese, Greece)," *Bollettino/Museo Regionale di Scienze Naturali Torino* 35, no. 1–2 (2019): 149–58.

79. Masseti, *Atlas of the Terrestrial Mammals*, 201.

80. Jacklyn Cock, *The War Against Ourselves: Nature, Power and Justice* (Wits University Press, 2007).

81. For an early announcement of this renewal, see "Chalki, the first Gr-Eco Island," in *Greek News Agenda*, November 29, 2021, www.greeknewsagenda.gr/chalki-the-first-gr-eco-island/.

82. Mary Annaïse Heglar, "Decolonizing Climate Coloniality," in Rebecca Solnit and Thelma Young Lutunatabua, eds., *Not Too Late: Changing*

*the Climate Story from Despair to Possibility* (Haymarket Books, 2023), Kindle, 31.

83. See "An Extremely Incomplete List of Climate Victories," in Solnit and Lutunatabua, *Changing the Climate Story*, 102.

84. When photographer Sebastiao Salgado inherited the family farm in Brazil in 1999, he was worn out and sick at heart after his work on a project about migrants and refugees. He'd lost faith in our species, he says, and was shocked to discover that the land, ravaged, and denuded by cattle ranching, was as wounded as he was. Then his wife, Lelia, said, "Let's rebuild paradise," and with help they did. The forest returned, the dry springs recovered, and the animals came back too. This story is told by Thomaz Milz, "Sebastiao Salgado finds hope in reforestation," accessed May 1, 2025, www.dw.com/en/in-brazil-photographer-sebastiao-salgado-finds-hope-in-reforestation/a-50877571. Then there are the individuals who quietly plant a forest over a lifetime, people like Jadav Payeng, the "Forest Man of India," who since 1979 has reforested an island in the Brahmaputra River, his action catalyzed by the sight of snakes that had died in the sand without shade. "When I saw it," he says, "I thought even we humans will have to die this way in the heat. It struck me. In the grief of those dead snakes, I created this forest." What an image. In the grief of those dead snakes. See Julie McCarthy, "A Lifetime of Planting Trees on a Remote River Island: Meet India's Forest Man," *NPR*, December 6, 2017, www.npr.org/sections/parallels/2017/12/26/572421590/hed-take-his-own-life-before-killing-a-tree-meet-india-s-forest-man.

85. Among many sources on the environmental impact of nurdles, here is one from a conservation organization in South Africa: "Nurdles: not your average ocean plastic," *Nature's Valley Trust*, October 9, 2018, https://naturesvalleytrust.co.za/2018/10/09/nurdles-not-your-average-ocean-plastic/.

86. Baptiste Morizot writes in *Ways of Being Alive*, trans. Andrew Brown (Polity Press, 2022): "I was sponge, bacterium, an ember among the embers. From every life form all around, a lineage of possibilities can be born" (136). Earlier, in the same chapter, he proposes: "We descend in a straight line from a sponge full of seawater. Metaphorically, this is our most constitutive ancestry from the point of view of the water that fills us" (115).

87. Joëlle Gergis, in Solnit and Lutunatabua, *Changing the Climate Story*: "When you realize that the 2020s will be remembered as the decade

that determined the fate of humanity, you will tap into an evolutionary force that has transformed the world time and time again. Recognizing you are part of a timeless tug of war for social justice electrifies the present moment in a way that brings meaning and purpose to our lives" (48).

88. Thanks to Sky Cope for introducing me to the remarkable story of *La ley del saludo* ("The Law of the Greeting") and its wonderful impact in terms of neighborhood solidarity and social capital, which is told in an essay by Robert D Putna, "What Makes Democracy Work," *National Civic Review* (Spring 1993): 101–7.

89. For J. Richard Gott's discussion of this, see J. Richard Gott, "The Mysterious Architecture of the Universe," the Royal Institution, July 12, 2017, YouTube, 1:06:12, www.youtube.com/watch?v=s9AuqxSVHUY. This presentation on the cosmic sponge was based on the argument in his book *The Cosmic Web* (Princeton University Press, 2016).

# CREDITS

Unless otherwise indicated, images are from the author's collection.

Page 13, *Skafandro*, 2017. Courtesy Michael Cope.
Page 8, Panormitis and Michael. Photographed by the author.
Page 76, *I Sfoungári I Tomári*. Photographed by the author.
Page 105, Lefteris and Julia. Photographed by Michael Cope.
Page 128, Goodbye to Symi. Photographed by an unknown tourist.
Page 142, *Petros*, 2019. Courtesy Michael Cope.
Page 189, Sakellaris Koutouzis, *Marine Pietà*. Photographed by the author.
Page 210, Kostantinos Dionysiu, *The Sponge Diver*, c. 1960s. Courtesy Kostantinos Dionysiu.
Page 225, On the hill. Photographed by the author.
Page 229, General Sponge Fishing Co Ltd, c. 1910. Courtesy Dimitris Zographos.
Page 258, Solar park. Photographed by the author.
Page 276, Zinovia with her late father, Gregorios Ergas, 2022. Photographed by Vasilis Kaimenakis. Courtesy Zinovia Erga.

Extracts from an earlier version of the book have appeared as the following essays:

"The Grocer, the Hunting Dog, and the Solar Park: 'This Web Radiating Out from Every Object,'" in *English Academy Review* (2023), DOI: 10.1080/10131752.2023.2282339.

"Hit by the Machine: Reading a Local Protest Poem on the Island of Symi, 120 Years Later," in *Current Writing: Text and Reception in Southern Africa* 36:1 (2024), 49–55.

"Life Goes On: Hard Bread and Lyricism on the Island of the Sponge Divers," in *Multilingual Margins* 10:1 (2023), 37–43.

**Julia Martin** is the author of *Writing Home*, *A Millimetre of Dust: Visiting Ancestral Sites*, and *The Blackridge House: A Memoir*. She collaborated with Gary Snyder on *Nobody Home: Writing, Buddhism, and Living in Places* and is the coauthor, with Barry Lopez, of *Syntax of the River: The Pattern Which Connects*. She is also the author of numerous essays on place, literature, and ecology. She lives in Cape Town, South Africa, and is a professor emeritus in the Department of English at the University of the Western Cape.

www.ingramcontent.com/pod-product-compliance
Lightning Source LLC
Chambersburg PA
CBHW020048170426
43199CB00009B/212